La Puerta

LA PUERTA

a doorway
into
the
academy

Edited by Carin Bigrigg, Mary Friedman, Karen McKinney,
Wanda Martin, Kate Warne, Rick Waters, and William Waters

KENDALL/HUNT PUBLISHING COMPANY
4050 Westmark Drive   Dubuque, Iowa 52002

Acknowledgments

Jane Caputi, "The New Founding Fathers: The Lore and Lure of the Serial Killer in Contemporary Culture." Jane Caputi, *Journal of American Culture,* 1990, vol. 13, no. 3, Fall 1990. Reprinted by permission.

Mark C. Childs, "Is This Urban Design?" Reprinted with permission from *Designer/Builder Magazine,* Vol. III, No. 2, June 1996. Subscription $28/year, 2405 MacLovia Lane, Santa Fe, NM 87505 (505) 471-4549.

Bryant Furlow, "When to Forgo the Joe." Reprinted with permission from *Psychology Today Magazine,* Copyright © 1996 (Sussex Publishers, Inc.).

Wendy L. Hansen and Thomas Prusa, "Does Administrative Protection Protect?: A Reexamination of the U.S. Title VII and Escape Clause Statutes." From *CATO Review of Business and Government, Regulation*, Winter 1993, p 35. Reprinted by permission.

E. A. Mares, "Los Alamos: Coming Down from the Hill of Certainty." *New Mexico Historical Review* 72 (January 1997) 47-56. Reprinted by permission. "Los Alamos: From Where the Zigzag Lightning Strikes." E. A. Mares, from *Albuquerque Journal Magazine*, August 6, 1985. Reprinted by permission of the author.

Kurt B. Nolte, "A $20 Life." Reprinted by permission of *The Western Journal of Medicine*, 1993: 159:96, "A $20 Life" by Kurt B. Nolte.

Wayne Oakes, "In the Mountains Dreaming of the Sea" and "Stare." Wayne Oakes, *Occur*, 1995. Reprinted by permission of Sputen Duybil.

Richard Rubin, "AMA." Eric Hillman, "AMA." First appeared in *Medical Muse*. Reprinted by permission of the author.

Scott Sanders, "English Grammar Rules . . . but not Clearly." From *Mirage*, Sprint 1992, by Scott Sanders. Reprinted by permission of New Mexico Alumni Association.

David Sklar, "Wrestlers and Doctors." From *Academic Emergency Medicine*, Vol. 1, No. 2, pp. 201-202, 1994. Reprinted by permission.

Sharon Oard Warner, "Christina's World." From *Learning to Dance and Other Stories* by Sharon Oard Warner, Copyright 1992. Reprinted by permission of the author. "In Defense of Writing What You Don't Know." From *Associated Writing Programs Chronicle*, December 1996. Reprinted by permission of *Associated Writing Programs Chronicle*.

David Wilde, "Snow on the Cactus." Reprinted by permission of the author.

Copyright © 1997 Freshman English Program
Department of English
Humanities Building
Albuquerque, NM 87131

ISBN 0-7872-3751-5

Library of Congress Catalog Card Number: 97-73449

Printed in the United States of America

10 9 8 7 6 5 4 3 2 1

*This book is dedicated to the students who have inspired it
and who will be the first to use it.*

Contents

Preface

It is not unusual for failure to give rise to success.

Back in October 1996, a committee of six English Department graduate students met to research and recommend a new reader for the English 101 Freshman Composition classes. Carin Bigrigg, the chair of our committee, had already sent out surveys asking UNM composition instructors to report the strengths and weaknesses of our present text. When she had received these surveys back, Carin arranged the answers, analyzed the results and came to our meeting prepared to provide us with the information that we needed to select a new text. All we had to do was select a text that met all the criteria of the surveys and that was inexpensive enough not to damage our students' financial well-being; then we could go home. Our task bordered on the mundane.

As Carin dropped her stack of surveys on the table and began to review the answers, we started to fret. Ten instructors thought we needed longer readings, 12 thought we needed shorter ones. Fifteen instructors wanted more fiction, 13 wanted less. Twelve instructors wanted more interdisciplinary readings, while 14 wanted more English-specific readings. In short, nothing added up. Our mundane task had become a horror show; suddenly we were faced with trying to find some kind of idealized text made up of myriad apparently unresolvable contradictions.

For the next two hours we weighed the merits and weaknesses of a half-dozen high gloss readers. None of them seemed adequate; the more we examined each text, the more we found writing that seemed distant and unapproachable, writing that "sounded" good but lacked substance, writing that too often privileged form over interest and relevance. Reluctantly, bullied by our fatigue and the impending darkness, we agreed upon a popular culture reader that seemed to address some of the issues and concerns that we had. But no one was really thrilled as we began to collect our notes and head out into the early winter night. Then, just as we were putting on our coats, getting ready to leave, William Waters said: "Why don't we just make our own book?" Everyone looked around, as if one of us would have the answer to that question, as if one of us would have the good sense to say "that's crazy." But no one did; instead, as the murmurs of "yeah, why don't we" grew, a small plan was hatched. In less time than it took for us to nod our heads in agreement, we had made a decision: we would recommend to the Freshman English Committee that instead of adopting another generic reader we would make our own.

Even then, no one heard the door begin to creak open.

When Carin took our suggestion to the Freshman English Committee, our small enthusiasm met a larger enthusiasm. Fortunately Wanda Martin had been planning a similar project for years but had never had the opportunity to implement it; now the time was ripe. So with the Freshman English Committee's blessing and with Wanda Martin's support and guidance, plans were made, committees formed, letters drafted, the process begun. Not surprisingly, though, as we took our project out of our imaginations and tried to bring it into the real world, we quickly realized that there was much we hadn't worked out. For instance, we knew what we didn't want: another high gloss generic reader. But what exactly *did* we want? And how could we get it? Here things weren't so clear.

We knew we wanted a book that would introduce our students to the kinds of writing and thinking that they would be expected to produce across all disciplines of the university, but not one that would be so far removed from their ken as to be inaccessible. We also knew that we wanted a text that would address contemporary issues in scholarship, issues that were questioning old dogmas while creating new beliefs, but not ones that were simply excerpted from other texts. And, most of all, we knew we wanted a text that would reflect the strengths and geniuses of our local talent, but not one that would exclude the beginner in favor of the professional. What we didn't know, on the other hand, was how we were going to collect all of these materials, organize them into a coherent whole, and then bring them to press within six short months.

At first we tried to work out a specific plan for the contents of the book. But then we realized that by doing so we would be limiting ourselves to only what we were already familiar with and therefore would lose some of the potential strengths of our project—the ability to learn about and include other disciplines, to see where they might illuminate our own. Putting all this together, slowly, committee meeting by committee meeting, revision by revision, we decided to invest in risk, to throw caution to the winds, make a call for papers, and see what might materialize.

What materialized was a windfall: we received more than 150 submissions from 13 disciplines and multiple campuses. From these submissions a selection committee, reading blind copies, carefully culled a wide-ranging collection of works that they felt would be both accessible and thought-provoking, arranged them into four chapters and then passed these 27 texts on to a pedagogical committee. Once the pedagogical committee received the texts, they carefully read each one, and interviewed each author for biographical background information as well as any other comments that might make their writing more interesting and accessible to our students. The pedagogical committee then, for each piece, wrote headnotes for the biographical information, endnotes for the additional information, and questions that could lead students into the text without interpreting it for them. Finally, these piles of papers and disks were passed on to a production committee that created a virtual copy of this hard copy of *La Puerta* that you are reading now.

Most miraculously, what materialized—after a thousand headaches, endless impossible decisions, computer crashes, ever shrinking time but ever lengthening "to do" lists, misplaced copy, and spilled coffee—was, in short, this book, but not just this book. Because *La Puerta* is a University of New Mexico product, a product of the efforts and expertise of our own students, staff and faculty; because a number of these authors have agreed to pursue closer contact with our program; and because the readers of this book will be able to meet with and talk to many of the writers of these articles—what materialized was what we had hoped for from the very beginning—'a doorway into the academy,' for us as well as for you.

La Puerta Editorial Board
Albuquerque, May 1997

Acknowledgments

The Editorial Board and staff of *La Puerta* wish to thank the following individuals, each of whom contributed their time and expertise in making this book a reality.

Adam Cohen
Harue Endo
David Fishgrab
Adam Grafa
Erica Landry
Dee Dee Lopez
Elizabeth Moorehead

Charles Paine
Andrea Penner
Jesse Peters
Annabelle Quintana
Scott Sanders
Jerry Shea

And, of course, the people at Kendall / Hunt.

There are two people who must be thanked for moving this project from ether to here:
Bill, without whom there would be neither beginning nor ending; and
Kate, who on the eve of leaving, stayed anyway.
You are both amazing.

JUST SAY KNOW

Consider Your Ending/
To Discover Your Beginning

William Waters

William Waters grew up in Massachusetts and took a bachelor's degree in English from the University of Maine. He did graduate work at University College in Galway, Ireland, before returning to the University of Maine for his M.A. After teaching two years in Maine, Waters taught English in Korea for almost four years. He is currently working on his Ph.D. in English at the University of New Mexico.

The heart, under
one roof,
searches every
direction
so that:

The sun burnt grain
becomes
fruit
in just such a way:

That the self
sees
within itself

A small green
growing
out of the dark
soil.

William Waters calls himself a professional poet. He is quick to add, however, that he does not mean professional *in a financial sense, but rather in the sense that he "professes" poetry. A linguist as well as poet, Waters asserts that it was while he was attempting to develop fluency in languages other than his own that he discovered that his writing students were not "fluent" in English. Waters claims that fluency in a language comes when the speaker or writer must explain something outside of speaking patterns, and he sees poetry as a way of breaking out of patterns. This poem came from trying to learn Korean. Waters says, "I had sudden phenomenal success learning* Hanja, *the Chinese characters used in Korean writing, and while learning words I found I could go to the etymology to learn a range of words." The four Chinese characters mean literally "think, fall, awaken, spring." Waters calls the poem a "transliteration" of these characters. In Chinese, the word "think" is made up of a field above a human heart. "Fall" consists of grain and fire. "Awaken" is from an ancient Chinese character, now archaic, that is made from the characters heart and self. The character for "Spring" is made up of a sun and a plant growing out of roots. Waters says of this poem, "the transliteration is true to the Chinese in such a way that one does not need to read Chinese." While discussing this poem, Waters observes "people cannot be adults until someone they know or part of themselves has died. Mortality is freedom."*

For Discussion

1. Think about what Waters might mean by his statement that "mortality is freedom." Read the poem again, then write about how the poem deals with the two notions of mortality and freedom.

2. This poem uses very little punctuation. Analyze the punctuation marks in terms of how they contribute to the meaning of the poem.

3. Teachers of poetry often tell their students to use "concrete images" in their poems. What such images are at work in this poem, and how do they affect your reading?

4. Read again what Waters says above about how he came to write this poem. Look carefully at the Chinese characters and explain how each represents the images Waters discusses.

5. In what sense is this poem a "translation" of the Chinese? You may want to combine your answer with your response to question four.

6. The final two stanzas of the poem show a consciousness of one's own development. Describe an occasion when you found yourself aware of a new plane in your own consciousness. How did you become aware of this condition? Did you feel any sense of loss along with the gain?

The Nature of the University

Richard Berthold

Richard Berthold took his bachelor's degree in history from Stanford University, and his master's and doctorate in history from Cornell University. At the age of 26, he began teaching at UNM, where he has been for the last 25 years.

Warding off pressures from the outside community, especially political interests, to alter its practices has always been a fact of life for the American university, which has mounted a steady and generally successful guard against such threats to its independence. Now, however, the very nature of the university is being challenged, as the proponents of new social trends have allied themselves with sympathetic and often powerful elements within the university itself. The traditional understanding of the university as an independent forum for the free examination of ideas is being attacked in favor of a concept of the university as an agency for direct social action, its prime concern no longer the search for truth, but immediate social utility.

The university has long been seen as an "ivory tower," isolated not from reality, but from the constantly changing political, social and economic winds of the outside world, from the forces that constantly seek to interfere with its central mission of seeking the truth. Its service to society has been indirect: the discovery of truth and the creation of educated citizens, who might then directly serve society's interests. In contrast, the new university is to serve society directly, participating immediately and directly in the social and economic developments deemed important by society and producing individuals educated to fill specific community needs. Curriculum is to be determined by social utility rather than intellectual curiosity, and if need be, truth must take a backseat to that utility.

In accordance with its traditional mission, the university has struggled, not always successfully, to remain apolitical and independent of the surrounding society, which inevitably seeks to impose its current vision of things on the university. Whether that vision revolves around Catholic theology, Nazi ideology, anticommunism or multiculturalism is quite irrelevant; the university must be free to chase ideas down whatever currently unpopular or offensive road they might lead. Nothing justifies the abridgment of this independence, and if the university is a state-supported institution, the taxpayers and government must understand that claiming and exercising any right to interfere is immediately harmful to the university's mission. Apart from managing the institution, the primary responsibility of a university administration is to protect it from such outside interference.

The current trendy vision of the university seeks to turn this all on its head and render the institution more, rather than less, dependent upon outside forces. Such cannot fail to politicize the university and limit its tradition of free inquiry, making it increasingly a voice of the people or more likely, of government, rather than the voice of truth. This is pernicious enough, but such a dependent relationship can only grow worse, as powers outside the university send in more tendrils, further undermining its autonomy. And a decade down the line those outside interests may no longer seem as benign or progressive, as the momentary concerns of a democratic society continually change.

Free expression, that most delicate and dangerous of basic rights, is central to the university, as it indeed is to a free society in general. But while limits on free speech will certainly injure society, they will with equal certainty kill the university—it simply cannot survive strictures placed on the free examination and discussion of ideas. Regardless of what society wishes at the moment, the individual on campus must be free to speak his mind, subject only to the single prohibition of not creating *an immediate physical danger.*

To limit expression, as proponents of the new university would do, on the grounds of offensiveness, psychological injury, perceived or real damage to society or simple unpopularity with the majority is to kill free speech. That the perpetrators may have the goal of improving society is irrelevant; whatever the motives, free speech is still dead, which must inevitably pave the way for those whose motives are manifestly unattractive. It is a tiny step from prohibiting offensive expression to prohibiting politically unacceptable expression, from banning criticism of a group to banning criticism of the government.

Also vital to the university is humanism, the assertion, first made by the Greeks, that human beings have a dignity and worth quite apart from heaven, that they are free to shape their destiny, and that the primary purpose of society is to serve man rather than God. And part and parcel of humanism is another curious idea discovered by the Greeks and under increasing assault in America: that of the individual. This is the notion, in theory fundamental to our society, that the individual has a value apart from the group and that he consequently ought to be judged according to his individual characteristics rather than those of the group.

Defending the individual and resisting the group judgments that are the foundation of tribalism and social oppression in their many forms is an unending struggle and one that is now being bitterly fought on the American university campus. The individual, whether student or faculty, is the basic unit of the university, the single mind that examines and debates ideas, and the group must suppress that individual in order to create a common voice for itself. Such subordination of the individual to the group, as history demonstrates, inevitably generates falsehoods, smothers new or different ideas and generally injures the pursuit of truth that is the prime directive of the university. Mr. Spock notwithstanding, in the context of the university the needs of the one far outweigh the needs of the many.

The university is a collection of individuals, not groups, each free to sing his own song, regardless of whether any harmonies result. It is by definition a contentious place, and a university where "consensus" reigns, even concerning the nature and mission of the university itself, is one that has failed. And a university that requires universal agreement with *any* idea has become its own antithesis. The university must defend the examination and expression of *all* ideas, even those that threaten it, or the free marketplace of knowledge will become a company store.

Insofar as the university constitutes a forum for the examination of any idea it is democratic, but the institution itself is not a democracy. It posits a basic inequality between the two groups that constitute it, faculty and students, and on the basis of that inequality assigns authority to the faculty. Students are free (and in fact should be encouraged) to challenge any idea propounded by the faculty and even challenge the competency of individual faculty members, but they can only be subordinate to the authority that is granted faculty by the institution. Students and faculty may separately organize themselves as democratic entities, but the classroom, where the two groups meet, can only be an autocracy, albeit one in which the individual is free to demonstrate the emperor has no clothes.

The university is not so much a thing or a place as a concept, that of the free exchange of ideas. The campus, with its classrooms, libraries and laboratories, is not the university, but simply a support structure. The university staff—presidents, provosts, secretaries, librarians, counselors, custodians, etc.—are not the university, but only its attendants, as it were, convenient for its functioning. Insofar as the university is a physical entity at all, it is the students and faculty, and all others serve the single purpose of facilitating the dialogue between the two groups. When Peter Abelard, fired from the twelfth century University of Paris, lectured students on his own in an open field across the Seine, he and they constituted a kind of minimalist university.

Unfortunately, for most Americans, especially the political and business leaders who most often control its economic fate, the university is simply an institution, another business in which the society invests resources in the expectation of a product. The university does not create an abstract sort of product—education—but understanding the institution as just another business leads inevitably to a demand for the immediate social and economic utility that is at odds with its essential nature. If we serve the university with our tuition, taxes and gifts, the argument goes, then the university ought to serve us by training new workers, creating jobs and contributing directly to the social and economic well-being of the community. And the result is the university becomes more and more a technical-vocational institute and an extension of the public school system, less and less a university.

The university does indeed serve society and provide a return on financial investment, but in an indirect and long-term way, by providing the forum for the free examination of ideas and by producing educated citizens. Whether those ideas or that education has any immediate or obvious utility to society is irrelevant. To demand otherwise is to create an institution that may be of benefit to the community, but which is no longer a true university.

While the university is most generally a free marketplace of ideas, its specific recognized purpose is education. Exactly what "education" means is of course the subject of intense debate, since the term can reasonably cover everything from forced political indoctrination to training a professional physicist to gaining the ability to survive in America's cities. Most would agree that the first and last of these are not facets of a university education, although both have appeared on the American campus, the first in the form of sensitivity training and the last in various outreach and popular culture programs. Training professionals in the arts and sciences is, on the other hand, a major component of the university's educational mission, and the graduate and professional schools are an accepted part of the university. Still, producing advanced degrees and professionals of all sorts is not the primary educational purpose of the university and in fact contributes to the current notion that the institution is simply a machine for filling the workplace needs of an increasingly complex and technological society.

The prime focus of the university's education mission is the undergraduate student body and a liberal education. In this context "liberal" is not to be understood as a political term, the opposite of "conservative," but rather as meaning "unrestricted" or "general," in contrast to the more specific and focused education of the graduate and professional student. A liberal education is in fact a general education, ideally one that provides the individual with a basic understanding of the universe, of the human experience and of himself. It also provides him the intellectual tools to explore further and to satisfy the basic—and in the eyes of many, dangerous—urge that lies behind the university, learning in general and indeed the very discovery of rationalism: curiosity. It is not too much to say that the university is in fact a monument to curiosity, to the spirit that drives humans to question and try to figure out why, all to the dismay of the ignorant, the complacent and the defenders of the established order.

Thus does the university serve society and ultimately humanity in two very important ways: it is the secure and free marketplace of ideas and it provides the liberal education necessary for a free and progressive society.

Professor Berthold is the president of the New Mexico Association of Scholars, a state chapter of the National Association of Scholars, which is dedicated to the preservation of the university in the United States. As he puts it, those within the group see themselves as academicians concerned with the direction that education is currently taking and desirous of conserving the more traditional liberal arts curriculum, where those outside the group see them as a bunch of frightened, old, white males who have a tendency to run screaming from progressive social trends. Further, with the exception of two important issues, Professor Berthold takes nothing too seriously (including himself), but rather sees myriad opportunities for finding humor in fallacious arguments, ideologies and stances (including his own). Two issues, however, which do not fall prey to his tongue are free speech and the Palestinian cause. Everything else is fair game.

For Discussion

1. Write a clear and concise definition of what Berthold believes "the nature of the university" to be.

2. Make two lists of the adjectives used in the last line of the introductory paragraph. List #1 is the adjectives used to describe how the university should be; list #2 is the adjectives used to describe how the university is becoming. By using the words he has chosen, what assumptions is Berthold making about the relationship between "truth" and "social utility"?

3. Pretend that Berthold's essay is the opening argument of a court case which will decide how universities are run in the future. As an *amicus curiae* (friend of the court), the judge has asked you to write a brief giving your opinion about this. Write a response to Berthold's essay which addresses your major concerns.

4. Explain the implication of the list in paragraph three: "Catholic theology, Nazi ideology, anticommunism or multiculturalism." How do these very diverse elements fit together? Or do they? What is Berthold implying by such a comparison? Do you agree?

5. In paragraph eight, Berthold makes a reference in the last two lines to *Star Trek*. From a rhetorical or writer's point of view, what are some of the benefits of enlisting pop culture to further an argument? What are some of the drawbacks to doing so?

6. Argue for or against Berthold's assertion that "in the university, the needs of the one far outweigh the needs of the many." Be careful to support your statements with examples from your own experience.

7. Compare the statement made in paragraph 15 about the goals of a liberal education with the detailed description of such in the companion essay, "The Content of a Liberal Education." Is it possible to have what Berthold calls "a basic understanding of the universe, of the human experience" and of yourself without a liberal education? If you argue yes, then give a detailed description of an alternate process which would give you those understandings. If you argue no, discuss your intentions for the next four years of your own college education. For both, why are you here at UNM?

The Content of a Liberal Education
Richard Berthold

Richard Berthold took his bachelor's degree in history from Stanford University, and his master's and doctorate in history from Cornell University. At the age of 26, he began teaching at UNM, where he has been for the last 25 years.

The foundation idea of a liberal education goes back to the medieval university, which was in turn heavily influenced by classical notions about the educated man. The content of that education will of course no longer do, since the early university existed in an intellectual environment dominated by Christian theology and an uncritical acceptance of classical ideas (at least those that did not conflict with Christianity). Both held the university in the confining grip of truth based on unquestioned and unquestionable authority, that of the ancients and especially that of the true faith. In addition to limiting academic freedom this fact of late medieval life created a basic curriculum that overemphasized some subjects, such as theology, and neglected others, such as the natural sciences. Fortunately, the decline of the Church and the rise of modern science, which broke the spell of the ancients, ultimately undermined the idea of authority-based truth, and the curriculum of the modern university has expanded into every conceivable area.

A modern liberal education has two essential components. The first of these is the clutch of intellectual skills necessary for any intelligent interaction with the world and the acquisition of further knowledge. The most basic of these tools, the ability to read and write, to calculate and to solve simple problems, are acquired in the process of primary education, though the sad state of American public education can no longer guarantee this. A liberal education should build on these skills and develop further the individual's ability to read analytically and critically and write clearly and persuasively. It should train him how to examine and approach logically any sort of problem or situation and how to argue and defend a proposition, whether in speech or in writing. In a word, a liberal education ought to teach one to think. If the university did nothing more than this, its existence would be more than justified.

The individual who can think, analyze and communicate is equipped to continue learning on his own, but a proper liberal education will also provide a second component: a broad basis of general knowledge that will give the student a leg up, as it were, in his further education. The emphasis here is on the broad and general, the acquisition of the information and ideas necessary for a basic understanding of how the world, both natural and human, works. From this one can easily proceed to a deeper understanding of any specific aspect of the nature of things.

A liberal education thus requires a grounding in both the sciences and the humanities. In the case of the sciences, the goal is not a detailed knowledge of any particular science, but rather an understanding of what the various sciences deal with, the important questions to which they seek answers and the general principles upon which they operate. More important to a liberal education than an expertise in any specific scientific field is a thorough understanding of *science* itself, what it is and is not and how it functions. Such an understanding of science and the fundamental principles behind our universe will allow the liberally educated individual to recognize and counter the pseudo-science, fantasy and general irrationality that constantly threaten to overwhelm the human race.

A similar goal is sought in the humanities, that is, a broad understanding of the human condition in all its aspects. Such an understanding requires some exposure to and basic familiarity with history, religion, philosophy, the political and social sciences and the arts. Again, the point is not to acquire knowledge in depth, but rather to gain a general understanding of the nature of these fields, particularly as tools for understanding the individual and society and making reasoned judgments about them.

Especially important in this regard are history and literature, both of which provide direct access to the human experience and thus contribute immediately to an understanding of ourselves. A study of the history and literature of the race will not only reveal the tremendous variety of human society, but in doing so it will also—and more importantly—illuminate the general human condition. To study the Greeks or Zulus or Chinese is simply to study ourselves from another perspective; to read the literature of Russia or India or Brazil is to see ourselves through different cultural eyes.

For the American university student study of the history and literature of Western civilization ought to be the starting point for this examination of human culture. This Western tradition comprises the values, perspectives and methodologies that have shaped our own society and thus has the most direct relevance to an understanding of ourselves, who are products of that society, regardless of superficial ethnic differences. It is necessary to comprehend the forces that shaped one's own point of view before examining that of others. And for good or for ill Western culture and its ideas have had and will continue to have a dramatic impact on the rest of humanity, making a study of the West a vital component of the liberal education of every individual, irrespective of his cultural origins.

A broad understanding of ourselves and the world around us and the ability to think analytically and communicate clearly, these are the goals of a liberal education. While not filling any specific workplace niches, a general education of this sort possesses a social utility far more important than that of any professional training. Common sense and the evidence of history demonstrate that the greater the portion of the citizenry that is generally educated, the better the society is able to solve its problems, employ its resources and improve its material and intellectual circumstances. Such is especially the case in a democratic state, which regularly asks it citizens to render political judgments, and it was the discoverers of urban-centered democracy, the Greeks, who first realized that a general education was a basis for civic virtue, that a general education was in fact a political education.

In the twentieth century of course political education has increasingly come to mean simply political indoctrination, which has rarely, if ever, been a benefit to any society. The political education of the liberally educated citizen, on the contrary, does not consist of a commitment to any particular ideology, but rather comprises a general understanding of society and history and the intellectual tools to employ that understanding in shaping his own political environment. A liberally educated citizen body is the most resistant to political oppression, the least likely to be taken in by appeals to emotion rather than reason. Democracy in particular rises and falls with the education of its electorate, and the voter who lacks an understanding of himself and his world is an easy target for demaguery and sloganeering, for the fear mongers and feel-good politicians. Indeed, liberal education is society's single most potent weapon in the unending struggle to preserve freedom.

One final note about a liberal education: it is work. While learning can be consistently interesting and frequently fun, it still requires discipline and effort. The acquisition of intellectual skills and knowledge demands mental exercise, memorization and practice. Interaction and dialogue are a vital part of education, but at its root learning is a solitary occupation of reading, writing and most important, thinking.

Professor Berthold is the president of the New Mexico Association of Scholars, a state chapter of the National Association of Scholars, which is dedicated to the preservation of the university in the United States. As he puts it, those within the group see themselves as academicians concerned with the direction that education is currently taking and desirous of conserving the more traditional liberal arts curriculum, where those outside the group see them as a bunch of frightened, old, white males who have a tendency to run screaming from progressive social trends. Further, with the exception of two important issues, Professor Berthold takes nothing too seriously (including himself), but rather sees myriad opportunities for finding humor in fallacious arguments, ideologies and stances (including his own). Two issues, however, which do not fall prey to his tongue are free speech and the Palestinian cause. Everything else is fair game.

For Discussion

1. Make a list of each of the following from the introductory paragraph: a) adjectives; b) adverbs; c) verbs.

Compare these lists with what Berthold is arguing. Then use your comparison to describe the subtext(s) or the underlying message(s) in this paragraph.

2. Starting with paragraph two, create an outline of the structure of the essay. Is this essay logically constructed? If you say yes, explain the progression of logical steps. If you say no, explain where there are steps missing.

3. At the end of paragraph four, Berthold writes that "pseudo-science, fantasy and general irrationality . . . constantly threaten to overwhelm the human race." Brainstorm a list of things that might fall into these categories which he describes. Then, explain why it might be dangerous for those things to replace the real science offered in liberal education.

4. In paragraph six, Berthold gives his explanation of the importance and relevance of the study of history and literature to humans. In your own words, define or summarize his position. Then, fit yourself into it; explain how you might see yourself through the eyes of another culture through literature and history.

5. On the flip side, consider how you see others through the lenses of history and literature. Others can include people outside of your circle, outside of your community, outside of your culture, outside of your country. Read "Snow on the Cactus," and the introduction section of "Urban Analysis." Who is the "other" in relation to you? Give detailed examples from your own experience.

6. What do you want out of your education here at UNM? What do you expect to know at the end of it? Who do you think you will be?

7. Read the poem "Consider Your Ending / To Discover Your Beginning." In what way are you, a student, "the self [which] sees within itself / A small green growing out of the dark soil"?

English Grammar Rules . . .
but Not Clearly

Scott Sanders

Since receiving his bachelor's degree in English in 1972 from the University of Arizona at Tucson, Associate Professor of English Scott Sanders has written numerous articles, books and poems, first as a doctoral student at the University of Colorado and then later as a teacher at several universities throughout the Southwest, including Colorado Women's College and NM Tech. Sanders has taught at the University of New Mexico since 1984, and during that time he has produced a wide variety of writing. Although his dissertation focused on Coleridge, Sanders has also written and published over 60 poems, and numerous technical and scientific pieces. Sanders is also the author of two books: Frontier Gothic: Terror and Wonder at the Frontier in American Literature *(with David Mogen and Joanne B. Karpinski, 1993) and* The Physics of Skiing: Skiing at the Triple Point *(with David Lind, 1997). Currently, Sanders is the chair of the English Department as well as the Director of the Professional Writing Program in the English Department. "English Grammar Rules . . . but not Clearly" was originally published in* Mirage, *UNM's alumni magazine in 1992.*

Principles of language usage may be less pristine than we've been led to believe.

In every city and town in the United States on at least one day or night a week, viewers watch the Starship Enterprise blast silently off into the infinity of the universe on its ". . . five-year mission: . . . to boldly go where no man has gone before." And someone in the viewing audience looks up from the screen and says, "Hey. 'To boldly go.' That's a split infinitive. How can they do that?"

Our fascination with usage issues, like the correctness or incorrectness of the split infinitive, may not match the ardor of our national passion for *Star Trek*, but Americans are fascinated by usage. That is, we are fascinated by proper—meaning correct—usage.

Humorist Dave Barry exploits this national preoccupation in his "Ask Mr. Language Person" columns, which give wildly ludicrous advice to readers' equally ludicrous questions. For example, consider the following that Barry attributes to "an actual reader," James F. Woods of Denver, Colo., who asks:

> In the song, 'Someone's in the kitchen with Dinah,' when it says 'Someone's in the kitchen with Dinah, I know, oh, oh, oh' does it mean that the singer knows that someone is in the kitchen with Dinah, or that the singer knows WHO is in the

kitchen with Dinah?'
Answer: Leading grammar experts have wrestled naked with this question for years.
—"Mr. Language Person Ready for Questions," *Albuquerque Journal*, 2 March 1992, B1.

The answer goes on at length from this promising start. The immediate target of Barry's spoofing is probably columnist William Safire of the *New York Times*, who regularly offers his readers advice on matters of usage.

While Safire may be Barry's immediate target, the field is crowded with other candidates. Perhaps because there is no officially sanctioned academy to define and protect the purity of English, each of us feels free to become an academy unto ourselves. And we do so. But the need to appeal to authority remains strong, and we want to know that our sense of what is correct matches the experts' cumulative opinions.

So we read Safire. And maybe Edwin Newman, the television-newsman-turned-grammar-maven and author of *Strictly Speaking* (a best-seller in the mid '70s) who once hosted a TV show where experts and laypersons wrestled (albeit not naked) with thorny usage questions.

So what about that split infinitive? I mean, it is wrong, isn't it? Well, not really. Students in my editing class research such questions and write reports. Their usage reports survey handbooks from different eras to determine when and where, if ever and at all, particular rules were laid down.

One student looking into the split infinitive controversy could find no unqualified statement that its use is incorrect. She searched 11 handbooks, ranging from Lindley Murray's *English Exercises* (1809; no mention of the split infinitive) to Kirszner and Mandel's *The Holt Handbook* (1986; "when . . . not awkward or ambiguous, the split infinitive is permissible").

The first edition of the venerable *Harbrace College Handbook* (1941) advises writers to "Avoid . . . awkward splitting of infinitives." This implies that gracefully split infinitives are acceptable, but no examples are given. By the mid '60s, the same *Harbrace*, then in its sixth edition (we are at 11 now, and counting), reprints the 1941 advice verbatim, appending this:

> Note: Although all split infinitives were once considered questionable, those which are not awkward are now acceptable. Americans seem to always be searching for something new.—*Newsweek*

The positive example helps rehabilitate this suspect usage, but "once considered questionable" suggests an abandoned higher standard, and the authority cited, *Newsweek,* is uncomfortably lowbrow. Did Milton, a student might ask (suspecting that the professor is more likely to read *Paradise Lost* than *Newsweek*), split infinitives?

While I don't know for a fact that Milton split infinitives (but I would bet that he did), in other matters of usage such as, say, past participles, he was quite creative. Readers of *Paradise Lost* will find such odd constructions, among others, as "have spoke," "had rode," and "was took." There's more going on here than the exercise of a liberal poetic license.

Clearly the rules of usage are not apodicitic; that is, they do not proceed from axiomatic principles such as a + b = b + a; many of the usage choices we make are not between correct and incorrect alternatives, in which making the wrong choice signals ignorance, willful or otherwise.

Where then do the rules come from? Drawing from Edward Finegan's very readable account of this story in his book, *Attitudes Toward English Usage: The History of a War of Words,* we can answer this question by looking at the historical development of rules of usage.

In a sense, it all began with William Bullokar's *Bref Grammar* (1582), the first book we know of devoted to the analysis of English. Bullokar noted the founding of the Italian *Accademia della Crusca* in 1582 and decried the "unruled" state of English.

Bullokar's voice was echoed by many over the next 150 years as, in succession, the French (1635), the Spanish (1713), and the Swedish (1739) academies were founded and English still had none. By 1694 the Italians and the French both had authoritative dictionaries to guide their writers and (more to the point) their printers.

English writers worked in a language whose usages, ranging from spelling to verb forms (Milton comes to mind here), varied wildly. Poet John Dryden (1679) asked plaintively "if it were possible, that we might all write with the same certainty of words, and purity of phrase." In 1697 novelist Daniel Defoe proposed an academy "to polish and refine the English Tongue, . . . and to purge it from all the Irregular Additions that Ignorance and Affectation have introduc'd."

Jonathan Swift's voice was the clearest and most widely attended on this issue. Swift wrote *A Proposal for Correcting, Improving and Ascertaining the English Tongue* (1712), in which he complained "that our Language is extremely imperfect; that its daily Improvements are by no means in proportion to its daily Corruptions; that the Pretenders to polish and refine it, have chiefly multiplied Abuses and Absurdities; and, that in many Instances, it offends against every Part of Grammar."

Capitalization aside, Swift's complaint should sound familiar to readers of Safire and Newman. The three share some underlying assumptions: without regulation, the language will be corrupted; and most, if not all, variation and change leads to decay, not to renewal. Swift wanted the language fixed—he wanted it to stop changing—and he wanted to do this by defining and then adopting immutable rules.

Remember that Dryden, Defoe, Swift, and the other writers of that time had before them the sobering example of Chaucer (who died in 1400). Chaucer's genius was perfectly clear, but his language, what we today call Middle English, was not.

How, wondered Dryden, Defoe, and Swift, had English changed so in a mere 300 years? Did this mean that in 300 more years their works would be read with difficulty equal or greater to the difficulty with which their contemporaries read (or could not read) Chaucer?

The answers to these questions would not come until the next century. For now, note that you probably did not stumble reading the citations from Dryden, Defoe, and Swift. Any two lines from the *Canterbury Tales* rendered here in Middle English would cause serious stumbling. The forces that changed Middle English into Modern English have not wrought similarly great changes in the language from 1700 to today.

But that is not because the language was codified by an academy. No officially sanctioned academy was ever established, in part because so many private dictionaries and grammars were published. The most important were Samuel Johnson's *Dictionary of the English Language* (1755) and Robert Lowth's *Short Introduction to English Grammar* (1762). In the history of English literature, Lowth's Grammar is a very minor event compared to Johnson's *Dictionary*. But in the history of English handbooks, Lowth's work is preeminent.

Lowth forthrightly judged "of every phrase and form of construction, whether it be right or not. The plain way of doing this, is to lay down rules, and to illustrate them by examples. But besides showing what is right, the matter may be further explained by pointing out what is wrong."

Lowth's emphasis on "pointing out what is wrong" has stayed with us ever since. Also, Lowth developed many of his rules by drawing analogies to Latin, which, unlike English, is both highly inflected and dead, making it at once more amenable to analysis and resistant to change. Largely to this practice of Lowth's we owe the notion that "It is I" is correct and "It is me" is incorrect, although the latter is certainly the more usual usage. Lowth cited many "abuses" of usage made by "some of our best Writers," including among those abuses the Miltonic past participles offered above.

Lowth's greatest disciple was Lindley Murray, an American by birth who emigrated to England in 1784. His *English Grammar* (1795) sold more than two million copies in more than 300 editions on both sides of the Atlantic over the first quarter of the nineteenth century.

Murray did not invent the tradition of "error-hunting," Lowth did. But Murray perfected it. Like Lowth, Murray offered readers both positive and negative examples, but he greatly preferred that students discover what was wrong in a sentence, an instructional method borrowed from, what else, Latin grammars of the day. Finegan suggests that Murray "bears major responsibility for the widespread misconception that 'grammar' is the art of adjudicating 'right' and 'wrong' forms among several score of divided usages."

At this point our story reaches a fork in the road. In the nineteenth century, the work of the Brothers Grimm led to understanding how languages change and develop from earlier languages. The gentleperson's study of language became the scholar's discipline of linguistics, and the Grimm's comparative methods became the basis of philological study in the humanities. Scholarly studies of usage became descriptive: the goal was not to prescribe correct usages, but to describe the variety of usages, compare them, and draw analytical conclusions about the underlying nature of the language itself.

As the scholars went their way, establishing the Ph.D. degree en route, popular grammarians and schoolroom grammar books followed the trail blazed by Lowth and Murray. It was the end of the century before professional societies tried to bring the insights of the century's language scholarship into the practice of teaching the language.

In the twentieth century the story gets more complicated, and I recommend Finegan's book to any who want more on the subject. In short, today we suffer misunderstandings about usage which stem from attitudes expressed 300 and more years ago and the continuing divergence of scholarly and popular concerns that began nearly 200 years ago.

Of course there are correct and incorrect usages. But those are not the usages which people dispute. Unfortunately, many divided usages are thought to be inviolate rules. Consider this one: Never end a sentence with a preposition. Winston Churchill purportedly said about this rule: "This is the sort of English up with which I will not put." Every college handbook published in the past 60 years will tell you there is no such rule, even as they will warn about "awkward" constructions that writers, misplacing a prepositional phrase, might end up with.

Perhaps this is the problem. Faced with too many students and too little time, teachers at every level may understandably recite recipes when they should teach rhetoric. It is easier to offer a rule, a template for correct expression, than it is to teach the taste and judgment needed to best address a given audience. Language arbiter Theodore Bernstein makes the same guess in *Watch Your Language* (1958). Writing about the preposition rule, he says, "We need not go the whole way with Miss Thistlebottom's rules—many of which were designed more for easy teaching than for better writing."

In many instances of what we thought was right or wrong, we now find choices between more and less appropriate usages. Choice is the key. Joseph Williams sums up the third edition of *Style: Ten Lessons in Clarity and Grace* (1989), by noting that:

> Because usage is largely a matter of personal taste—idiosyncratic, individual, unpredictable—I can offer no broad generalizations, no global principle by which to decide any given item. . . . Finally, I think, we choose among these items less on the basis of their real or supposed correctness than according to a sense of our own personal style. . . . The shalls and wills, the whos and whoms, the self-consciously unsplit infinitives—they are the small choices that let those of us who wish to do so express that sense of linguistic conservatism that many believe testifies to their linguistic precision.

Where do you place yourself in the liberal to conservative continuum implied by Professor Williams? If you've read from the beginning to this point like a good reader should, you have encountered many doubtful usages—a score of sentences beginning with conjunctions, sentences ending with prepositions (one with not one but two), a disagreement in number between pronouns, one split infinitive, incorrect uses of "which" and "that," a misused "like" for "as," a comma splice, even a sentence fragment—and those are only the "errors" I have intentionally put in.*

Begging my editor's pardon, but surely there are still more unintentional usage "errors." Did any startle you? Cause you to stumble as you read? What makes a usage incorrect, anyway? This question gives us something to think about. Usage is much more than memorizing rules.

*Not all are highlighted. Enjoy the hunt!

When you ask Sanders about his relationship to writing, he laughs and says, "the only enjoyable part [of writing] is running the printer," which means, of course, that the writing is finished. Such an admission is surprising, given Sanders' experience as a writer. To Sanders, the key to writing is to avoid facing a blank computer screen; to insure that this doesn't happen, Sanders likes to organize and collect his ideas on paper before sitting down in front of the computer. Because so many of his ideas result from the process of reading, Sanders takes detailed notes while he reads so that his ideas may later be used as starting points in his writing process. When he actually begins to write, Sanders finds that the best way to avoid writer's block is to start writing in the middle, and save writing the more difficult sections, like the introduction, until the end. As a teacher, Sanders seeks to both delight and instruct his students about the art of writing well. He encourages his students to find wonder in ideas that we often take for granted, such as the rules of grammar that we are all expected to follow when we write. He says that when he teaches his senior-level students about grammar, he encourages his students to question and challenge the rules of grammar, rather than simply follow them. Indeed, "English Grammar Rules . . . but not Clearly," which is based upon a lecture Sanders has delivered to his students since 1985, challenges its readers to become active participants in the debate concerning usage. This article originally appeared in Mirage, *UNM's alumni publication, and reflects Sanders' desire to write a piece which would be humorous as well as play with the idea of what English teachers normally teach in their classrooms.*

For Discussion

1. In paragraph one, Sanders uses an example from *Star Trek* to support his point concerning split infinitives. Why do you think that Sanders chooses to use an example of pop culture to support his point? What kind of tone does it set for the rest of the essay?

2. Summarize what Sanders means by *usage* in the essay, using specific references to the text to support your points. How does Sanders's definition differ from your own definition of *usage*?

3. Why are Americans so preoccupied with issues of usage, according to Sanders? Why is correct language so important?

4. What happened when Sanders' students began researching the split infinitive? What does this example tell you about usage?

5. Describe the historical context that Sanders gives in his essay. Why does he provide this context? How does it work in his essay?

6. Look at the grammar manual that we are using in this course. Write a short response comparing and contrasting it to the manuals Sanders describes in his essay.

7. This essay was originally printed in *Mirage*, UNM's alumni magazine. In the original essay, several errors in the essay were circled in red ink. Why do you think the editors decided to do this? What effect might this have had upon the readers of an alumni

magazine?

8. In paragraph 22, Sanders admits that he has salted his essay with errors. Circle the errors that you noticed while reading the essay. How does this confession support Sanders' argument concerning usage and audience?

9. Describe a time when someone pointed out to you that you were incorrectly using language? How did that make you feel?

10. One aspect of language usage is that language is constantly changing. Yet some say language ought to remain the same. What evidence can you offer from your own experience to support the idea that language changes? For example, compare your language to your parents' language. How is it similar; how is it different?

11. What rules of language usage have you learned and whom did you learn them from?

12. Look at Berthold's essays describing the university and the content of a liberal education. How does grammar usage influence one's ability to fit into an academic setting? Use your own experience to support your points.

Fragnet

Jerry Shea

An alumnus of the University of New Mexico's doctoral program in American Studies, Associate Professor of English Jerry Shea has had a wide and varied teaching career: he has taught at Colorado State University, Illinois State University, the University of Albuquerque, and the College of St. Francis, in addition to teaching at UNM since 1977. In recognition of his dedication to teaching, Shea received UNM's Outstanding Undergraduate Teacher Award for the school year 1990/91. Shea is the co-author of Thought To Essay: A Process Report, *and has written numerous essays which have appeared in* Century, New Mexico Magazine *and* Southwest Storyteller's Gazette. *When he is not teaching his students the fine points of grammar, Shea works as what he describes as a "practicing storyteller."*

This is the city, Albuquerque, New Mexico, home to half a million people—rich, poor; young, old; ambitious, defeated. They all have stories to tell, and there is enough illiteracy around to keep me awfully busy on any given day.

My name's Shea. I carry a Ph.D. I'm a grammarian.

The captain's name is Noam Chomsky; my partner is Chris Buchalter. We were working the day watch out of UNM Precinct, heading west on Zuni, when the wake-up call came crackling in. Residential address on Washington NE—meter reader had observed young white male using a semicolon in a note to his mother and got on the the hotline (223-4726: "BAD GRAM"). If the fellow was underage, as suspected, he was in big trouble.

He was in a peck of it. An ID check confirmed that he was only 17, so there was a clear 506 (Use of a Semicolon by a Minor). A perusal of the note showed the wisdom of the law—suspect had misused that semicolon ("Although I'm spending the afternoon at Muffy Smith's; I'll be home in time to mow the lawn." Buchalter blanched, but I've seen it all, too many times). So now he had a 611, a third degree felony, to tack onto that misdemeanor. Suspect's name was Chip Thornton. He seemed a decent enough lad, but we had to book him. How do they go wrong?

We took Thornton downtown and spent the rest of the morning in mobile surveillance: billboards, the occasional private sign ("4-Sale": have they no shame?) and bumper stickers ("Don't laugh, its payed for!": three for one! I felt like a Scrabble winner), writing tickets like a couple of rookies or, rather, just as a couple of rookies would. We managed a quick lunch at one of our favorite spots, Manny's Coney Island Dogs. We checked the menu for orthographical slips and comma splices, but more out of habit than anything else. Manny runs a clean operation; he's one of the thousands of hard-working, good people in this Duke City on the Rio. "Don't take any wooden commas," he called out as we left. We both grinned, not at the banal humor but at the bonhomie behind it.

One-eleven p.m. We got a call concerning a complainant in a walk-up off San Pedro. We arrived to find a very upset older woman, a Mrs. Stefanson.

"I'm just a stupid, stupid old biddy. Might as well have run out in the street and forced that $500 on the first stranger to have come along!" (She'd lost her peace of mind and a pot of money, but one had to admire those subjunctives. Buch and I exchanged an appreciative glance.) "He was so friendly, looked just like my favorite nephew. Said he had just finished up a big paragraph renovation in the neighborhood. Said he had all these phrases left over. Shame to waste them, give them to me for a song." (Her syntax was crumbling around our ears but, hey, even grammarians can look the other way. Sometimes.)

"Yes, ma'am. He took your money and had the goods delivered later, phrases you'd be ashamed to use in an idiot's rought draft."

"How did you.....?"

"Drink this water, Mrs. Stefanson (and watch those ellipses). Oldest scam in the book, I'm afraid. Our beat is grammar, not rhetoric, but let me guess: "viable parameters"? "at this point in time"? "misspoke"? "downward monetary adjustment"?

"Yes, and . . . oh, more and worse."

"That's government surplus stuff, tired tropes and bafflegab. You wouldn't let your parrot use it. He probably paid $10 for that garbage at auction."

Now she was in tears and the con artist probably in Los Lunas. Buch had radioed the rhetoric bunko squad. We slipped out while Mrs. Stephanson was blubbering a statement for them. Tomorrow, some other victim in some other town: these vipers and vultures really sicken one.

Outside, Buchalter and I squinted in the glare and hit the sun-bleached streets again. Chris has been on the force for half a dozen years now. She's aces as a grammarian and incorruptible as a pair of parentheses. She came to the job in a fairly typical way. After a master's degree, she was going to become one of those hotsy-totsy "creative writers." Tiring of that goal, she decided she was going to make big bucks in advertising. (This all spilled out one night when we were staking out a counterfeit colon operation.) One fine day she was walking down one of our broad avenues, dreaming about the big bucks, the Porsche, and the condo in Sandia Heights, when she overheard one little tow-headed tyke say to another, "If I would of had twenty more cents I could of bought a milkshake."

Sure, she could have kept walking. Most people would have. But Christine Buchalter isn't most people. Before she got to the next corner, she knew that there could be no good life to enjoy in a world where nine-year-olds (nine-year-olds!) put "would" in their conditional clauses and think "of" is a verb. A week later she was in the Academy; six months later she was on the street with a shiny new badge, a badge she has always lived up to.

The next hour was almost siesta time on these mean streets. We kept our eyes open, but chatted mostly about the pennant race and good restaurants. Buch set me a poser about Middle English preterites after the Great Vowel Shift (you can take the kid out of grad school, but you can't take grad school out of the kid) just to see if the old man can still cut the mustard.

He can.

It was turning into a day that we could file away with most of the others, and there was only about an hour left on the clock when, so to speak, the pronouns hit the fan. A new office building at Louisiana and Southern had a beige expanse of stucco that practically begged to be written on. And some joker had just accepted the offer.

But this wasn't your run-of-the-mill joker, your garden-variety vandal. The deranged grin and the vacant eyes told us immediately that this was a type that we're seeing more and more often in this pressure-cooker world: the true linguipath. Growing up where grammar isn't respected, with sometimes not a handbook or even a dictionary in the house, he (or sometimes she!) has no respect for grammar. Your linguipath will split an infinitive and enjoy a good meal five minutes later: he wouldn't know remorse if it bit him.

And there he was, up on the baseline pediment with a fine-stream pressure can of Sherwin Williams #006 Teal Blue, taking liberties with language that made even me almost lose my lunch. Point of view shifts, pronoun disagreements, fragments, comma splices, dangling modifiers—you name it and he was doing it. He was flaunting this desecration, daring us to stop him, spitting his hate at us and the world. I tried to smother rage with pity.

"Stop right now, son, before you go way beyond white-out."

"Why don't you and some army try to stop me, grammar pig?" He was still writing even as he spoke, and right before my eyes he used "them" to refer to "somebody."

"How do you like *them* apples, grammar nanny"? My guts churned and tightened. He was toying with us. Our instincts told us both, somehow, that his next outrage would be an unwarranted tense shift. I was on the edge, but when I look over at Chris, alarms went off.

She had slipped her regulation-issue Biro Broadtip from its sheath. These new Biros are Japanese engineering in a sleek Scandinavian shell, beautiful correcting machines.

"Use the past tense and you're history, scumbag!" She was losing it. It was in her voice.

"Chris!" I barked. "Live up to that badge! We're not judge and jury!"

"Damn strait, missy. Listen to your buddy here," the miscreant smirked.

"That's 'straight,' you ignoramus!" Now I was almost losing it.

"I can't wipe that smirk off your face, mister, but I can tell you a couple of things. No, we're not judge and jury; we're just syntactical footsloggers doing our bit toward keeping this old city intelligible, toward keeping your sort off the streets. You probably don't know them, but there are thousands of decent people all around you in this desert metropolis, people just around the corner or just up the street or jostling past you on the sidewalk. I'm talking about people who would misplace their grandmothers before they would misplace a comma, people whose pronouns always agree, people who would never dangle anything. Those are the people we serve. They don't all know Buchalter and me by name, but they know about us and dozens like us and they know that they sleep just a little more soundly because we never—I said 'never,' mister—slack off on our job. They know that a duly appointed judge and jury will put you in the grammar slammer at least until the century is out, and inasmuch as smirking is the only diversion you'll get behind bars, I guess you can practice all you want."

My little talk had had one good result: Buch had got behind the subject and deftly wrenched the can out of his hand. He surrendered and we cuffed him. The bad element always slips up, as surely as there are two *u*'s in "minuscule," and somewhere in the city, perhaps, a tyke was dreaming about being a grammarian when he grew up. at least we grammarians can dream, too.

****

ON SEPTEMBER 23, 1995, TRIAL WAS HELD IN SUPERIOR COURT, DISTRICT SEVEN, IN AND FOR THE COUNTY OF BERNALILLO. THE SUSPECT, WILLIAM SHADRICK MEGELSON, WAS FOUND GUILTY AND REMANDED TO THE NEW MEXICO GRAMMAR CORRECTIONAL FACILITY IN CLAUNCH, WHERE HE IS CURRENTLY WRITING SEVEN MILLION TIMES, "I WILL ESCHEW GRAMMATICAL SLOVENLINESS."

When Jerry Shea attempts to think of a way to describe himself, one apt description immediately comes to his mind: "language freak." Shea is fascinated by language and the way we use it to communicate our ideas. Perhaps more importantly, Shea is dedicated to helping his students become better at using language effectively in their own writing. Shea's love of teaching becomes apparent when he speaks of his own experience as a student in Freshman Composition at LaSalle University. Shea says that as a student, he longed for his English teacher, Mr. Fitzgerald, to tell him not only what he should do when writing an essay, but why to do it. This desire to know why certain techniques improve a piece of writing has inspired Shea to attempt to provide his students with the same understanding he desired as an undergraduate. To Shea, writing is like teaching: when we write, we seek to inform our audience and teach them something. As a writer, then, Shea often creates essays explaining a certain aspect of writing that his students are unsure about. Shea describes his writing process as one which begins in confusion and uncertainty. He says that when he begins to write, he rarely knows exactly what he's trying to say until he has written for some time. Like so many writers, Shea says that the most difficult part of his own writing process is simply beginning to write; to help make starting easier, Shea likes to begin with a question which he attempts to answer in his writing. As Shea begins to answer the question he has posed, he allows the ideas to feed into one another until he finally discovers exactly what it is that he wants to say. From there, Shea moves into the process of revising, as he discards his preliminary writing, and focuses on writing about the topic itself. Although Shea often writes for his students, he says that "Fragnet" was not originally written with his students in mind. Shea says that when he wrote "Fragnet" in 1987, he did it for fun, but also because he wanted to reveal what it's like to be an English teacher. In short, Shea took his love of language and decided to play with it in his writing.

For Discussion

1. How would you describe Shea's style of writing in this essay? List specific words and phrases in the text that support your description.

2. In paragraph five, Shea describes Chip Thornton, one of his "suspects." How does Shea depict Thorton? What other stereotypes are used in the essay and why?

3. Does the grammarian in Shea's essay emerge as someone worthy of respect or as someone worthy of parody? Cite specific examples from the text to support your points.

4. As you read this essay, you may not understand all the "errors" being described. Use your handbook to decipher these "errors," and then evaluate them. Do they seem like major or minor errors and why?

5. In an interview, Jerry Shea mentioned that when he writes, he often does so in order to explain a grammatical concept to his students. What do you think Shea is trying to teach you in this essay? Use specific examples from the text to support your opinion.

6. Is Shea breaking any of his own rules in his writing? For example, think about the rules you have learned concerning how to write a paragraph. List those rules, and then

look at the paragraphs in Shea's essay. Are there any paragraphs which break the rules you've learned? List them. Why does Shea break those rules, and what effect does it have upon his essay?

7. Near the end of the essay, Shea describes confronting a graffiti artist who insists upon using bad grammar. What is Shea saying about the relationship between those who study grammar and those who don't? Write a paragraph in which you discuss how Shea depicts this relationship, using the confrontation between Shea and the graffiti artist to support your points.

8. Shea ends his essay by writing, "at least we grammarians can dream, too." How does the tone of the essay change with that sentence? What do grammarians dream of, according to Shea? How does that dream affect student writers?

9. Write a response in which you discuss grammar with Shea. What questions would you ask? How would you respond to Shea's critique of those who use "bad" grammar?

10. In "English Grammar Rules . . . but not Clearly," Scott Sanders discusses how issues of language use often preoccupy speakers and writers of English. How are Sanders' ideas reflected in "Fragnet"? Use specific examples from both texts to support your ideas.

"So, If You Want to Really Hurt Me, Talk Badly about My Language": Language(s) and Identity(ies)

Carmela Delia Lanza

Carmela Delia Lanza was born on Long Island, July 8, 1959, where she spent her entire childhood. She attended Emmanuel College in Boston, Massachusetts, for her B.A. in English and then UNM for her M.A. in Writing and is currently in the Ph.D. program specializing in American Literature. She has taught two years of high school in New York City and Santa Fe. She has taught at UNM for seven years and is currently teaching at Crownpoint Institute of Technology, Crownpoint, New Mexico.

> *Cyborg politics is the struggle for language and the struggle against perfect communication, against the one code that translates all meaning perfectly.*
> *—Donna Haraway, "A Cyborg Manifesto"*

inscribing

In her essay, "Talking Back," the African-American writer, bell hooks, describes an eventful moment in her childhood when she was first introduced to the name "bell hooks" (her great-grandmother), which she later took on as her writer's name, as her own identity of voice. She had just "talked back" to an adult which meant she had talked "as an equal to an authority figure" and was told that she was just like her great-grandmother, bell hooks.[1] Her great-grandmother was the kind of woman who "spoke her mind" and was "bold and daring" in her speech (hooks, 9). Because of this belief and expression of strong speech, bell hooks made a childhood connection to her great-grandmother that survived into adulthood. That moment in her childhood shaped her life as a writer and theorist:

> That initial act of talking back outside the home was empowering. It was the first of many acts of defiant speech that would make it possible for me to emerge as an independent thinker and writer. In retrospect, 'talking back' became for me a rite of initiation, testing my courage, strengthening my commitment, preparing

me for the days ahead—the days when writing, rejection notices, periods of silence, publication, ongoing development seem impossible but necessary. (hooks, 9)

hooks makes the decision to transform herself "from object to subject" through the act of speech and its relationship to one of her ancestors. hooks made the choice to not feel ashamed of her behavior or ashamed of this strong-minded great-grandmother. Why did she choose the journey of empowerment through writing, through speaking, instead of cultural shame and female silence? She was certainly not encouraged as a child to speak out in whatever way she wanted; she was not encouraged to have autonomy, to feel this right to express ideas that differed from her family and her community:

> I was never taught absolute silence, I was taught that it was important to speak but to talk a talk that was in itself a silence. Taught to speak and yet beware of the betrayal of too much heard speech, I experienced intense confusion and deep anxiety in my efforts to speak and write. (hooks, 7)

But hooks will not allow herself to be engulfed by this construction of acceptable behavior within her childhood world of family and community. In fact, she believes that her growing up difficulties made her more determined and more capable to deal with the rest of the world:

> Certainly, when I reflect on the trials of my growing-up years, the many punishments, I can see now that in resistance I learned to be vigilant in the nourishment of my spirit, to be tough, to courageously protect that spirit from forces that would break it. (ibid., 7)

In his essay, "The Order of Discourse," Michel Foucault examines these forces that may break the spirit in his exploration of discourse and "systems of exclusion."[2] Foucault argues that in Western civilization there is an underlying fear of allowing discourse to express itself without authority and master constraints:

> It is just as if prohibitions, barriers, thresholds, and limits had been set up in order to master, at least partly, the great proliferation of discourse, in order to remove its richness, the most dangerous part. . . . No doubt there is in our society, and, I imagine, in all others, but following a different outline and different rhythms, a profound logophobia, a sort of mute terror against these events, against this mass of things said, against the surging-up of all these statements, against all that could be violent, discontinuous, pugnacious, disorderly as well, and imperilous about

them—against this great incessant and disordered buzzing of discourse. (Foucault, 1164)

Talking back. Causing disorder. Moving from "object to subject," takes self-awareness, analysis, the ability to perceive linguistic censorship (hooks, 9). For an individual who as a child does not speak the discourse of mainstream society, who is taught that education is valuable and, at the same time, threatening to his or her identity and sense of belonging, learning the language, talking the talk of mainstream society, is no simple matter. Foucault's call of disarming the signifier is a challenging theory, but for people from working-class, immigrant, and minority backgrounds the challenge is multilayered and full of contestation. It is a house of mirrors, full of shadows and half-images regarding identity, loss of identity, community, loss of community, revolutionary acts in speech, and acts of conformity and choosing to remain part of the group.

voices

> If you and your students are from different cultures, you may have quite a bit to learn about how they see teaching styles and nonverbal communication. . . . This is not to say that your students' culture and the culture that you are representing to them are totally unlike each other, of course. Nor does it mean that all members of a particular culture are exactly the same in what makes them feel comfortable or uncomfortable.[3]

In Richard Rodgriguez's book, *Hunger of Memory*, he poignantly describes his experiences growing up in an immigrant, working-class home and living within the contested site of language and how language shapes self-identity, worldview, the sense of belonging to a community, the sense of alienation, and possibly loss. Rodriguez explains:

> For me there were none of the gradations between public and private society so normal to a maturing child. Outside the house was public society; inside the house was private. . . . I'd hear voices beyond the screen door talking in Spanish. For a second or two, I'd stay, linger there, listening. Smiling, I'd hear my mother call out, saying in Spanish [words]: 'Is that you, Richard?' All the while her sounds would assure me: *You are home now; come closer; inside. With us.*[4]

Rodriguez connects Spanish to his home, his private, intimate life and cannot imagine that intimacy, a sense of belonging, can be imposed superficially by introducing another language into the public world of the classroom. For some, Rodriguez's ideas on bilingualism and education connote racism, binary thinking, and perhaps elitism. There was considerable debate that *Hunger of Memory* supported the familiar argument that it is necessary to sever oneself from family and community (and to leave Spanish behind) in order to succeed in the world of academics. But I do not see Rodriguez's text privileging one language over another or claiming that he had to reject Spanish in order to achieve at Stanford. Rather, he is admitting to the experience of change with language when an individual moves from a private language of family to a public language of institutions. Like hooks, Rodriguez is opening, challenging the discourse of speech and stating that "intimacy is not created by a particular language; it is created by intimates" (Rodriguez, 32). He does not want his identity or his history to be owned by a particular language because it cheapens authentic intimacy and connectedness within a community. For Rodriguez his private language of Spanish will remain the language of belonging, of his parents, of his grandmother, of the noises of the street. But that doesn't mean that anyone who is taught Spanish in school or is hearing their home language in school will receive instant intimacy and a sense of belonging. For Rodriguez what is private is private and what is public is public, and he finds dignity and autonomy in that space:

> The communication of intimacy passes through the word to enliven its sound. But it cannot be held by the word. Cannot be clutched or ever quoted. It is too fluid. It depends not on word but on person. (Rodriguez, 36)

It is not enough that I can translate some Italian expression that my grandmother used or my relatives may still use and I hear my brother-in-law imitating. What is necessary, what is needed to really understand, is to sit at my grandmother's table and eat her food. Or to sit in my mother's kitchen on a Sunday morning, listening to the "Italian Hour" on the radio and watch my mother get the sauce ready for Sunday lunch.

> Some days I feel my writing wants to break itself open. Speak in a language that maybe no 'readership' can follow. What does it mean that the Chicana writer if she truly follows her own voice, she may depict a world so specific, so privately ours, so full of 'foreign' language to the anglo reader, there will be no publisher. The people who can understand it, don't / won't / can't read it. . . . In Spanish, 'compromiso' means obligation or commitment. And I guess, in fact, I write as I do because I am committed to communicating with both sides of myself.[5]

Rodriguez does not want his private language to be commodified or publicly gutted of all of its flesh. It is not the word but the person. And for Rodriguez, the person will leave and take with him or her the intimacy. He mourns for himself: the small boy who walks outside, the screen door slamming behind him, leaving one world and entering another. He is acutely aware of the fragility of his life within his immigrant family and close community and his entrance into the public world of English, the institution of education, of becoming part of a different crowd. In his journey towards English, Rodriguez admits to his difficult dance between the public and the private. He will not call Spanish his family language and yet in leaving that language of the home, he is admitting to loss of intimacy. It is an act of negative capability:

> Intimacy is not trapped within words. It passes through words. It passes. The truth is that initimates leave the room. Doors close. Faces move from the window. Time passes. Voices recede into the dark. Death finally quiets the voice. And there is no way to deny it. No way to stand in the crowd, uttering one's family language. (Rodriguez, 39)

Here is Rodriguez's house of mirrors. He is mourning the temporal nature of intimacy in his private life and insisting it cannot be contained, preserved within a particular language, and yet he is grasping for those ghost images, half-images, trying to hold on to those intimate sounds by listening to a song, or reading a poem aloud in his bedroom. It is his way to escape the public world for just a while. And his bittersweet return to what he believes is lost is his way of privileging the lost Eden, what Donna Haraway describes in her essay, "A Cyborg Manifesto," as the "wholeness imagines of the self, the tragedy of autonomy, the fall into writing, alienation."[6]

"Tell me in Italian," I ask my mother on the phone. And she can't because she has forgotten the Italian words for what she is trying to say. I feel angry with her because of this loss.

In her book of theory, poetry, and visions, *Borderlands/La Frontera: The New Mestiza*, Gloria Anzaldúa spends a great deal of time examining her language and speech as a Mestiza with a "wild tongue." She begins her chapter, "How to Tame a Wild Tongue," with a story. She is having a dental examination and the dentist tells her, " 'We're going to have to control your tongue,'" and she wonders, "how do you tame a wild tongue, train it to be quiet, how do you bridle and saddle it? How do you make it lie down?"[7] Anzaldúa, like hooks, looks at her position as a person who lives "in a country in which English is the reigning tongue but who [is] not Anglo;" as a person who cannot identify with Standard Spanish or Standard English, and she sees a landscape of creative possibility, of finding her own strengths and challenging the mainstream discourse. Unlike, Rodriguez, Anzaldúa is not in mourning. She is very aware of the ramifications of the violent, destructive act of losing a language, but she refuses to see her language as a loss or in the state of losing. For Anzaldúa, her language is rather a "border tongue," and she feels quite comfortable and strong in the space of a weblike, borrowing, breathing language. Anzaldúa acknowledges the private language of her family, but she connects it to a multitude of tongues—the media, school, interacting with Mexican immigrants, a variety of relatives (her brother married a Mexican woman and they rarely mix English and Spanish), California Chicanas. She is taking on Foucault's idea of "monster" which is an individual who is not speaking within the rules of an established, constrained discourse. Anzaldúa is not in mourning; rather she is the cyborg, the monster, the border-crosser. She is supporting Donna Haraway's request that we seek "a dream not of a common language, but of a powerful infidel heteroglossia" (Anzaldúa, 181). Anzaldúa empowers herself with this evocation weaving the contradictions into a network of possibilities:

> I will no longer be made to feel ashamed of existing. I will have my voice: Indian, Spanish, white. I will have my serpent's tongue—my woman's voice, my sexual voice, my poet's voice. I will overcome the tradition of silence. (Anzaldúa, 59)

Anzaldúa joins the group of:

> illegitimate cyborgs, not of Woman born, who refuse the ideological resources of victimization so as to have a real life. These cyborgs are the people who refuse to disappear on cue. (Haraway, 177)

I am the axe hatching out of her egg
to tell a story that will kill me someday,
I hold up my sign in front of libraries, banks,
asking if I can break down doors
and I want to define my life, not exploit it.
I change my clothes and the pronunciation of my name;
I am a harsh accent while I fall in love
with Burger King and my blonde boyfriend,
cruising my transoceanic dream,
letting my hair down over the Appian Way,

Like Rodriguez, Anzaldúa asserts that identity with culture cannot be trapped or inscribed within a language. For Rodriguez identity connects with the people in his life, with his parents' insistence on keeping family life private and their disgust of people talking on television about their divorces or marriages. For Anzaldúa identity is also connected with people and with sensory experiences that are non-speech and yet are significant events or happenings:

> For me food and certain smells are tied to my identity, to my homeland. Woodsmoke curling up to an immense blue sky; woodsmoke perfuming my grandmother's clothes, her skin. The stench of cow manure and the yellow patches on the ground; the crack of a .22 rifle and the reek of cordite. (Anzaldúa, 61)

Patricia Williams describes a similiar non-speech act that creates meaning and presence in the space of absence. In her book, *The Alchemy of Race and Rights*, she poignantly recounts tending and feeding her godmother, Marjorie, who has suffered a massive stroke and who can no longer speak. Williams writes:

> The physical act of holding the spoon to her lips was not only a rite of nurture and sacrifice, it was the return of a gift. It was a quiet bowing to the passage of time and the doubling back of all things. The quiet woman who listened to my woes about work and school required now that I bend my head close to her and listen for mouthed word fragments, sentence crumbs. I bent down to give meaning to her silence, her wandering search for words.[8]

presence in absence

Richard Rodriguez insists that language does not create or destroy intimacy, yet he does offer many powerful personal stories of his relationship with Spanish and his family life. He does not see any overlapping or mutating going on within this process. What is spoken in the home is private and cannot be commodified, and what is spoken out there in the world is public and can be commodified. Therefore Rodriguez does not fully support any regulated program requiring children to learn Spanish within a school system. He feels when educational people contend that children who hear Spanish in school will feel "more at home," they are trivializing his specific, private culture. Rodriguez is asking us not to accept superficial, easy answers to the questions of language(s).

hooks, Anzaldúa, Williams, and Haraway, on the other hand, would most likely insist that participating in and/or creating a weblike system of language(s) does not mean the individual is choosing "low status varieties" but instead is opening up the discourse in a Foucaldian way, allowing the disorder and the disruptions, to "call into question our will to truth, restore to discourse its character as an event, and finally throw off the sovereignty of the signifier" (Foucault, 1164).

In a sense all of these writers are bell hooks, as a small girl, "talking back" and in talking back, they are all gaining another layer of identity through re-connection, re-membering, and re-inventing language(s).

Notes

1. bell hooks, "talking back," *Talking Back: Thinking Feminist/Thinking Black* (Boston: South End P. 1989), 5-9, esp. 5.

2. Michel Foucault, "The Order of Discourse," *The Rhetorical Tradition: Readings from Classical Times to the Present*, ed. Patricia Bizzell and Bruce Herzberg (Boston: Bedford Books, 1990), 1154-1164, esp. 1158.

3. Earl W. Stevick, *Teaching and Learning Languages* (Cambridge: Cambridge UP, 1986), 6.

4. Richard Rodriguez, *Hunger of Memory: The Education of Richard Rodriguez* (New York: Bantam, 1983), 17.

5. Cherrie Moraga, *Loving in the War Years: lo que nunca paso por sus labios* (Boston: South End P, 1983), vi.

6. Donna J. Haraway, *Simians, Cyborgs, and Women: The Reinvention of Nature* (New York: Routledge, 1991), 177.

7. Gloria Anzaldúa, *Borderlands/La Frontera:The New Mestiza* (San Francisco: aunt lute, 1987), 53.

8. Patricia Williams, *The Alchemy of Race and Rights: Diary of a Law Professor* (Cambridge: Harvard U P, 1991), 229.

Lanza's writing process is very much connected to what she is writing. Since she is a poet, as well as a theorist, she often plays different roles at her writing desk. She has discovered that she never has a definite thesis or controlling idea before she starts writing, whether it is a poem or an academic paper. She plays around with quotations, visual images, bits of conversation, dreams. It is a circular process that involves the layering of images and ideas. Often she has no idea where the journey will take her. She has used pieces of her poems in academic papers and pieces of

*her academic papers in poems. In this essay she writes about language and identity.
She is particularly interested in the relationships between ethnic and working-class
identities and the dominant, upper and middle class cultures of America. Since she
is from an immigrant (Italian-American), working-class family, she is intrigued by
how our languages shape our public and private identities. She is also interested in
how ethnic writers, who are often from working-class culture, are frequently
marginalized within the educational system. Her essay, which includes voices of
theory, personal narrative, and poetry, attempts to show a playful, creative re-
visioning of language and identity.*

For Discussion

1. What is the thesis of this essay? Indicate the spot in the essay where you think Lanza
is presenting her thesis, and write in your own words what that thesis is.

2. Make a list of the sources that Lanza uses in her essay to support her thesis. Describe
how each source helps to support the thesis.

3. Lanza uses several different kinds of writing in her essay. List the different kinds of
writing that Lanza uses. What effect does this create in the text and how does it help to
support her thesis?

4. How does Lanza's personal experience fit into this essay? Mark the spots in the text
where she includes her personal experience and discuss the effect that her personal experience has upon the text.

5. An epigraph is a quotation placed at the beginning of a piece of writing that helps to
establish the focus of the writing. Study the epigraph Lanza includes in her essay. How
does the epigraph predict what is going to come in the essay?

6. In paragraph one, Lanza cites bell hooks, who adopted her grandmother's name after
learning that her grandmother "spoke her mind." Think about your own name. Whom
are you named for and why? What point is Lanza making about the power of names,
and how does your own experience allow you to expand upon what Lanza is saying?

7. In paragraph two, Lanza cites bell hooks, who writes about what was considered acceptable behavior in her family. What "rules" existed in your family as you were growing
up, and how did they influence how you acted and behaved?

8. Lanza uses a series of longer or block quotes in her essay to help support her argument. Re-read the essay, skipping over the block quotes. How is Lanza's essay different
without the quotes?

9. Lanza writes a great deal about the difference between public and private language in her essay. How does Lanza define the two terms? Think about your own use of language. When do you use public language and why? When do you use private language and why?

10. In paragraph eight, Lanza discusses how her family often communicates using a "language of food." What is Lanza saying about ways of communicating? What other forms of communication, besides "traditional" spoken language, exist in your family?

11. In "Fragnet" and in "English Grammar Rules," issues of language use are raised. How do issues of grammar and usage amplify, support, add depth to what Lanza argues for in her essay?

12. By now you've read three essays focusing on language, each taking a very different style and approach. Analyze the styles employed by Sanders, Shea and Lanza in their essays. How are their styles different and/or similar? What effect does style have upon a discussion of language use? Use specific examples from each of the essays to support your ideas.

In Defense of Writing What You Don't Know

Sharon Oard Warner

Sharon Warner was raised in Dallas, Texas. She earned her B.A. in philosophy at the University of Texas, Austin, and her M.A. in English and creative writing at the University of Kansas. She now teaches English and creative writing at UNM. Sharon Warner claims she had a "tumultuous" education. Because her family moved considerably during her childhood, she attended 16 different schools, all of them in Dallas. At age 17 she was attending Sonoma State and took a senior philosophy course in Marx and Engels, which led her to study philosophy. Warner feels there were big gaps in her education because of the frequent moves. She has tried to fill in these gaps through reading, and it was by reading others' work that she learned to write.

Maybe you've had a similar experience. When I was in my early twenties and a junior or senior in college, people often inquired about my plans: "So, what do you want to do with your life?" You know the question. It's a more abstract version of "what do you want to be when you grow up?" Confronted with this query, my impulse was to lie or to laugh. You see, I hadn't approached higher education with any practical aims in mind. So far as I could tell, my major in philosophy was preparing me for two things—to think deeply and live cheaply. If relatives asked about my plans, I made noise about going to law school. But with strangers, I told the truth: I wanted to write. In fact, I was already writing short fiction, and, one way or another, I hoped to make my way through writing. Invariably, these curious strangers responded to my confession by doing something I found inexplicable at the time—they launched into a story.

Sometimes, the story was short, but most often it was long and tedious, and the person telling it was earnestly involved and absolutely certain that he or she was doing me the favor of a lifetime. These encounters usually ended with the storyteller reaching across the table or the seat of the airplane to pat my hand. "You can have it," the stranger would say, as though bequeathing me a great gift. In truth, I was being given something valuable, a confidence, but I was too young and impatient to appreciate that fact. Instead, my internal response went something like this: "Don't they think I have my own stories? What's the point of writing if you're only going to tell other people's stories?"

Indeed. I've come around to thinking that writing fiction is all about telling other people's stories. Not just anybody's stories, but the stories that make you catch your breath, that make you stop and think, that make you want to crawl into another person's skin and hold still until a stranger's heartbeat becomes your own. What would it be like to grow up with two parents who are blind? Why does someone become a beekeeper, a bus driver, a child abuser? How does it feel to adopt a child, divorce your husband, deliver a baby or shoot a stranger? What do we talk about when we talk about love?

Josephine Humphreys has said that stories are "the writer's response to the most important question he can ask." She goes on to explain that "the question is simple and nearly always the same." Here, she is probably referring to those large, philosophical queries, the kind that crop up when we're children and plague us until we're old. But she would likely agree that fiction is about smaller questions as well. Simply reading the newspaper or watching the news is likely to provoke any number of such questions: Why do gang members send policemen their photographs? How can you rob a bank without a gun? What woman in her right mind would attempt to carry eight babies to term? Writing fiction is a way of satisfying our curiosity about such things. If we succeed in our quest to find out, we may well answer the questions of our readers, or else urge them to questions of their own. As a genre, as a way of life, fiction is primarily exploratory; it's an approach to understanding the world.

Back in the days when I was announcing to strangers that I wanted to be a writer, I conceived and wrote a story called, "An Exercise in Understanding." Recently, I dug it out of the file cabinet and took another look. All things considered, it isn't very good. Certainly, I wrote it knowing that it was in some sense an exercise, a way of learning, hence the title. I never tried to publish it, and I haven't thought about it in years, but I still remember the impulse that led me to write it. My Aunt Rene was my godmother, my mother's sister, a wonderful woman I learned to love when I was a small child. It turned out that my Aunt Rene was also a schizophrenic. Though she functioned well enough in my early childhood—taking me to the circus to see the trapeze artist and to the park to frolic with her little pug dogs—as I got older, she retreated into mental illness.

Later in her life, when I was beginning to live on my own, Rene had to depend upon the care of others. Sometimes, she lived with her parents, other times in the state hospital in Terrell or in a halfway house or a nursing home. By the time I was 20, I'd been to visit her in all of these places. Occasionally, she greeted me with a warm hug and smile, but often she had only a blank stare to offer. Those were the worst times, when she didn't recognize her visitor, when the things she muttered made no sense to me, regardless of which way I held them up to the light.

Once, when she was cognizant, Rene told me about a job she had folding surgical jackets. My aunt had been trained as a nurse, but she could no longer work as one. By the time I reached adulthood, that part of her life was over. If she worked at all, it was at some menial task like folding clothes, which only required that her fingers still be under her control. A few times in my life, I have loved others with an unreasonable devotion, and my aunt is one of those people. I wrote the story "Exercise in Understanding" to try to understand what it was like to be Lorena Curtis, a person whose life had narrowed and narrowed until she was left with only the thread of daily routine. Surely, part of my impulse was defensive. Schizophrenia runs on both sides of my family, and other mental illnesses plague my near and dear. As an adolescent, I was sometimes paralyzed by the fear of going crazy. Now, as a mother, I sometimes worry that mental illness will descend on one of my children.

Looking back on the story, I find little to remark about. It risks nothing in the way of plot—let's face it; it doesn't have a plot—and I certainly had a lot to learn about prose style and paragraph structure. Many of the sentences begin with "there is," an expletive construction I now mark in my student's stories. But what I still value about this attempt is the experiment itself. As the title suggests, I was attempting to enter my aunt's head. How did she think? What was a day in her life like, anyway? Could I go there and be her for a few moments?

No. Rereading the story, I realize that I did not go there. I did not find out what it was like to be Lorena Curtis. But I did do something useful, both as a writer and as a human being. I made the attempt to leave my own life and enter someone else's. In this case, I tried to find out what it was like to wake in the morning, not knowing how the world would arrange itself on that particular day, not knowing whether the people around me would be familiar or strange, and on the best of these days, to go to work at a center for the disadvantaged and fold surgical jackets. What would be the compensations in such a life? Rereading the story, I see that I was looking for them. I notice that the narrator of the story is "graced by the light from the window and the warmth it creates on her scalp." That's something, a small something, and so I still value the attempt.

One of the old saws that writing teachers haul out at the slightest provocation is this one: "write about what you know." I don't know who said it first, and if you do, please be sure and tell me. In any case, it's a well-worn maxim, nearly as revered as "show, don't tell." Beginning writers chant it to themselves and to each other. Write about what you know. Write about what you know. Said rapidly enough, the maxim could serve as a mantra, lulling one into a deep trance, a false relaxation. But what does it mean to write about what you know? And is it useful advice?

Most of us probably take it to mean that we should write about what's familiar and close at hand. Since I was born and raised in Texas, I should write about Texas. Having lived in Iowa for seven years, I might reasonably set a story in Iowa. But a story about New Mexico might be premature, even risky. I've only lived in Albuquerque for a year and a half, and we can all agree that such a short length of time is barely enough to learn how to spell the city name—all those *u*'s and *q*'s are certainly tricky. And what if I were to write out of a setting that's entirely unfamiliar? Well, that would definitely be flouting the maxim. And yet I've done just that, and so far, no one has thought to complain.

I began the story "Christina's World" because I was fascinated by Andrew Wyeth's painting of a woman sprawled in a field, staring up at a house on a hill. Who was Christina, anyway, and what was she doing sprawled in that field? In a quote about the painting, Wyeth said, "The way this tempera happened, I was in an upstairs room in the Olson house and saw Christina crawling in the field." If he knew why she was there, he never said. (Painters are curious, too, but their curiosity runs in different directions. "I search for the *realness*," Wyeth has said, "the real feeling of a subject, all the texture around it. . . .")

When it came to "Christina's World," my initial impulse was to make it all up, but a little research led to a little more, and pretty soon I was writing something I've heard referred to as "faction," part truth and part fiction. (In that wise, bub, I'm no different than Oliver Stone.) I learned, for instance, that Christina Olson was stricken with polio as a child, and as she went into adolescence, her frail legs could no longer support her weight. Rather than resort to a wheelchair, Christina got around by way of a regular kitchen chair, hitching it across the room with an awkward jerking motion. Her brother, Alvaro, who loved nothing more than the life of a fisherman, gave up the sea to care first for his father and later for Christina. They were a proud and isolated family, too poor to do repairs on the house. When the glass broke in the windows, they stuffed the holes with rags.

On their mother's side, Christina and Alvaro were related to Nathaniel Hawthorne, the writer, and to John Hathorne, the chief judge of the Salem witch trails. All this information fascinated me. By the time I was finished with interlibrary loan, I had the details I needed to bring the story to life and convince readers of the setting, Cushing, Maine, a place I've only been to in my imagination.

But my research didn't provide any answers to my initial questions: why did Christina crawl into the field; what was she trying to see? Here, I was working from the same impulses that led me to write the story about my aunt; only this time, I had considerable experience in writing fiction. This time around, I was able to immerse myself in Christina Olson's world and dream up plausible answers to my questions, and because of that, I consider the story a success.

In his profound and opinionated book, *The Art of Fiction,* John Gardner advises writers with regard to the maxim of writing about what you know:

> Let us suppose the writer has mastered the rudiments. How should he begin on fiction? What should he write about, and how can he know when he's done it well?
>
> A common and usually unfortunate answer is "Write about what you know." Nothing can be more limiting to the imagination, nothing is quicker to turn on the psyche's censoring devices and distortion systems, than trying to write truthfully and interestingly about one's own home town, one's Episcopalian mother, one's crippled younger sister. For some writers, the advice may work, but when it does, it usually works by curious accident: The writer writes well about what he knows because he has read primarily fiction of just this kind—realistic fiction of the sort we associate with *The New Yorker*, the *Atlantic,* or *Harper's.* The writer, in other words, is presenting not so much what he knows about life as what he knows about a particular literary genre. A better answer, though still not an ideal one, might have been "Write the kind of story you know and like best—a ghost story, a science-fiction piece, a realistic story about your childhood, or whatever."

While Gardner's advice is certainly sound, I agree that his answer isn't ideal. By and large, writers automatically stick to the genres they know and love the best. The only reason to do otherwise is to try and make a quick buck. I've known literary writers to dally with romance and mystery for just this reason, particularly given the climate in the present-day marketplace. By and large, though, we tend to write the sort of thing we read, or at least we do our damndest. Thus, I want to offer what I hope is more pointed advice. (Yes, I'm quaking in my boots. It's difficult to dispute Gardner, though he's left us for loftier lodgings. Even now, I feel his spirit hovering over my computer.) Here goes: rather than writing about what you know, or the kind of story you like best, write about what you *want* to know. Write about what you yearn to understand, what you're dying to experience, what you seek to explain. Write out of your own deepest longings and out of your idle curiosity. Write out of your guts rather than out of your memories.

During the summer of 1993, in the midst of the great flood that turned the Midwest into a sea fit for Noah's Ark, I attended a reading at Prairie Lights Bookstore in Iowa City. About then, Iowa was on the verge of complete submersion. Both exits into Iowa City were blocked by water, and in some parts of the city only the roofs of houses were still visible. The basement of the building where I was teaching was flooded. All day every day, volunteers labored to stack sandbags in a make-shift barricade around the Union, where I was staying. Each morning I awoke and rushed to my window to see how high the river had risen overnight.

Even so, the business of publicizing a novel goes on, and Mark Richard had come to town to read from his new novel, *Fishboy.* Considering our circumstances, the title was fitting, and a large crowd showed up to hear him. It would be the last reading of the summer at Prairie Lights Bookstore. Access to the airport proved too undependable. Much of the rest of the summer the highway would be completely under water.

In any case, Mark Richard was clearly pleased to have made it to the scene of a disaster area, and in keeping with the local atmosphere, he decided to read a short story from his collection, *Ice at the Bottom of the World.* The story is called "On the Rope" and it's about the aftermath of another great flood, this one in Louisiana. It's been a while since I heard his explanation of the story, but I believe I recollect the gist of it.

Before he began reading, Mark Richard told us he'd written the story to better understand an uncle, one of the walking wounded, a man who was most often distant and depressed. Despite the uncle's difficult personality, people in the family treated the man with kid gloves. As a boy, Mark Richard had no idea what had happened to his uncle, but as he grew older, he began to piece the story together. As a young man, the uncle had bought a wooden power boat, and he spent considerable time and money putting the boat in prime condition. The boat was his pride and joy and he'd just completed work on it when a devastating hurricane hit the coast. After the storm passed, the Coast Guard put out a call for volunteers with boats. The uncle volunteered, thinking he would be rescuing survivors, but, in fact, he was put to work recovering bodies. The dead numbered in the hundreds. Mark Richard's uncle motored out on the water in his beautiful boat and stayed out for three days straight, hauling bodies over the side and returning them to shore. And when the work was finished, some part of the uncle was dead, too.

Mark Richard wanted to imagine what the experience had been like for his uncle, so he wrote a story. The story he read to us wasn't something he knew beforehand; rather, it was something he wanted to know, something he needed to understand. And evidently, he got it right because when his uncle showed up unexpectedly at a reading in Louisiana, Mark Richard screwed up his courage and read "On the Rope." Afterward, the uncle lumbered up and gave his nephew a pat on the shoulder. "That's just the way it happened," he said.

Now, Mark Richard doesn't have psychic powers, at least none he told us about that night. If he'd admitted to being a psychic, we would have asked him just when it was going to stop raining. So when the author's uncle said, "that's just the way it happened," I don't think he was referring to the specific details, the chronology of events or the actual bodies described in the story. Rather, he was referring to the cumulative effect of those three days, the toil and the horror and the disbelief. Those are things the story describes in a very matter-of-fact way. Mark Richard used his imagination to recreate the scene and his heart to imagine the consequences. Thus, the story rings true, even to the one who actually lived through it.

Lately, it's come to my attention that fiction writers aren't supposed to write fiction. The whole, wide world isn't open to them, the way it once was. At least so my students tell me. Each writer has his or her territory, a sort of culturally-dictated, gender-specific plot of land where he or she may graze contentedly. But if the writer happens to look up and notice the far-off mountain, if the writer jumps the fence and hauls ass for points west, then all us of are allowed—nay, obligated—to frown on the offender and refuse to buy his books. Basically, this attitude amounts to a sort of subject segregation: it's no longer just a suggestion that you write about what you know; it's a dictum. You *will* write about what you know; you *will* write about who you know; you *will* write about your own culture, your own gender, your own class. And if you don't, we'll kick up such a ruckus you'll wish you'd stayed where you belong.

Surely this attitude is an outgrowth of the politically correct times we live in, and perhaps my awareness of it is exacerbated by the fact that I teach at the University of New Mexico, where the mix of ethnicities is such that the writers in my classes come from a variety of cultures: Hispanic, Anglo, Native American, African-American, among others. In any case, workshop discussions often end up in sharp difference with regard to the issue of "appropriation." If you look up the word "appropriation" in the dictionary, you'll find a denotation that mentions *stealing, seizing, taking without permission*. What does all this mean in the province of fiction writing?

Just a week or so ago, a middle-aged Anglo woman sat in my office on the verge of tears. Cynthia is an extremely intelligent and accomplished person; in fact, she has a Ph.D. in literature, and is now taking undergraduate writing classes as a way of learning the craft of fiction. She's a serious and dedicated writer as well as the mother of two young children, one of them an adopted Korean. Thus, she has a vested interest in the mingling of various cultures.

This semester, she wrote a story called "Butterfly Woman," about a young woman from the San Felipe Pueblo who adopts her cousin's baby. When the class discussed the story, the tension was palpable, and reading the journal entries, I noted that several students took exception to Cynthia's story. They thought she had no business writing about Native Americans, and they let her know it:

"You have taken on controversy by writing about a culture you do not share," one student wrote. "I have read enough 'ethnic' writing both good and bad to tell that you are not Native American. In other words, your writing doesn't give me the sense of an entire culture behind it (it never could), which automatically brings your intent under examination." Another student was even more to the point: "I don't care how good a writer the author is or how many Ph.D.s, I can't stand white middle-aged women writing about Indians or Hispanics." (It's worth noting that neither of these students is Native American or Hispanic.)

"So what do I have left?" Cynthia asked me. "Can I only write about a little white girl in New Jersey who grew up with a mentally-ill mother?"

Good question. My answer is no. No, no, a thousand times no. If I answer yes, I am exhorting Cynthia to write only out of her own life. In other words, I am sentencing her to write non-fiction. And that's not what she wants to do. In the case of "Butterfly Woman," she is writing out of her guts and out of her experience as a mother, but she's also writing to find out. She knows what it means to love someone else's child so much that the child becomes her own. But she doesn't know what it means to do so without a paycheck to take her from one week to the next, or to do so when she already has a whole houseful of children clamoring for her attention. She doesn't know, and she wants to find out. In addition, she wants to find what it's like to be a Native American on a pueblo in New Mexico and not a little white girl from New Jersey. And what better place to learn than on the page? Now it's incumbent upon her to do her research, to ask questions, and accept criticism, and in the final analysis, *to get it right,* but it is not incumbent upon her to write about herself, her history, her gender, her culture. It can't be; otherwise, we have to give up on the art of fiction, and in so doing, we may have to give up on ourselves as well.

In 1966, Joyce Carol Oates read an article in the March 4th issue of *Life* magazine called "The Pied-piper of Tucson." Although the article might have been written today, about any number of other serial murderers, in many ways it is an artifact of the sixties. The murderer, Charles Schmid, went by the name of Smitty, and he yearned to look like Elvis Presley. Only five foot three inches tall, Smitty was so self-conscious about his height that he stuffed an extra-large pair of boots with rags and beer cans to appear taller, stumbling about "so awkwardly while walking that some people thought he had wooden feet." But the boots weren't his only affectation. He also dyed his hair black, wore pancake makeup, and sported a grease paint beauty mark. In a golden jalopy, he cruised the local teen hangouts, and despite his crude makeup and his madness, girls flocked to him and bleached their hair blonde for him and in the end, three of them died for him.

Joyce Carol Oates used that article to write her famous story, "Where Are You Going, Where Have You Been?" Perhaps you've read Oates' story. It's arguably her most widely-read piece of fiction, anthologized in many introductory literature texts and praised by every writer I know. I've read it numerous times myself, and I've also read the article from *Life,* and recently I thought to ask myself why Oates wrote the story. Why write about this particular murderer? What was it Joyce Carol Oates wanted to know? (It's worth noting that the title of the story is itself a question, or rather two questions. Where are you going? Where have you been? The order of the questions suggests that where you're going depends on where you've been.)

Of course, I can only make educated guesses about Oates' motives, but the story itself provides a number of clues. The story is about *the before*—before the murder, when life was still possible for our protagonist, Connie. It begins the day before Connie is abducted, taking us through the evening, when Connie and her friend sneak over to the town's hangout, a drive-in shaped like a big bottle. There, she is spotted by Arnold Friend. "Gonna get you, baby," he said, and drew an X in the air.

And as those of you who've read the story know, he did get her. But we can't help wondering why. Why does he get her? Why does she let him? Why doesn't she slam the door on him; why doesn't she run? Lord knows, he couldn't catch her. Like Smitty, Arnold Friend stuffs a lot of junk in the bottom of his boots. Throughout the story, he wobbles and lurches and leans. During his encounter with Connie, Arnold Friend also struggles with his wig and his makeup and his pesky friend, Ellie. Clearly, the man is more facade than fiend. And yet when it comes to abducting, raping, and murdering able-bodied girls, Arnold Friend doesn't have any trouble at all. Why do these girls die so willingly?

The story provides the answers. In the first paragraph of "Where Are You Going, Where Have You Been?" we are told that Connie "had a quick nervous, giggling habit of craning her neck to glance into mirrors, or checking other people's faces to make sure her own was all right." And later in the same paragraph, Connie is described as looking right through her mother, "into a shadowy vision of herself as she was right at that moment: she was pretty and that was everything." Connie is so concerned with the way she looks, to herself and to others, that she doesn't notice the first thing about anyone else.

When Arnold Friend shows up at Connie's front door on Sunday morning, he is wearing mirror sunglasses, and what Connie sees when she looks in his eyes is herself reflected back. She doesn't see Arnold Friend, at least not until he has his stuffed boot in the door, not until he's so thoroughly frightened and confused her that she's hollow with fear. It's easy to manipulate young girls who have grown-up exteriors but child-like interiors, girls who are seduced by music and the right clothes and attention paid to their looks. After all, the culture tells them to concentrate on appearance—their own and everybody else's. It was that way in the sixties, when "Where Are You Going, Where Have You Been?" was written. It's even more that way now.

In writing her story, Oates must have discovered the ways in which a young girl can be seduced to her death, and in reading it, we discover them, too. As appalling as it is, we have to understand that our culture is complicitous with serial murderers, that we are all in some sense responsible. The messages we send teenage girls debilitate them, sapping their strength and reducing them to putty in the hands of any two-bit manipulator. Arnold Friend exhorts Connie to behave "because what else is there for a girl like you but to be sweet and pretty and give in?" Let's face it: he's only telling her what she's heard before—from the songs on the radio, from the movies and the magazines. We can't save Connie or the real girls Charles "Smitty" Schmid killed. But if we ask the right questions, of ourselves and the culture, we can save our daughters, our nieces, ourselves. The story points the way.

So here's my response to students who tell me about a writer's small plot of land: I urge them to keep jumping the fence. If men can't imagine what it's like to be a woman, if whites can't imagine what it's like to be black, if young people can't imagine what it's like to be old, then we're all in a whole heap of trouble. If we don't have the capacity to understand and empathize with one another, then all the Affirmative Action legislation, all the Equal Rights Amendments, all the marches and petitions and boycotts we can muster won't take us to a better, more equitable world.

I refuse to believe it. I argue that it's the fiction writer's job to prove the contrary, to prove that imagination is as large as experience, that indeed, imagination is one way of achieving experience. In her wonderful book, *Writing Fiction: A Guide to the Narrative Craft,* Janet Burroway says that fiction is an emotional experience we don't have to pay for. I agree. But I would add that fiction is a way of transcending our own narrow experience. If readers are expected to step into another world—the world of the book—and emerge changed, why not writers, too? All those years ago when strangers bequeathed their stories to me, I made the mistake of thinking in terms of *yours* and *mine*. Now, I argue that there's no such thing as *yours* and *mine*. It's a mark of generosity to share stories, but in the final analysis, they're *our* stories; they're human stories.

Warner says she always has possible places in mind to send the things she writes, whether it is her fiction or writing about writing. She has backlogged ideas of things to write, and her work is often inspired by classroom discussions. Warner says the question of appropriation often comes up in her classes, and claims that people are more sensitive to this issue at UNM than elsewhere. This essay came about as a result of student response to a class assignment. Students were to look for articles in the paper and base a short story on what they found; Warner wanted her students to write about something besides their own lives and experiences. With much to say about the issue of appropriation, Warner gives her interest in gay and lesbian literature as an example. Is it appropriate for a heterosexual scholar to write about gay issues and literature about AIDS? Warner insists that our interests motivate what we choose to write about, and that we need to be willing to take criticism and learn from our mistakes.

For Discussion

1. What tone does this essay take from the very beginning, and what specific words tell you this?

2. The language suggests the author expects the reader to share some common experiences with the writer. How does the personal appeal to the reader's own experience affect your reading?

3. Does it seem odd to you that the writer observes "I hadn't approached higher education with any practical aims in mind?" What "practical aims" (apart from finding a job) do you have in mind for your education?

4. In paragraph three the writer describes how she understands the process of writing fiction. To what kind of stories does she refer? Analyze the implications of Warner's metaphor. Imagine yourself applying Warner's method, and describe the experience of writing your own fiction.

5. In the final lines of paragraph four, Warner lists three aspects of fiction to explain why we read and write it. Identify those aspects of fiction, then discuss your agreement or disagreement.

6. Examine in three paragraphs the motivations for writing "Exercise in Understanding" as presented in paragraphs seven through nine. Develop each of your paragraphs through careful references to the relevant passages from Warner's essay.

7. Why does the writer quote John Gardner at such length in paragraph 16? What do you think of Gardner's advice?

8. How closely does the experience of the writer Mark Richard match that of Warner, and what point is made when the uncle says "[t]hat's just the way it happened"?

9. What is the influence of "Political Correctness" that Warner notes in paragraph 25, and have you experienced any of this here? Is "P.C." a problem? How well do you think we get along at UNM, and can you offer suggestions for change? How should this affect what we write about, read, and discuss in our classes? Compare your answer to what Professor Berthold says in his essays about what the university should be. Make reference to both Warner and Berthold in your response, as well as your own experience here.

10. Write a detailed response to the writer's assertion that it is the writer's job "to prove that imagination is as large as experience, that indeed, imagination is one way of achieving experience."

Christina's World

Sharon Oard Warner

*Sharon Warner was raised in Dallas, Texas. She earned her B.A. in philosophy at
the University of Texas, Austin, and her M.A. in English and creative writing at the
University of Kansas. She now teaches English and creative writing at UNM.
Sharon Warner claims she had a "tumultuous" education. Because her family
moved considerably during her childhood, she attended 16 different schools, all of
them in Dallas. At age 17 she was attending Sonoma State and took a senior
philosophy course in Marx and Engels, which convinced her to study philosophy.
Warner feels there were big gaps in her education because of the
frequent moves. She has tried to fill in these gaps through reading,
and it was by reading others' work that she learned to write.*

*The way this tempera happened, I was in an upstairs
room in the Olson house and saw Christina crawling in
the field.*
—*Andrew Wyeth*

I. 1928

Christina enjoyed watching the girls' hands as they fingered the shells—picking them up, turning them over slowly, putting them down again—always cautious, as though they couldn't trust their hands to do their bidding. These were well-mannered little girls whose mothers had taught them to safeguard the possessions of others, and so they were cautious, though there was no real need to be. Plump and steady with palms pink and soft as kittens' paws, the small hands held the shells to ears, to the light, and out to Christina. She declined them. Her own hands had dropped so many shells she didn't dare pick them up anymore. Not that the shells were valuable, though some were rare enough in this part of the world, but they were a legacy of sorts, something to remind generations to come that theirs had once been a sea-faring family. Besides, Christina didn't like the girls to see that her own fingers were stiff as winter twigs. While she didn't pretend that she could walk or do things she couldn't, she did stay put when the girls came to visit. If they wanted something to eat or drink, she let them rummage about for themselves. They liked being trusted to do things.

One of the girls was named Betsy, and she was Christina's favorite. Dark eyed and somber, Betsy loved the color blue and wore it nearly every day. Her dresses were starched stiff and shiny, the deep blue of Forget-me-nots or the soft blue of the summer sky. Sometimes she wore navy with a white linen collar, which made her look pale and a little somber. Christina tried not to favor, but to her, children were like cats, some easier to love than others. If Betsy had been a cat, she would have been the sort to curl up in Christina's lap and go off to sleep, a warm pulsing ball of fur.

But she was a girl, and so she sat cross-legged on the floor near Christina's chair, a nautilus resting in the pouch her dress made. In the fading afternoon light, the blue of Betsy's dress became a pool for the nautilus to float in. Christina narrowed her eyes and imagined she saw the shell drift. The room was so quiet she could hear the ins and outs of Betsy's breath. The other little girl was across the room, busying herself with arranging long lines of shells. Christina watched her for a moment, then turned back to Betsy, reaching out with one thin hand to touch the top of the child's head. Betsy's hair was warm where the sun had been shining on it and soft. Each year it grew longer and smoother. The first summer Betsy had spent in Cushing she was eight, and her hair was short and snug on the head like a cap. Right away, Betsy had been fascinated with Christina's hair, which she wore knotted loosely at her nape. Only a few weeks after they'd met, the little girl began to come over in the late evenings to comb it. Betsy told Christina that she wanted her own long hair, but her mother said no, not until she was old enough to care for it herself. Combing and braiding Christina's hair would serve as practice.

Long and coarse, Christina's hair fell to her waist, and when it was left hanging, looked for all the world like God's leftovers—red, black, grey, blonde—all sewn onto one poor head. Betsy thought it was the most beautiful hair in the world, and she came over every evening to comb, braid, unbraid, twisting the long straight strands around her sturdy fingers, trying vainly to curl them. Christina sat very still during these sessions, a little bird of happiness in her throat. Sometimes Betsy pulled the hair so tight that Christina's temples pulsed with blood, but she was careful never to betray any discomfort. Often, Betsy's fingers would stray across the back of Christina's neck, and when this happened, memories of Christina's mother would rise like vapors in the room.

Her mother had been dead for a year, but her ghost did not pass easily. At thirty-five, Christina was still more her mother's daughter than she was anything else, and so she resisted letting go. This room, this museum to the sea, had been her mother's creation. The shell picture frames, coated with dust now, had been hers. She had hung the lace curtains in the window and made sure every visitor got the grand tour. During summers, there had often been more visitors than family living in the house. Now it was only Christina and Alvaro and their father in this huge house meant to hold so many more.

Kate Hathorne Olson had been the artistic sort, and though others often questioned the quality of her work, Christina had always admired her mother for having the courage to create. She remembered the days her mother had devoted to the little shell table, days spent kneeling on the floor, surrounded by old newsprint, bottles of glue, and piles and piles of tiny shells. One by one, she'd stuck them on, covering and recovering, until finally the table was so thoroughly encrusted it appeared to have been made entirely from shells. Since then, Christina had overheard several people call it tacky. In fact, Fred's wife had once wondered aloud about the point of a table that you couldn't put anything on, but Christina knew comments like these missed the point. Her mother had left something behind besides children, which was more than most would ever do. Folding her hands in her lap, looking away from the table, Christina wondered what she might leave for others, certainly not tables or children, maybe nothing at all.

Betsy's friend was wandering about the room, her hands clasped behind her back, as though she'd decided not to touch another thing and was going to make sure her hands didn't try any tricks. Christina could see that the girl was about to say it was time to go, and then Betsy, always obliging, would stand and return the nautilus to its place before saying good bye. Once the girls were gone, the house would be unnaturally still, and Christina would feel the sort of loneliness that only came when those she liked had just closed her door.

"Do you like stories about witches?" Christina asked loudly in the girl's direction. "Did Betsy ever tell you about my ancestor? He was the chief judge at the witch trials in Salem."

"Witches?" the girl asked, turning from the window. She looked over in Christina's direction, but avoided meeting her eyes. Round, white and blank, the girl's face was like a fancy china plate, pretty but empty. Christina couldn't help not liking her very much. "Do you believe in witches?" the girl asked and then added, "My momma says there's no such thing."

"Your momma's right, dear," Christina replied. "Most people today know better than to believe in witches, but back in 1692 lots of folks believed in such things, especially folks in Salem."

"We learned about it in school," Betsy said, nodding her head importantly.

"We did too," the girl said quickly, her hand edging across the table until it found a shiny purple shell, shaped like a clam, and just the right size to fit inside the girl's palm. She closed her fist around it. The shell was one of Christina's favorites, and she sighed, wishing the girl hadn't picked it up.

"The whole thing began so innocently with a group of bored girls who wanted to know whether the future held anything in store for them." Christina paused to see whether she had the girls' attention before going on. "They wanted to know whether they would find husbands and have children, whether they had any happy gay times to look forward to. Salem was a very cold and solemn place, you see. Seems there was this servant who could tell fortunes from looking at tea leaves in the bottom of a cup."

"Really?" Betsy asked, and Christina could see that she would have been the first to believe.

"Who knows if it was true, but it was enough for the girls because the servant told them happy things that they wanted to hear. Whatever sad things she saw in those leaves she must have kept to herself." Christina smiled, thinking she told a good story. "Sooner or later, though, they were bound to be caught at their mischief, and it was the preacher himself who discovered them." Christina shook her head. "Oh, it was an awful time in Salem. To keep from being punished for doing something their parents saw as the devil's mischief, the girls said they'd been enchanted. . . ."

"What does that mean?" Betsy's friend asked.

"Under a spell. The girls said others had been making them do these things. It wasn't true, of course, but the girls were so frightened that they might well have believed it. The girls didn't set out to hurt anyone, and neither did my ancestor John Hathorne, but many innocent lives were destroyed. Those who were responsible had to pay, even their families, and those who came so much later, born far from Salem, were still somehow paying penance."

Betsy's face went from knowing to bewildered, and Christina regretted her words. The child would never understand, not even if Christina had been able to explain. Two hundred years had elapsed between the trials of Salem and the birth of Christina Olson. To claim a connection was more than silly; it was the same sort of nonsensical thinking that had brought about the trials in the first place. Still, the feelings persisted.

"Did I ever tell you about Samuel Sewall, Betsy?" Christina asked.

The girl shook her dark head. Christina watched while Betsy's friend slipped the purple shell on the window ledge and moved over to sit down beside them. She'd obviously forgotten her intention to leave. Looking down into their faces, so serious and expectant, Christina knew exactly how the whole problem in Salem had come about. No one is more open to suggestion than a young girl who's begun to feel hormones racing through her blood and the nubs of breasts rubbing against the starched front of her dress. Everything becomes at once possible, delightful, and frightening. The whole world reflects the mystery taking place in her body, a mystery no one ever bothers to explain. Was it any wonder those girls in Salem huddled together and read tea leaves to discover the future? The present was a closed box they were trying to break out of.

"Samuel Sewall was a chief juror in the witch trials," she said, looking away from their glowing eyes to the window and what she could see of the darkening sea. The waves were gathering strength, swelling as they approached land, then flattening themselves on the shore. If she stared too long, she'd begin to feel the house rock, a hapless ship at sea. Pulling her eyes away, she trained them again on Betsy and her friend, who was sniffing the air, as though something in the kitchen were burning or would be soon.

The girl is determined to keep me off balance, Christina thought, then, with sinking heart, launched into the rest of her story. "After the girls' hysteria had run its course and the hangings had stopped, sanity came creeping back to Salem, and the people who took part in condemning the innocent were filled with the most horrible remorse. Samuel Sewall was stricken worse than the rest, though only God knows why. I'm sure my ancestor John Hathorne must have suffered too, but certainly not nearly as much as Mr. Sewall. The poor man had fourteen healthy children when the trials began, but as soon as they ended, a horrible plague descended on his family. One by one his children were taken from him. A son fell to smallpox and then a daughter, too. The next year his youngest boy was thrown under the wheels of a wagon, and Mr. Sewall had only just buried him when another daughter, not much more than a child herself, died in childbirth. And if that wasn't enough misery, that summer Mr. Sewall's eldest son was shot under mysterious circumstances." She paused, weighing whether or not they were old enough to be told that a woman was involved, a married woman at that, decided that they weren't and went on. "Mr. Sewall had lost more than most of us ever will in a lifetime, but he still had a family to gather round him when his youngest son was lost in a blizzard and froze to death. Poor wandering soul. I think of him when the whole world outside is white and the wind is beating against the walls of this old house, trying to get in. One of the blessings of not being able to walk is that I'm bound to die right here in my own house." Christina's voice faded away, and all three pairs of eyes were drawn to the window. Outside, the sky was streaked with purple, a summer sky, but beneath it they imagined a boy wandering lost in a world of white. Christina felt guilty for telling them such a sad story. She knew she shouldn't before she began, but she couldn't stop. They deserved better, but hadn't Samuel Sewall's children deserved better, too? None of it made sense. There was no lesson to be learned, so why burden the children with it? In fact she could no longer remember who had told her about Sewall and his children. Perhaps she'd even dreamed it. Sometimes she had the strangest dreams. Still, in her heart, she knew it was as good as truth, wherever it had come from, and that once she had started, she had to finish it.

"Eventually," she said, pretending interest in the sunset, "they were all gone, poor darlings, all fourteen children and his wife, too. It was Mr. Sewall's misery to watch his entire family die."

"But why?" Betsy asked. Her friend was tracing her name on the dusty floor, no longer listening.

Christina only smiled at Betsy and shook her head, as if she didn't know.

II. 1935

On the first day of November, Christina woke early, even before the light that rose like a mist around the house, coloring the world around them in shades of gold, and green, and gray. Usually, she slept for several hours after dawn, but on this morning she woke in the dark, and was so chilled that she wanted only to get into the kitchen by the stove. Later, she realized her waking had been more than chance. Not that she'd known what Al intended to do, but she had noticed the restlessness in his body when he'd come through the front hallway the night before, stood in the half light so she couldn't see his eyes or mouth, and asked, "Are you certain you don't want it, Anna?" She was certain.

He only called her Anna when he meant to be formal or distant, and last night he'd meant to be both. Since their father's funeral he'd been keeping to himself, going up and down the stairs, in and out of the rooms on the second and third floors, pulling doors closed behind him with final-sounding clicks. He seemed to be looking for something, but if it was what she thought, he'd never find it in the house. What he was looking for had been gone so long he could no longer remember what it felt like. Al was a tethered animal on a long leash, and Christina was the stake that held him.

For the last fifteen years, he'd had the both of them to hold him, their father crippled with arthritis and Christina by polio. The two of them had been reason enough for Al to give up fishing for farming, to spend his days hauling wood and cutting hay, but now that Al had lifted his father from his wheel chair into his casket, she alone would be keeping him from the sea.

Since childhood, she'd trained herself against wondering what might have been: the doctors in Boston had told her she'd never get better and she'd had sense enough to believe them. What had become of that sense now? For ten nights, ever since their father's funeral, Christina had been having the same dream, a dream in which she was completely, remarkably well. She woke each morning to a damp pillowcase, and got up early to get away from it. During the day, she kept her eyes away from Al, afraid that if she caught his glance, she would know for certain what he was feeling. He roamed the house and the fields, and she watched him go, his slender, already stooped figure, going up the stairs and out the door.

"I'll be going out now," he told her on the morning of the eleventh day.

She was still making her way to her chair, and she never spoke to anyone until she was situated. The exertion often left her breathless, and when it did, she would rest in her chair until she could speak without panting. Al always busied himself with something until she was ready to talk.

"Breakfast?" she asked.

"Had a little bread and some coffee an hour ago, thank you." He was looking out the window at the season's first snow fall. Ten days ago, when they'd made their way from the house to the family graveyard down the hill, the ground had been dry, even dusty. Christina had conceded to ride in her father's wheelchair, and she remembered seeing the dirt rise in small clouds around the turning wheels. On the way down the hill, it had seemed more like autumn than winter, but as she'd sat at the gravesite, listening to the rise and fall of the preacher's voice, she'd felt the bite of wind from the north, wind so damp and chilly it was bound to bring snow. Even she, housebound most her life, knew a winter wind when she felt it. Shivering, the sharp bones of her elbows knocking against the metal arms of the chair, she'd tried to deny the joy she felt at being out-of-doors. The wind tugged at her hair, pulling it free of the neat bun one of the sisters-in-law had fashioned for her. Christina felt chill bumps rising on the skin of her arms and legs, and she sighed deeply out of happiness. The low drone of the preacher's voice brought her back for a time, but she couldn't bear to waste these precious moments mourning her father. She'd have to rest of her life for that and besides, he was out to sea now. Turning her face south to the bay, she opened her mouth to the damp salt air. How happy he must be, she thought. Afterwards, Christina sat alone in her chair at the table and felt the sea air drying her skin, pulling it taut. That night she'd had the dream for the first time.

Al went on standing at the window. He was waiting for her to say something, but they'd always kept their secrets, and she thought it best they go on keeping them. "Looks like we could get several more inches of snow," she offered, and when he didn't respond, she pulled the white cloth from the dishes on the table and draped it across a chair. If Al had been thinking of her, he'd have brought her a cup of coffee, but his mind was out to sea.

She waited, thinking he might turn and leave, but when he didn't, she hitched her chair across the floor to the stove, taking care not to put more strain on the chair's legs than she had to. Christina knew she was foolish to refuse the wheelchair, but everyone was granted a certain amount of foolishness, weren't they?

By the time she'd poured her coffee and had drank enough of it so that she could inch back across the floor without slopping, Al had left the window. She could hear him in the front hallway, knocking about and pushing the chair this way and that. It had a squeak that no amount of oil would silence. While her father was still alive, most of the time parked in the front hallway with his back to the sea, Christina had learned to ignore it, or rather to incorporate it into the small group of sounds she associated with her father: sudden yells and snorts; the gentle wheeze that meant he'd fallen asleep in the chair; that deep, despondent laugh; and the squeak, squeak, squeak of his chair. Now, without the other sounds to accompany it, the squeak was an affront to her, and she was relieved when Al opened the front door and pushed the chair outside. When he slammed the door, her cup rattled in its saucer, and she picked it up and took another sip. In a moment, she could see him from the window, coming around the side of the house, pushing the chair in front of him. He looked so strange out there in the snow, pushing that empty wheel chair. If anyone from the street had seen him, they might have thought he'd lost his senses. Briefly, it occurred to her that he had, but she pushed that thought aside and went on with her coffee. He didn't look in at her as he passed but kept his eyes on what lay ahead. She fixed hers on the tracks he was leaving. Children might have danced between them.

Four times each year, Christina got out of bed, made her way to the window, and looked out to see children playing in the fields outdoors. In the winter, they rolled huge balls of snow and carried sleds up the hill. In the spring, they dashed about wildly, picking flowers and weaving garlands. They came only once each season, and this regularity reassured Christina, who knew they weren't real. Once or twice, when they'd first begun coming, she'd called Al to the window without telling him why. He'd only looked out and then back at her with a puzzled smile. She didn't offer an explanation but went on watching the children run and shout. It disappointed her that she couldn't share them with Al. After a while, Christina stopped worrying that she was the only one who could see them, and came to regard them as the children who should have been: her mother's brothers and sisters, her own children and Alvaro's.

Today was surely the start of a new season—fresh snow outdoors and a frigid chill inside—but the children stayed away. Maybe it was her father, newly buried, that kept them from coming or maybe it was wild-eyed Alvaro, pushing the empty wheelchair God knows where. The children would have to come soon. She could see her breath in the kitchen. Surely that meant the end of fall, no matter what the calendar said.

In winter, their house was nearly as cold as the outdoors. The man who helped them cut wood occasionally once remarked that heating the Olson place was like heating a lobster trap, and Christina supposed he wasn't far from wrong. To conserve heat, they kept the second and third floors closed off. Some of the panes in the upstairs windows had been broken, and Al had stuffed balls of rags the size of someone's head in empty places, but the wind whistled right through them. Christina had seen the balls for the first time last summer when Al carried her outside to see the flowers. Because she fretted and felt guilty, he never told her when things broke or wore out. She thought they should be taking better care of things. The house had been left to them and year by year they were letting it fall apart. So he'd kept the balls of rags to himself, and when she'd caught sight of one in the upstairs window, she'd screamed loudly and tried to jump out of his arms. Already weary, Al had lost his balance and they had both fallen heavily to the ground. Neither was hurt, but Al didn't offer to carry her outdoors again, and she didn't ask.

He was halfway between the house and the shore when Christina realized that he meant to shove the wheelchair into the water. "What's got into him?" she asked herself, keeping her eyes on the small brown spot moving steadily away. Leaning across the table to get a better look, she knocked the dishes in front of her off-balance. The cup of coffee toppled in the saucer and as she leaned further, crashed to the floor. Christina didn't look after it. Al was down at the water's edge, and she wanted to see him push the chair in. It didn't go easily. When he reached the end of the dock, he lifted the chair as high as he could before heaving it out to sea. It hit the water with a splash that drenched him, but he went on standing there, stupidly watching while the chair bobbed on the surface of the water and then slowly sank. "Come back you fool," Christina yelled, banging feebly on the glass. He couldn't hear her, of course, and she could do nothing except wait until he turned and walked slowly toward the house. When he got inside his coat and pants were no longer wet; they were frozen.

"Take off your clothes and stand by the stove," she begged him, hitching off in the chair for a blanket, but by the time she got back with it, he had gone to his room and closed the door. Al lay in bed for two days, but on the third, when Christina was on the verge of panic, he got up and asked her for a cup of coffee. Neither of them mentioned the wheel chair, but Christina often thought of it. She wondered whether it had stayed in the spot where it sank or whether the currents had carried it off to sea.

III. 1939

Betsy had grown up. Christina didn't know when it had happened or why she hadn't noticed it before, but the Betsy standing before her was no longer a girl. When she and the strange young man had first come in, Christina had smiled happily at them, but now she was so sad she felt heavy in her chair and could think of nothing to say.

Betsy and her family had been coming to Maine every summer since Betsy was a young girl, and always when she showed up on their doorstop after a nine months' absence, Al and Christina would be shocked. The girl that stood patiently on the step, waiting for them to ask her in, was never quite the Betsy they remembered. She'd be taller; her hair would be longer or sometimes shorter. Each year the roundness of her childish face gave way a little more, but once she came in and dropped into Al's rocking chair, suddenly she became herself again, no different really than she had been the year before.

Christina recalled those other summers clearly. June evenings in Maine were still cool enough for sweaters, and Betsy's mother always sent her daughter off with one draped over her shoulders. More absentminded than dutiful, Betsy left her sweater exactly as her mother had arranged it on the walk over, but once inside the house, she'd shrug it off onto the table or the nearest chair. Often, it slipped to the floor and a cat curled up in it. When the visit was over, Christina stooped from her chair to retrieve it. After brushing the sweater thoroughly, she would replace it on Betsy's shoulders and send her off with strict instructions to walk quickly. In this way, Christina had hoped to convey to Betsy's mother the love she felt for her child.

Today, Betsy wasn't wearing a sweater. The unfairness of it welled up in Christina so that she had to turn her face away. Just when Betsy's family had seen fit to buy a farmhouse up the road and move to Maine on a year-round basis, Betsy had turned into a young woman. Christina would still love her, of course, but adults and children were as different as dogs and cats. People had their preferences, and hers were for cats and children. Children knew how to relax and be natural around her. They didn't have to pretend that she was like everybody else because they usually didn't notice she was any different. Adults and dogs tried too hard to be friendly and made everyone uncomfortable in the process.

Christina had to admit that the young man Betsy had brought with her was an exception. He didn't seem to be trying at all, and in fact acted as though he were sitting down with family or close friends, which was all the more odd since Christina knew he'd only just met Betsy as well. His name was Andy, and he was all eyebrows and nose and wide grin. Al was smiling too, and Christina supposed she should at least be pleased for her brother. He so loved a bit of company, no matter who it was. Christina decided she should try to forgive Betsy for bringing this scarecrow of a man. After all, it wasn't her fault she'd gone and grown up on them.

"I'm going out for a pipe," Al said, grabbing his cap and ducking his head to Andy. "Care to come?"

Christina smiled at Al. She knew he wanted both the smoke and the company but that he wanted the company more. If Andy didn't agree to go along, Al would go out on the porch and smoke alone, but he'd be wishing the whole time that he were back inside where the talk was. He'd puff, puff, puff and make himself sick to be done with a bowl full. On the other hand, if Andy were to sit out with him, he'd nurse that same bowl until dusk.

Andy didn't seem to have heard the invitation. He was standing with his back to them stroking the wall, which was nothing more than bare planks. Christina wanted to tell him to watch out or he'd have a hand full of splinters, but she could tell already he wasn't the sort to worry about splinters.

"Be glad to, Al," Andy finally said, just when they were beginning to think he'd forgotten all about them. "Mind if I do a few sketches of the house?" Turning, he shone that wide grin on the whole room. "I don't know how it happens, but some houses come alive with their own characters and histories. There's so much you can learn from a house like this if you're only willing to sit quietly and listen." He shrugged and looked apologetic for having made a speech. For the first time, Christina looked closely at him.

"Help yourself," she said.

When the men were gone, Christina and Betsy sat quietly, listening to the squeaks of the porch and the drone of the voices outside. Al seemed to be explaining something to Andy.

"Still going off to college, are you?" Christina finally asked.

"Oh, yes," Betsy replied, nodding repeatedly. "It's all I ever think about."

"Well, it's a wonderful opportunity," Christina said, knowing that it was but wishing all the same that Betsy wouldn't take it. "I don't hear them talking out there, do you? Where do you suppose they've gone?"

Betsy got up and peered out the window, then laughed and motioned for Christina. "Come look," she said.

Sighing for show, Christina hitched her chair over until she could see out. Al was no where around, but Andy was perched on the roof of his car, legs crossed Indian-style, a sketchbook in his lap.

"He's an odd one," Christina said, thinking how like a cat it was to climb up on something to gain a vantage point. Dogs never thought to do things like that.

"He told me this morning he's a pre-med student at the University of Pennsylvania," Betsy said in a voice Christina had never heard. When she trailed her hand across Christina's shoulder, the touch was so casual and warm Christina was reassured. Maybe she would get used to this new Betsy.

"Phooey," Christina said, reaching up to pat her hand. "You've got to stop believing everything you're told."

IV. 1948

One summer morning Christina looked out the window and saw bumblebees burrowing in her flowers, silly creatures buried up to their wings with only the fat tips of their bottoms showing. They looked so ridiculous with their round yellow and black bodies and those tiny transparent wings. Who would have thought they could fly? When one buzzed in the open window she couldn't imagine being frightened and shooed it away with the back of her hand. Offended, the bee stung, and a knot the size of a thimble rose on her wrist. Christina pressed a cold cloth to it, and when Al came in from lunch she hid it from him. She knew he'd just go to fretting about screens for the windows, something they couldn't afford. Besides, Christina liked being able to stick her arm out whenever she wanted to feel the outdoors, and the open windows allowed the cats to come and go as they pleased. For the cats, going out was considerably easier than coming in. The windows were too high off the ground for them to leap right through. Instead they had to jump and grab with their front claws for the window ledge, then scramble up the side of the house with their back legs, scraping and scratching away whatever paint was left. Christina liked to catch them at that moment when they gained control and made the leap inside. Always, their expressions turned serene, even haughty. She liked that about them, that they could immediately forget the struggle.

Sometimes at night, Christina would lie on her pallet downstairs and imagine herself as a cat prowling in and out of the upstairs rooms, many of which had been closed off for so long she could no longer remember what they contained. Probably, they were only bare and dusty, but she liked to think of curling her sleek cat body around dark heavy furniture before leaping onto a thick, soft mattress. She believed cats were God's most fortunate creatures: fearless, graceful, and completely independent.

Lately, a porcupine had taken to coming in, too, though obviously not through the window. On nice evenings, Al left the kitchen door open, and one night a fat little porcupine found his way inside. Lumbering across the room, he headed for the pantry, ate his fill of whatever had been dropped on the floor, then wandered back outside again. "Well, I'll be," Al had said that first night. "Looks like the animals aren't going to wait until the house falls down to start rummaging around in it."

Christina looked forward to the porcupine's visits, and took to dropping more than her share of food on the pantry floor to make sure he came back often. Once, she dreamed she touched him, and the quills weren't at all as she had imagined them to be. Not rough and prickly but smooth and polished, like hard wood toothpicks. In her dream, the porcupine even sat on her lap; he kept his quills back, and she stroked them softly and evenly. When she'd awakened from this dream, she had the sensation of doing something no one had ever done before, and she had lain very still to hold onto the pleasure it gave her. Finally, opening her eyes, Christina had stared at the ceiling, dark slabs of wood nobody had ever bothered to paint. In the half-light, the wood looked so waterlogged and heavy that she rolled out of bed and crawled as quickly as she could to the door. She'd decided then to go outside and see the house for herself.

A week passed before she could gather her energy and quiet her nerves. She went out of the house so rarely and never alone. In preparation, she surveyed all the first floor windows and decided which way to go. The front of the house faced the road and the back the sea. Either way, she was likely to be noticed. The alternative was to go instead toward the family graveyard, off to one side of the house. That direction, too, led to the sea, but she had no intention of dragging herself that distance. All she wanted was to get as far as the wild blueberries, and if Al happened to see her, she would tell him she'd come out to see how the crop was doing. He wouldn't expect an explanation, but she would give him one to keep the air clean between them.

The hardest part of going outside was getting out the door. The porch steps had all but rotted away, and there was a sizeable drop from the porch to the ground. Christina felt like one of the cats struggling to pull its hind legs onto the window sill. She had to slide slowly and carefully out the door and then off the porch to keep her legs from being rubbed raw.

By the time she reached the edge of the yard, she was panting for breath. Frightened by the pounding of her heart and the rattling of her lungs, she lay back on the ground and rested. When she stopped gasping for breath the air was suddenly filled with smells both familiar and strange: grass, ripening berries, the sea, and something else she couldn't put a name to.

No longer aware of the lumpy ground beneath her hips or the burning of her palms, Christina opened her eyes to the field that stretched all around her. Witch grass and goldenrod waved first this way, then that, and what most astonished her was the sound it made as it moved, the swish of the wind and the low moan of the grass in return. Everything made a sound, even if it were only a stirring, and everything was alive. Pushing herself to a sitting position, Christina moved out into the field. She kept her movements measured—first one arm, then the scooting forward with her hip—rather like the caterpillars that inched among her flowers. The wind loosened her hair, and it too was swept from side to side and sometimes into her mouth. Nothing bothered her now; she had never felt stronger.

Once, she stopped and put her head to the ground, listening to the silence of the earth with one ear and the whirring of the cicadas overhead with the other. She remembered when the boys used to pitch tents in the oak grove beyond the house. Girls stayed only until dark; then they walked slowly home together, chittering and twirling in the grass. The noise of the cicadas was all around; they felt the nervous intensity of insects in their bloodstreams. Christina had been like the other girls then, walking with a limp but needing only a little help. None of them ever wondered where they came from but only where they would go. She recalled they had all expected to go somewhere.

When she had pulled herself as far as was necessary, but before she looked up toward the house, Christina closed her eyes and tried to recall a photograph taken of the family in 1907. She'd been seven years old then and so proud of the dress she was wearing. The whole family had been hooked and tied and wet combed; then their mother had pushed them out the door to stand in front of the house. It had been a different house in 1907, just as they'd been different people. Painted white, with tall pines growing behind it, the house had loomed large and proud in the picture, dwarfing the family so that no one who looked at the photograph noticed the clean frilly dress Christina was wearing or Al's combed hair. The house was what was important to preserve for history, the real living entity in the picture.

Christina wondered whether it would still be so, forty-one years later, and when she opened her eyes her heart was pounding, not from the exertion but from the fear. For her whole life she'd been living inside this house, and like a soul that cannot really understand the weaknesses of the body it inhabits, she expected the house to endure, to be there even when she and Al weren't. Only recently, she'd begun to worry that it wouldn't be, that maybe the whole structure would cave in, even before she and Al were gone, and that they would have to crawl out of the rubble, like rats. She wanted to leave something behind, if not children or tables then at least this place where she had spent her entire life.

Leaning out across the field, stretching herself toward it, Christina opened her eyes. The house looked a good deal smaller from where she was sitting than it had in the photo and a good deal more fragile as well. The white paint had worn completely away, and the pine trees too, had disappeared, though she couldn't remember how. She thought they might have gone for fire wood. Now the house was a weathered gray, somehow sad and ghostly looking. These days were a far cry from the hey days when it had been the Hathorne house, and there had been a continual round of parties and weddings and births. She and Al were a humbler lot, not expecting much of their house or themselves except endurance. And she could see that it had endured and would go on for some time, shabby or no, without her.

Sighing, she turned her attention to the waning of the day, to the sounds in the grass and the smells in the air. One thing she had always been proud of: she took very little for granted. For a moment, she thought she saw a face in one of the upstairs windows, and wondered whether Andy were up there painting again. He didn't knock anymore. Like the porcupine, he just lumbered in and found what he needed. For all she knew, Andy might have been working upstairs all day. After a while, Christina forgot Andy and Al and the house and lay back to enjoy the warmth of the sun and the breeze that brushed her face and neck with the dampness of the sea.

Warner says she always has possible places in mind to send the things she writes, whether it is her fiction or writing about writing. She has backlogged ideas of things to write, and her work is often inspired by classroom discussions. Warner says the question of appropriation often comes up in her classes, and claims that people are more sensitive to this issue at UNM than elsewhere. Asked about literary influences, Warner says she has trouble answering because there are so many. She mentions Flannery O'Connor, Raymond Carver, and "the Russian writers" specifically.

For Discussion

1. The story begins with a quote by painter Andrew Wyeth describing how he came to paint a particular painting. Explain how the quote influences the writing of Warner's story.

2. Why are the shells important in the opening of the story?

3. What does the portion about the Salem witch trials contribute to the story?

4. The story is divided into sections according to time, from 1930 to 1948. Why are these dates important, and what effect does Warner achieve by breaking the story into these sections?

5. What overall theme pervades the story?

6. Describe Christina's motivation. What makes her act as she does in this story?

7. Explain the title by carefully describing Christina's world. Be sure to make reference to relevant passages from the story to support your response.

8. Read "In Defense of Writing What You Don't Know," a nonfiction piece about writ-

ing by the same author, Sharon Warner. In this essay, Warner describes how she came to write the story "Christina's World." Compare what Warner says in the nonfiction piece to your response to the story. How does the essay influence your appreciation of the story?

A Poet Hears Voices

Michelle Pierce

Michelle Pierce, a New Mexico native, took her bachelor's degree in English litera-ture from the University of New Mexico, after which she taught English in Yokohama, Japan, for two years. She has returned to Albuquerque, where she will begin her master's in Creative Writing in the fall of 1997.

The ghosts outside
rake the leaves,
say I am careless
and untidy. I wish
I could laugh
believe it was a dream.

Some can control their dreams
ask the trees questions
when confused. I wonder
if the answers are spoken
in the same way
when warning one another
about the gypsy moths or the soil.

A lost girl had said
she learned to fly there
in her dream, not with the
swiftness of a war hawk
but in a way that enables her
to travel to Andromeda
without aging.

My dreams haunt me
as if I were wheat,
the dream a tractor
progressing toward me

while I am rooted and blind
but able to hear the
sounds of metal rakes
across concrete slabs

or sometimes, I am sanctioned
to speak my mother's language
only I am no longer
one body
just two voices conversing
about the migrant rain

and many times, I have stood
silenced, watching a woman left
without her clothes
without her face. And the ghosts
laughing.

Pierce, who will focus on poetry as her main interest in the master's program, does not believe that there is one single reading of a given poem. Rather, she believes that the reader brings her own background (education, experiences, emotions) to each poem, and finds meaning filtered through her individual lens. In this way, it is possible to have as many possible readings as there are possible readers. Further, Pierce finds that the accidents which occur when elements of a poem collide in unexpected ways give birth to unanticipated meanings, and that these are often more powerful than contrived connections which lose power because they are forced. Ultimately, she believes that one must strive to be in a space where one participates with the poem, rather than judges it, and for this reason, she refuses any investment in her own personal "misreading" of her own work.

For Discussion

1. Identify the voice of the poem, and decide to whom that voice is speaking. Support your decision with particular instances from the text.

2. Examine the images which Pierce uses in each part of the poem, and the way she shifts from one image to the next (i.e., smooth, abrupt, reasonable, odd, etc.). What impression are you left with? Write an interpretation of this poem's imagery, using pieces

from the text to support your statements.

3. At the end of the third stanza, Pierce makes a reference to Andromeda. First, look this word up and briefly summarize all of the definitions given for it. Then, examine each "denotation," or explicit meaning, and think about how the "connotation," or implied meaning, shifts depending upon which definition for Andromeda you focus on. Afterward, write a paragraph explaining the use of the word for each definition (denotation/connotation) that you have come up with.

4. Pierce uses the word "dream" five times in the poem; references to "ghosts" and being haunted appear several times as well. Question the reality underlying the poem: is the "I" of the poem waking or dreaming? Or is she somewhere between? Support your position with specific examples from the poem.

THINGS THAT GO BUMP IN THE NIGHT

Urban Analysis
Paul Steiner

Paul Steiner was born in New York City in 1951 and grew up in the neighborhood described in this piece, New York's Lower East Side. He dropped out of high school at age 16 and moved to Santa Fe to live in a commune. During the following years, he did quite a bit of writing, publishing chiefly in underground presses. He has made his living working in construction, but is now enrolled as a freshman at UNM and is majoring in architecture.

Introduction

I grew up in a place and at a time when one could walk a couple of blocks, if you dared, and enter an alien world. My own block was a mix of pre-Civil War brick townhouses and Old Law tenements. The tenements were full of Puerto Ricans recently off the island, and on their side of the street men with berets and sleeveless undershirts played dominos on folding cardtables set up on the sidewalk and transistor radios beat out Tito Puente and even Perez Prado. I didn't cross the street much. At the corner to the east began the projects and I never went that way, and neither did the Puerto Ricans. The projects were black. Two blocks to the west were the Ukrainians. The blacks from the projects did not walk west, at least not on Seventh Street, although they were allowed into the Odessa Coffee Shop which had the best *pirogis* in the city. The Odessa faced Tompkins Square Park and across the park lived the slightly seedy gentry of the neighborhood, in four story brownstones with stained glass transom windows over French doors and wonderful wrought iron handrails on the stoops.

The park was a shared world, but not a mixed one. The old Ukrainian men played chess in one corner while their short square women with their hair tied up under bright printed scarves took the sun and gossiped. At the fountain in the center the Puerto Ricans brought out their conga drums and cowbells and watched sharply over the mothers watching their kids in the playground. The blacks had the opposite corner and the basketball courts but respected the chain link line of demarcation between them and the Italians in the handball courts. The winos and junkies stumbled through it all, ambassadors of brotherly love and bad breath.

Physical Forms (see Figure 1)

Edges—the edges were contextual, not physical. Each group had its own edges, streets they didn't enter, corners they didn't turn. Everyone knew which was which but there were no physical boundaries like freeways or rivers or major transportation corridors.

Paths—edges marked where you couldn't go, paths where you could. Within a gridded city block overlay I have no idea why people make a path of one set of streets and not another. I always walked west on St. Mark's Place (Eighth St) and east on Seventh. If there was a reason I can't imagine what it was.

Nodes—again, different groups had different areas which became foci for different activities, age groups, sexes, etc. The distinction between nodes and districts seems dependent on the size of the area being analyzed. If the Lower East Side is a district, then the shopping area on Avenue A is a node, but if the separate neighborhoods of the Lower East Side are each called districts, then the Avenue A shopping area is another district (or something. Maybe it's a noodle).

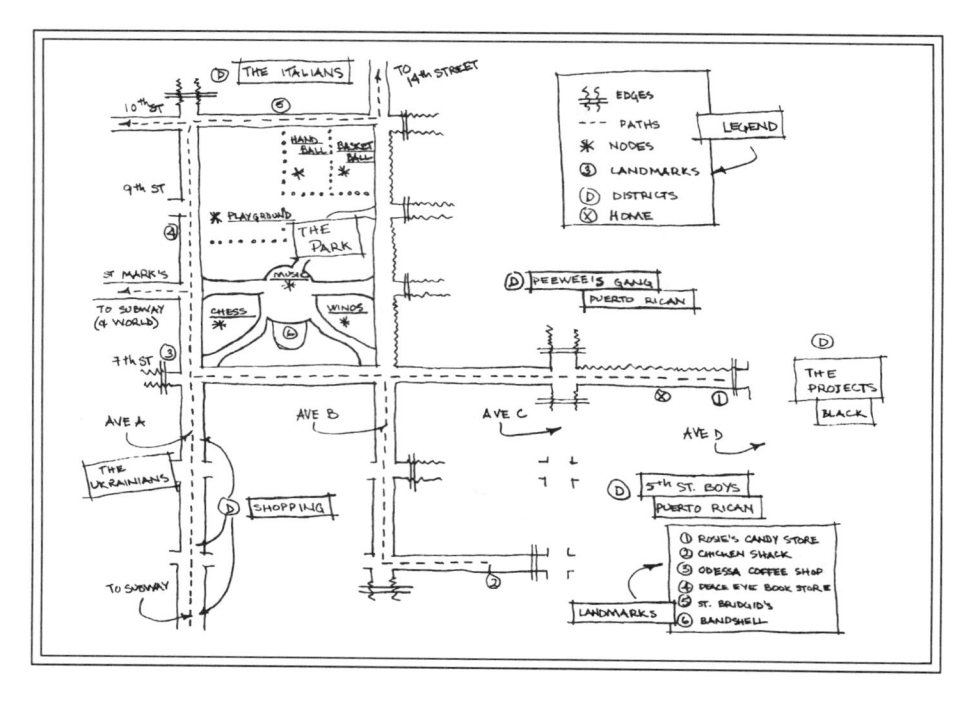

Figure 1

Districts—problematic (see above), or open to various interpretations depending on size and significance. I described the districts racially rather than purely in spatial terms, although the races, for the most part, did segregate themselves spatially. I think this is the way they were generally experienced.

Landmarks—as significant markers or points, which sometimes also function as edges or nodes, but which seemed, to me, to provide specific guideposts or references.

Conclusion—it appears to me that Kevin Lynch is proposing that we work towards making our cities legible and coherent, not that they already are. He now prefers to describe patterns (sense, vitality, fit, access, control) rather than the more rigid forms that he used in *The Image of the City*.

Lynch also says that he is limiting himself to physical objects and disregarding "the social meaning of an area, its function, its history, or even its name."[1] This would make my own analysis, which is based on all these things, a flop. But I would argue that physical objects are only "legible and coherent" if their meaning is taken into account. I don't know what legibility could refer to without meaning. And clearly no one, even in Jersey City, perceives an image of his city, sharing it with "a significant number of citizens," without sharing some sense of history, function, etc. The idea of stripping forms, or images, of their meaning may be too postmodern for me. Or it may just be silly.

Appendix: Albuquerque

To approach a city, or even a city neighborhood, as if it were a larger architectural problem, capable of being given order by converting it into a disciplined work of art, is to make the mistake of attempting to substitute art for life. As Jane Jacobs observes in *The Death and Life of Great American Cities*:

> The results of such profound confusion between art and life are neither life nor art. They are taxidermy. In its place, taxidermy can be a useful and decent craft. However it goes too far when the specimens put on display are exhibitions of dead, stuffed cities.[2]

And as V. B. Price writes in *A City at the End of the World*, "Albuquerque is a city with amnesia, a place with a fascinating past and almost no collective memory."[3] Most people living here are not connected to or aware of the past of the place. Nor is the past readily visible. Its remains, and certainly its effects, are few. Price talks about it as a case of "cultural lobotomy."

The search for legibility which is at the heart of Lynch's description of urban life will certainly continue whether people know and share in the history of where they live or not. People do derive meaning from their environment. Or maybe they create it. But whatever movies are showing in their minds as they get themselves from one place to another, the movies are certainly as important in getting them there as the cars. How this works, or doesn't, as generations grow up who have never lived in or experienced traditional urban life (in other words, as those of us who negotiate by nostalgia disappear), is an interesting question. And one to which I have no answers. I think we may need not just a different vocabulary but a new grammar.

The late J. B. Jackson said, "a landscape tradition a thousand years old in our Western world is yielding to a fluid organization of space that we do not entirely understand, nor know how to assimilate."[4] It seems likely to me that people will create villages to live in, as they always have, in one form or another. When the Middle Ages proclaimed "city life makes men free," most people pulled tight the hides which covered the openings of their dark and filthy huts, and waited for things to settle down. A very few went out, not just to the cities, but from the cities to New Worlds of one sort or another. Perhaps many will now withdraw into the womb of the World Wide Web and get their understanding of their environment from the hosts of talk radio and satellite TV.

Hart Crane's "To Brooklyn Bridge" puts it:

> I think of cinemas, panoramic sleights
> With multitudes bent toward some flashing scene
> Never disclosed, but hastened to again,
> Foretold to other eyes on the same screen.[5]

Notes

1. Kevin Lynch, *The Image of the City* (Cambridge, MA: Technology Press, 1960), 6.

2. Jane Jacobs, *The Death and Life of Great American Cities* (New York: Random House, 1961), 373.

3. V. B. Price, *A City at the End of the World* (Albuquerque, NM: University of New Mexico Press, 1992), 53.

4. J. B. Jackson, *Landscapes* (Amherst, MA: U of Massachussetts P, 1970).

5. Hart Crane, *The Complete Poems*, ed. Waldo Frank (New York: Doubleday, 1958), 3.

Steiner was quite surprised to hear that his piece had been selected for this book, as he wasn't even aware that it had been submitted. "Urban Analysis" was an assignment for Steiner's Architecture 101 class that called for him to use Kevin Lynch's scheme from The Image of the City *in order to describe an area of Albuquerque. Steiner is the son of a writer, and thus grew up believing that writing was just what one did when one was an adult. His own writing process involves an initial period of reading and research, followed by taking notes on index cards (although he often loses them). He begins to write at a specific point, when he knows instinctively where his piece is heading, even if he is not yet aware of the entire shape of the piece. As he revises, he tends to consciously break some traditional grammar or style rules, but he likes to consult a style manual in any case, so as to be aware of the rules he chooses to break.*

For Discussion

1. Chances are the structure of this essay is very different from what you are used to reading. List and describe the purpose of the four sections Steiner uses to organize the essay, beginning with the introduction.

2. List the physical forms Steiner uses to organize the Lower East Side of Manhattan. Steiner says in paragraph two that the park is a shared world but not a mixed one. Describe what each form says about the behavior of the people in the neighborhood.

3. What does Steiner mean by "alien world"? List the kinds of "aliens" and summarize how they are described in the text.

4. Reread paragraphs eight and nine. Steiner writes "I would argue that physical objects are only 'legible and coherent' if their meaning is taken into account." What harm might there be in divesting physical objects of their meaning? Who is Steiner arguing with and what is the opposing argument?

5. Based on your discussion of physical forms, look at the map and write a summary of how the neighborhood is organized.

6. Write your own urban analysis of a place following Steiner's format. In your appendix identify your place within this analysis. Discuss the everyday effect of living within this place.

7. List and describe several different social groups in your high school. How do you think others perceived your group? Were their perceptions accurate?

8. How does classifying/stereotyping both aid and hinder our understanding of ourselves and others who are not like us?

9. Based on your knowledge of Albuquerque, write an argument supporting or refuting the claim in paragraph 10 that it is "a city with amnesia" suffering from a "case of 'cultural lobotomy.'" Use examples from your own experience to support your argument.

10. Steiner suggests in paragraph 11 that we need to "share in the history of where" we come from because "people do derive meaning from their environment." Consider the place you come from and its history. Based on your own experience, do you agree or disagree with this statement? Why? Why not?

Snow on the Cactus

David Wilde

David Wilde was born in Wales in 1944 but moved soon after to London. Following the end of WWII, Wilde and his family moved to Leicester, the setting for "Snow on the Cactus." Wilde is a classical musician, and studied French horn at both the Cardiff College of Music and the Royal Academy of Music. He taught music at the University of Loughborough before attending the University of Lancaster in 1980. Following this, Wilde worked on an oil rig in the North Sea before coming to America. He arrived in San Francisco and hitchhiked to Albuquerque, arriving in the middle of the night during a blizzard twelve years ago. Wilde currently works at Zimmerman Library's Center for Southwest Research and is studying Portuguese.

It began in the time of the second World War, and when my dad came out of the army. We lived in London, my eldest brother and sister being born there, and I was the youngest. The war ended, like most human things, and my dad had bought a house in Leicester, where there was said to be a lot of work. So, into the furniture van we all piled, and headed for Leicester. At the very first arriving in Lorraine road, we were branded as gypsies—because of the house being so dirty, we had to stay in the van (removal van) to brew tea, and eat our dinner. It took a good lot of cleaning and eventually we could move in and settle down, for the next decade, or so, provided another war didn't immediately break out. Those human beings were pretty good at starting wars, and all that hullaba-loo, over race, ethnicity and land—yours, or mine?

Well, we lived up to the neighbors' expectations, and pretty soon, we had dogs, cats, ferrets, and over 200 rabbits, which we ate, or made gloves out of. My mother would kill them, by holding the ears and walloping them behind the head with a baton, or heavy wooden stick. Then they would be skinned and cooked, whilst the skins would be laid out to dry. This operation took place in our cellar, where the gypsy-police wouldn't find us. In the coronation of 1953, our street celebrated with tables in the road, like all the rest of the country was doing, and hired the local hall at St. James, for a "knees-up." We were very surprised to see a pram—perambulator—(strangely, just like the one in our back-garden), being wheeled into the hall, supporting an adult-baby, which belonged to the citizens (the hoi-polloi) of our neighbors, and realizing that, indeed, the pram belonged to us. Not very nice, we thought—but it was the coronation, and everyone was happy with the princess, now, God help us, a queen.

We had our allotment—our bit of sod—to grow vegetables and rhubarb—a pie-making essence difficult to forget, or digest—with custard. And mint, so plentiful we felt like gypsy aristocracy, the bearers of The Royal Mint, Lorraine

Road, suppliers to the empire—or what was left of it in the 1950s. A new queen, and a new allotment, for keeping us at the helm of a rather different world than before.

My dad worked at the post office, in Campbell Street (I think it reminded him of Scotland), and we did our best to get smart, at the local school, where boys and girls wore a cap and a blazer, to show where we belonged in society—even as gypsies. Occasionally, our aunts and uncles would visit us, from The Rhondda (Glamorgan—South Wales), Coventry and from America—the GI who had faithfully followed previous generations of Welsh or Irish immigrants to the New World, seeking fame and fortune. They didn't just go to Leicester. Oh, no, they had to sail half way around the world to get that out of their systems; and, who knows, perhaps they did.

In Lorraine Road, we were glad of our rabbits, and allotment, and rhubarb pie, even though we were still gypsies—the humble aristocracy of post-empire tea-brewers, not about to give in to neighbors, nor the hoi-polloi. My grandmother came once, and I recall sitting on the brown-covered kitchen table, getting my knees washed. That was the last time we ever saw each other. Later, after I had left home, for a period of training with the government—following in my father's footsteps—my mother spent some time with her, and then she died. Not very old, but a sad life by all accounts—two marriages and disastrous consequences. That's the reason my mother was sent as a boarder at St. Vincent de Paul. Probably why she liked to pose as an educated public (private) school type, instead of as a gypsy queen.

One day we all got on board the special, to go to the zoo, at Whipsnade, with brown paper bags full of sandwiches: cheese and onion, spam and cheese, and large slices of rhubarb pie—without the custard. The ride was exciting, everyone was trying to talk at once, making a great noise—the sound of freedom, from work and domestic uniformity. We sat crowded into small railway carriages, enough to make one miserable, or sad, according to how one felt about the social order of things, and ate our sandwiches and drank our "pop," or emptied the brand new thermos flasks of tea. At the station, a general rush to get off was regarded by staring citizens, with both amusement, and horror at our tidy but ambitious looks. We all made it, but some slower folk, who didn't see the need to compete, took a more gentle approach, rather like Edwardians in a Thomas Hardy novel. We had never heard of Thomas Hardy, but we had heard of zoos and wild animals. We were working-class, blue-collar folk and we made no bones about proving it—to any one who wanted, or didn't, to know it. Most people, in those distant days, didn't care—either way. Perhaps a false sense of pride—or perhaps not! Leicester, at the heartland of industry, and Whipsnade, at the heart of zoo-country—for the gypsy hoards. And the rhubarb pie with custard. A full day was spoilt when after wandering around for some lost hours, it was with horror that I found I was lost, and every one of the others had left for home. Luckily, the private car-owners, from the same district, found me, and fortunately reunited me with my mother and father, and brothers and sisters, back in the Heligoland of industry, and home, Lorraine Road. No scolding, only happy faces and thankful voices, for a lucky and safe return.

We had our first communion at St. Edwards, a small Catholic church on the main road, running through our part of the town, our neck of the woods. And when the big day arrived, we set off in all our scrubbed, and polished, and ironed, finery. My new Christian name was to be "Paul," because I liked the name: my older brother's was to be "George." I never did learn the origin, or root, of that particular attachment, unless it was our neighbor's son, George, who even at that early age, of six, or seven, had a penchant for disappearing, and who, eventually set off to trek across the globe (just like our GI uncle), to see how the other nine-tenths of humanity managed to stay out of trouble. My older brother didn't quite get that far, or inspired—or interested—because he settled into a quiet but rustic routine in the Southwest, preferring the humble life of a farmer to the exigencies of travel. Dangerous in a less matter of fact sort of existence, than hitch-hiking across the Gobi Desert. All that I recall of the ceremony of my first communion was kneeling at the altar and getting uncomfortable with the cleanness of everything—the gypsy blood, rebelling at such spiritual order— and then the late breakfast, as we couldn't eat before the ceremony, which made us so hungry—out of all proportion—that it was some time before the exercise of confessing and receiving forgiveness was repeated again.

My father only agreed to this event (as a non-practicing Christian) to keep the peace, at the behest and express wish of my mother, who, it will be noted, had been a boarder at St. Vincent de Paul, and had, it also will be remembered, been properly trained in the holy order of that institution, so we knew it was OK to take part (officially) in this rite of initiation. And it also kept the peace at our little hamlet, in Lorraine Road, to the extent that both the boys and the girls (by now there were even more of us—like the rabbits), agreed to be as good as gold, and not fight like cats and dogs when our parents were absent, or not available for inflicting corporal punishment, or dispensing summary justice. (We occasionally had the feeling we were recruits, to be shipped off at the first signs of trouble, to the front line, or the first hint of an uprising in the colonies—Wales). Sunday afternoons found us, in rubber Wellington boots, too big, or too small, odd or even—before the estates were built—walking like a band of "you-know-whats," to the small copse, or woods, in easy walking distance for us country-dwellers, where I promptly got my foot stuck in a tree, whilst attempting the "long-step" method of tree-scaling (for boys), and failing, because my too-large rubber Wellington boot—size "wrong"—had stuck in a "Y," and wouldn't let go. Can I ever get over the agony—again—of being left behind, whilst the rest contentedly pursued their leisurely stroll—their post-prandial meditations?

Wilde is self-published, and Zimmerman Library holds many of his works. He began writing as a young student, and claims that his composing process stems from his musical background. He responds to language as a musician, focusing on the musical sense of his writing rather than on the literary sense, and thus he is concerned with the idea of an authentic and unified voice. He sees revising as interrupting that authentic voice, but self-criticism often drives him to revise anyway. He often writes on the themes of emigration, travel, and the human condition, as in "Snow on the Cactus." Although his family were not gypsies, their ancestors had been and Wilde himself identifies with the label, in that it ties to his feelings of still being a foreigner in America.

For Discussion

1. Rather than fully describing his childhood, Wilde gives us snapshots capturing significant moments in his life. Draw a map tracing the places and activities Wilde writes about, starting at the beginning. Is his organization confusing or easy for you to follow? Why? Why might Wilde have chosen to organize his narrative in such a way?

2. What tone of voice does Wilde use in discussing his childhood? Reread the essay and write a list of words or phrases that illustrate this tone.

3. Wilde refers to his family as gypsies. Using an encyclopedia or other reference book, write a one-paragraph definition of *gypsy*. Be sure to include the name and publication year of your source.

4. Wilde tells us that he and his family were "branded as gypsies." List at least 10 words that you associate with the word *branded*. Using the words you came up with, write a three to six sentence definition of the word "branded." Why do you think Wilde chose this word rather than *labeled* or *called*?

5. List or circle all of the places in the narrative where the author uses the word *gypsy*. At each place, what is he saying about gypsy life? How did being "branded as gypsies" affect Wilde's childhood?

6. Describe a time when you were falsely labeled or falsely labeled someone. Why do you think it happened? What were the results?

7. Although Wilde is describing snapshots of moments in his life, the common theme of gypsy life ties his narrative together. Think about your own life. Make a list of labels or descriptions that might have fit you or your family. Choose one and use it to write a story in which you describe moments of your life that are separated by time, but seem to you to have an underlying thematic connection.

8. Both Paul Steiner and David Wilde write about the effect of environment on identity. In what ways are their essays alike? In what ways are they different? Consider structure, tone, point of view and thematic elements.

Mari Llwyd and *Kelpies* and *Pookas!* Oh My!

Carin Bigrigg

Carin Bigrigg grew up along the Central Coast in California and earned her B. A.
in English at California Polytechnic State University at San Luis Obiso, where she
wrote "Mari Llwyd and Kelpies and Pookas! Oh My!" for a 300 level composition
class. She moved to Albuquerque in 1992 to continue her studies at the University of
New Mexico, where she is currently employed as a teaching assistant and is working on her Ph.D. In addition to studying Twentieth-Century Literature and
Renaissance Drama, Bigrigg is interested in the theatre and has directed several
plays at the Vortex, including Caryl Churchill's Cloud 9 and David Mamet's Speed-
the-Plow.

CARIN: Laura! You look terrible! What's wrong?

LAURA: Thanks a lot, Carin. I can always count on you to be honest. You're
right, though, I do look pretty miserable, but after last night, nobody could look
good!

CARIN: OK, you've got me. What happened last night?

LAURA: Well, I went to bed late, like normal, but it took forever to fall asleep,
and when I finally did, I had one nightmare after another. The worst was the
first, of course, so I had trouble going back to sleep. After falling asleep, the
first thing I remember is walking and running for a long way. I was stumbling,
falling, and tripping because I kept looking over my shoulder. When the clock
struck midnight, I ran as fast as I could, but I knew it wasn't fast enough; I fell
again and as I got up, six tall figures in long, black, hooded cloaks surrounded
me and closed in until all I could see were skeletal faces and hands. They picked
me up and carried me to this run-down old church. When they laid me on the
altar, I saw whips, chains, knives and thumb-screws. The last thing I remember
was the feel of the knife on the side of my face.

Nightmares, like Laura's, aren't unusual. Everyone has had a nightmare that
frightened him/her into wakefulness, with adrenaline pumping, heart racing, and
lungs gasping. Maybe our nightmares weren't as vivid, intense or psychotic as
Laura's, but we have them all the same. Adults dream of the loss of security,
like a job or a house; adolescents visualize falling and dying or the latest slasher
movie, while children often dream of the monster-under-the-bed or the
boogeyman. As a matter of fact, the mischievous behavior of children must be
world-wide because all societies have some form or another of the boogeyman

to frighten children into staying indoors at night and behaving "or the boogeyman'll get you." In many instances, these nightmares have a common background in folklore. This is particularly true of the Celtic people. The Welsh have the *Mari Llwyd*; the Scots, *kelpies*; the Irish, *pookas*.

The Welsh *Mari Llwyd*, or Grey Mare, is one version of a Celtic boogeyman. She takes the shape of a horse, composed only of bones, and seen only at night, which chases, plays with and then eats people. She has a special liking for naughty children.

> It was the skeleton of a giant horse, staring with the blind eye-sockets of a skull, running and leaping and prancing on legs of bone driven by ghostly muscles long rotted away. . . . Silently it overtook them, head turned, grinning . . . . The white bones of its great rib-cage glittered . . . . It tossed its dreadful silent head, and red ribbons dangled and fluttered like long banners from the grinning lower jaw.[1]

With her horrifying appearance, she is, in effect, a night mare, and she holds a prominent place in Welsh children's stories. Most children hear tales about the *Mari Llwyd* from parents and grandparents warning them to obey or "the *Mari Llwyd* will take you." The disobedient child who refuses to listen to his/her mother is often portrayed running off to the fields or moors to play. Once the child moves away from the house, the *Mari Llwyd* appears, usually with death as the outcome of her appearance. However, there are stories where the *Mari Llwyd*, while playing with her meal like a cat with a mouse, outsmarts herself, and the child escapes; but happy endings are few and far between.

Like the Welsh, the Scottish boogeyman takes the shape of a horse. While there is only one *Mari Llwyd*, there are many *kelpies*, or *each uisge* in Gaelic, and they live in lochs and rivers. The *kelpies* are shapechangers, like werewolves, and while they usually take the form of horses, folklore and children's tales also depict them assuming the shape of humans. Despite their malleability, they prefer the horse shape and appear immaculately groomed and magnificently accoutered. Without a rider, such a horse attracts attention, but when the admirer pats or touches or strokes the shining coat, his/her hand becomes permanently stuck. With the human attached like a fly to flypaper, the *kelpie* retires to its loch and enjoys a nice leisurely meal.

> In Sutherland, not so very long ago, there was a number of children playing beside a loch, when into their midst there came a beautiful, and apparently, owner-less horse. Before long there was a string of lads mounted . . . and other boys there were hanging on to the beast. . . . But one boy there was, who had heard about

kelpies and their ways; and, as soon as he remembered, he tried to take his hand away; but, strive as he might, the hand of him clung. Fortunately, the boy had sense enough to recognise that the loss of a hand was as nothing compared with the loss of his life. So, out came his knife, and off came his hand. And no sooner was he free, than up rose the *kelpie* . . . high into the air it went, right over the loch, and down into the waters, carrying its human load and the amputated hand with it. And never more were those boys seen again.[2]

Despite the *kelpies'* predilection for horse shape, folk tales also have them appear human for seduction reasons. While the individual realizes the mistake soon enough, one does wonder about the motive of a *kelpie* assuming human shape. For though the real human feels and fondles the *kelpie*, the human is never physically attacked or eaten. In these instances, maybe *kelpie* are interested in breeding stock, not food.

On the other hand, the Irish *pooka, recte Puca,* while able to shapechange like the *kelpie* (and werewolves), are unable to take human form, appearing only as animals, and though the *kelpie* prefer horse shape, *pookas* have many shapes: horse, ass, bull, goat, eagle. While werewolves are believed to change only during the full moon, *pookas* can change shape at will. Contrary to the nature of the *Mari Llwyd, kelpies,* and werewolves, *pookas* don't eat their prey and are more mischievous than vicious. *Pookas* can be good or evil, helpful or hurtful, and though they are capable of killing, they do not use this ability often. Rather than eating naughty children, their primary function in children's stories is to warn children about the dangers of playing cruel tricks on animals or venturing forth at night to explore.

'[Y]ou can catch fast hold of the reaping-hook that's sticking out the side of the moon, and 'twill keep you up.' 'I won't then,' said I. 'May be not,' said he, quite quiet. 'If you don't . . . I shall just give you a shake, and one slap of my wing, and send you down to the ground, where every bone in your body, will be smashed as small as a drop of dew on a cabbage-leaf in the morning.' . . . so giving him a hearty curse in Irish, for fear he'd know what I said, I got off his back with a heavy heart.[3]

Despite this eagle's fierceness, *pookas* have been known to befriend humans; however, with their changeable and mischievous natures, it is usually better to politely refuse; unless, of course, a trip to the moon is the desired result.

Whether in nightmares or children's stories, the *Mari Llwyd, kelpies,* and *pookas* all have starring roles, especially for young children.

"[I]t had you. . . hypnotized."

"Ah," Bran said. "The original Nightmare, that thing. . . . when I was very small . . . I saw the *Mari Llwyd* and it frightened the lights out of me. Terrible. Screaming nightmares for weeks." (Cooper, 178)

Notes

1. Susan Cooper, *Silver on the Tree* (New York: Collier Books, 1977), 177.

2. Ronald MacDonald Douglas, ed. *Scottish Lore and Folklore* (New York: Bonanza Books, 1982), 115.

3. T. Crofton Croker, "Daniel O'Rourke," *A Treasury of Irish Myth, Legend, and Folklore* (New York: Gramercy Books, 1986).

Bigrigg credits much of her love of writing to her love of reading, which, she says, can be traced back to the many afternoons she spent out on the porch pouring over westerns, like Louis L'Amour novels, with her grandfather. In the fifth grade, she began writing horror stories for fun and to this day she prefers informal, personally relevant writing to formal assignments. For Bigrigg, the most important, and the most difficult, part of writing is getting all of her ideas down in some kind of form she can work with and discuss, then organizing them so that they all relate to some point. She advises having a second reader for every essay, or at least trying to be an objective reader of your own piece: "red ink gets me into a critical mentality. It gives me distance and allows me to read my paper like it is no longer a part of me— it's just something on the page."

For Discussion

1. Restate the thesis in your own words. How does each paragraph support the thesis?

2. List the characteristics of a "good" essay conclusion. Does Bigrigg's conclusion meet these requirements? Which ones? Is it a "good" conclusion? Why? Why not?

3. Bigrigg begins her essay with dialogue: what effect does this have on the reader?

4. Based on Bigrigg's descriptions, draw *Mari Llwyd*, a *kelpie*, and a *pooka*.

5. At the beginning of her essay, Bigrigg tells us that everyone has nightmares. In the third sentence she uses the pronouns "our" and "we." Why does she do these things? What affect is she trying to have on her reader? Rewrite this sentence substituting different pronouns for the ones Bigrigg uses. How might using different pronouns change the tone of the beginning of this essay?

6. Reflect back on your own childhood. Write an essay in which you tell a boogeyman tale specific to your culture or experience. What lesson were you supposed to learn from this tale? Was it effective? Did you learn the lesson?

7. Make a list of "grown-up" hobgoblins and boogeymen. Consider figures from television, film, and books, or "real life" figures like Jack the Ripper. Choose one and write a brief description. What does this person look like? What happens to the victims? What motive drives this person? What lesson is the audience expected to learn from the story?

8. List the differences between our childhood boogeymen and the more adult myths that you discussed in the above question. Based on this list, draw some conclusions about the purpose of each of these kinds of myths.

9. Bigrigg suggested in an interview that myths like those discussed in this essay "serve to inculcate traditional values, such as Christianity and respecting your parents." Using your list from either or both of the two previous questions, write an essay in which you describe the connection between several myths and the cultural values they seem to reinforce.

10. Take your response to question seven and compare it to what Jane Caputi writes in "The New Founding Fathers: The Lore and Lure of Serial Killers." What lesson does she think we learn? Do you agree or disagree? Support your response with specific references to Caputi's work.

A $20 Life

Kurt Nolte

After receiving his B. A. in biology at the University of Pennsylvania and his M. D. at the Albert Einstein College of Medicine, Kurt Nolte served his residency in anatomic pathology at Pennsylvania Hospital. From 1983 to 1984 he worked in general practice for the Public Health Service Indian Hospital in San Carlos, Arizona. In 1990 he began work in the Office of the Medical Investigator at the University of New Mexico as a forensic pathologist. Nolte has published numerous other articles, among them, "'Cookie cutter' Bullet: A Unique Projectile" (Journal of Forensic Sciences, 1991) and "Death and Dignity: The Case of Diane" (New England Journal of Medicine, 1991). "A $20 Life" was first published in the Western Journal of Medicine in 1993. The article is based on an experience Nolte had while working as an associate medical examiner in Connecticut.

The sound of gunfire was not unusual in the drug-ridden neighborhood. The car lurched forward and stopped against a utility pole, a young man slumped over the steering wheel. A woman exited the front passenger door and fled down the street. Then, all was quiet.

Birth and death are the coinage of existence. In my practice as a forensic pathologist, violent deaths are a common occurrence. Despite their frequency, I am still amazed by the often trivial precipitants. A man once shot his wife and daughter because they had persisted in serving him pork chops, which he could not chew because he lacked teeth. Another man shot his best friend in a drunken argument over how many dams there were on the lake where they were fishing. Life is cheap. Nowhere is this more obvious than in the competitive "business environment" of drug dealing.

I examined the young man from the automobile in the stillness of the autopsy room that Saturday morning and noted a small round entrance gunshot wound over the left temple. A simple hole. Surrounding the wound were the punctate abrasions of gunpowder stippling. "It's an intermediate-range gunshot wound," I told the detective, "a distance generally less than two to three feet."

The detective narrated briefly the story given by the woman passenger, who was a prostitute. The young man was a corrections' officer who had just received his weekly paycheck. To celebrate with a night on the town, he first picked up the young woman. Together they drove to another neighborhood to purchase some cocaine. The young man circled a block several times while pricing the drug with various curbside dealers. He eventually settled into negotiations with one dealer and agreed to purchase 11 bags of cocaine at $20 a bag. He pulled a wad of $20 bills from his wallet, counted out 11, and handed them out through the window into the darkness, to the dealer. The dealer handed him the cocaine and counted his money. "Hey, man! I'm short $20," he exclaimed. "No you're not, I gave you 11 twenties," replied the young man. The argument lasted 10 seconds until a supervising dealer stepped forward from against a building. "What's happening?" "He shorted me $20," said the curbside dealer. "Shoot him," authorized the more senior partner.

The detective had been at the death scene earlier in the morning, before the autopsy. I asked him what he had observed. "Not much, Doc. Just a $20 bill in the gutter."

Nolte admits that he was not particularly interested in writing early in college, but this changed when he realized he had to improve his grades to get into medical school. When he began to understand that writing well would benefit him in all of his classes and would be an essential skill for his occupation, particularly if he wished to publish, he sought out "wordsmiths," who could look at and criticize his writing objectively. He notes that, for him, the skill of writing is not really writing, but critical reading and revision. Reading critically, Nolte suggests, means "not getting so invested in your work that you can't see it or take criticism." He has, in fact, become an enthusiastic "wordsmith" himself and notes that as a forensic pathologist, where, among other requirements, he must write a report on every case he investigates, composing is a daily activity. It is, in fact, a fundamental means of sharing his work with the medical community. He points out that "the end product of research is writing. If you can't write, you can't publish your results."

For Discussion

1. In paragraph two, Nolte says that "birth and death are the coinage of existence." What does this mean and how does he illustrate it in the essay?

2. What is Nolte's attitude toward the drug buyer? Toward the drug dealer? What value does he place on their lives? Are some people's lives more valuable than others?

3. Our president has a team of secret service agents ready to protect his life with their own. For the sake of argument, assume that the president's life is the most valuable life in the country. In light of this, consider how we "value" other lives (for example, of the homeless). Placing the president at the top, list, in order of importance, people whose lives might be valued differently. Then write a justification for each person's ranking on your list. What makes one life worth more than another?

4. In this essay, Nolte describes a drug deal gone bad. What is his point? Be careful to

support your answer with specific examples from the text.

5. Use the first paragraph of this article as the beginning of your own narrative. Try to mimic Nolte's tone and style as you write a story which could have followed from such an introduction.

6. Rewrite your narrative from the above assignment as a letter to your mother as if you were speaking of someone you both know. Describe the tone of each of your essays. How does your tone change to reflect your audience? How might the tone change if the event you describe were a topic on a talk show or the subject of a sermon?

7. Make a list of a people, both historical and contemporary, whose lives became more interesting once they were dead. Choose three or four and describe how and why their deaths made them more popular. Be specific in your use of examples to support your points.

8. Write your own obituary. When you are gone, what will people say about you?

9. When discussing the function of a forensic pathologist in an interview, Nolte said of his profession that "the reason we examine the dead is to help the living." Do you think this article helps the living? Describe in detail why or why not.

10. Consider Wilde's essay, in which he talks about the effects of being labeled and valued as a gypsy. In light of this, what can you write about Nolte's characterization of the people involved in the murder?

MTV and the Co-opting of a Revolution

Sarah Janeczek

Born in June of 1976, Janeczek grew up near Louisbourg, West Virginia, but she moved with her family to El Paso in 1990. She came to the University of New Mexico in 1994 and is currently studying creative writing. Although she is most interested in writing short fiction, Janeczek admits that she enjoys essays that allow her to express her own thoughts and opinions.

I have spent the last couple weeks with the illness that is currently plaguing the students and faculty of UNM and the residents of Albuquerque, that evil cold that just won't go away. As I have lain moaning on the couch, surrounded by tissues and vitamins, I have viewed more television than I have in a long while, dismissing reading assignments for Montel Williams and MTV. I am exhausted from the war waging inside of my immune system, and from the physical pain of watching TV. I rationalized it in the sense that I was doing what I call "research" for what I feel is my duty as an American citizen: to stop people from watching MTV. The past few days have done no less than reinforce my opinion that MTV is the root of all that is evil and malign.

These are not merely empty accusations; they are rooted in my belief that in terms of sexism and racism, MTV's ideologies are utterly hypocritical. I have seen several ads urging Generation MTV to embrace diversity and multiculturalism. These ads use such hip, urban imagery that it is almost as if the network is trying to sell it in a bottle of CK One. Stylish, attractive, young "generationers" sell multiculturalism and equality.

These ads are sandwiched between reruns of "Spring Break," "Beach MTV" and "MTV Jams," a show which supposedly showcases among various slow-jam songs, the newest and freshest hip hop. It is my opinion, however, that these shows do nothing but perpetuate the sexist and racist stereotypes that MTV claims to be against.

For those who are sheltered enough (and I do mean that in a positive sense) to have never seen "Beach MTV," it is a show laden with cheesy Sigma Phi boys and scantily clad girlies gyrating to the newest Ace of Base hit.

"MTV Jams" is of little better quality: the only "hip hop" shown is that which glorifies the life of a "player," featuring young thugs driving pimped-out Range Rovers; the poetic content can be equated to that of the archetypal 1970s pimp movie, where the lyrical scripts follow that same old tired story: man meets ho, ho wants man's money, man puts ho in check, all the while defeating other sucka MCs. This degradation of women and pigeon-holing of black men as violent criminals certainly goes against the liberalism that MTV is trying to sell.

"Spring Break" takes place in South Padre Island, Daytona Beach and the like, and basically glorifies the drunken testosterone-laden antics of frat guys and their sorority girlfriends. Highlights include "The Grind," the "Club MTV" of the 1990s, on the beach, complete with girls in bikinis shaking their thonged groove things to the top 10 dance hits and scandalous camera angles.

"Beach MTV" is hauntingly similar. Highlights of this show include the bikini contest, supposedly open to amateurs only, but one has to wonder how a college freshman learned to prance around in six-inch white heels and if she used her student loan to buy a sequined thong bathing suit. In fact, such bikini contests have received criticism for using strippers to add a little bit of raunchiness to such a "wholesome" event. Again one must ask, how can a network simultaneously claim to support feminist issues and feature women in such degrading roles?

In days past, such ugliness lapsed for two hours every afternoon in the form of "Yo MTV Raps." Hosts Dr. Dre and Ed Lover filled my living room from 3:00 to 5:00 p.m., easing my teen angst and tormenting my mother. "Yo MTV Raps" features all kinds of hip hop, not just the typical West Coast hard-core stuff featured on "MTV Jams." Now, "Yo MTV Raps" has been pushed back to a most unfortunate time slot: Friday night "Yo" can be seen from 1:30 to 3:30 a.m. I am now forced to stay up way past my bedtime to catch a glimpse of the newest and best rap videos.

But my frustration does not merely rest here. I am not simply annoyed that I cannot get drunk on Friday nights for fear of passing out and/or forgetting to watch "Yo"; this annoyance goes deeper into the recognition of the racism that lies behind this corporate decision.

Allow me to elaborate. The average non-rap fan and the corporate MTV joe would probably argue a similar point: plenty of rap is shown on MTV. They would talk about the immense popularity of gangster rap and the enormous amount of media play it receives. This, however, would only further my point— gangster rap is popular because MTV makes it popular. For much of today's youth, MTV defines popular culture and dictates who and what is cool in the music business. Most young people discover new music through MTV.

"Yo MTV Raps" showcases all of the genres lumped under the "rap" label, and is certainly not limited to West Coast style hard-core rap. Much hip hop displays much more poetic versatility and musical originality, but since it is pushed back to a 1:00 a.m. time slot, it remains obscure to the typical viewer.

Think about the genre that MTV pushes onto primetime viewers: a form of media that actually glorifies black-on-black violence. Again, I implore the network executives: how exactly does this celebrate and promote multiculturalism? *Vibe* magazine has actually called for a complete boycott of MTV due to what it calls, and I agree is, the racist hypocrisy of the network.

If MTV corporate heads must be the oppressors, let them be so without the sheath of liberalism. This needs to be pointed out to our younger brothers and sisters who kneel down to the MTV god every day. If we cannot stop them from watching altogether, we can at least give them the tools to view critically, and to recognize that the network is not as revolutionary as it claims to be.

Janeczek gets many of her ideas for topics from her journal, which she has kept since she was a child. She says that being interested in her topic is the key to writing well for her. Once she has scribbled down her thoughts, she uses an outline to organize them; "otherwise the writing is a mess." The next step is sitting with pen and paper or at the computer to write out a complete draft. She says that often she prefers to write on paper because she likes "to see the word on the page." "MTV and the Co-opting of a Revolution" was her response to an assignment in an advanced writing class. She says she chose to write about MTV because her "generation grew up on music videos—they feed you a whole way of thinking, trying to tell you what you should be." "MTV and the Co-opting of a Revolution" is, Janeczek admits, a good essay, but she would still like to do more with it. Given the chance to revise, she would develop the description of "Spring Break" in more detail and would expand the section on rap with more examples of the kinds of "hip hop" she believes should receive more air time on MTV.

For Discussion

1. Look at the introduction to this essay. Circle words or phrases in the first paragraph that connect with your own background or experience. What effect does the mentioning of these things have on you as a reader? Why do you think Janeczek begins this way?

2. Who is the audience for this essay? List the words and phrases that led you to this conclusion.

3. In paragraph eight and following, Janeczek argues that "Yo MTV Raps" is a better show than "MTV Jams." List the support she gives for this argument. Pretend you have never seen either of these shows. For someone who does not watch MTV, would this be a convincing argument? How so? Which pieces of evidence are the most convincing?

4. Janeczek writes in paragraph 10 that "for much of today's youth, MTV defines popular culture and dictates who and what is cool in the music business." Write an essay in which you agree or disagree with this statement. Be sure to use examples to support your claim.

5. Why does Janeczek think it is her "duty as an American citizen . . . to stop people from watching MTV"? In other words, what is the point of her argument? Describe the places in the text where you see her making this point.

6. How, according to this essay, are MTV's ideologies "utterly hypocritical"?

7. Watch one hour of MTV and write a response to Janeczek's argument based on and using examples from what you see.

8. When asked in an interview what she thought of popular culture, Janeczek responded by saying, "I like the culture . . . if I didn't like it so much I wouldn't worry about it so much." Write an essay in which you illustrate your concerns about a particular aspect of popular culture and suggest how it might be improved. Be sure to discuss why it is worth improving.

9. Find a set of ads that feature women (for example, if you buy this car, you will attract a beautiful wife, become independent, successful, beautiful . . . the possibilities are endless). Define the role of women in American society based solely on the explicit or implied messages of these ads. Then, in your own words, describe what is accurate or inaccurate about the images portrayed in them.

The New Founding Fathers: The Lore and Lure of the Serial Killer in Contemporary Culture
Jane Caputi

Jane Caputi, Ph.D., was born in Brooklyn, New York in 1953 and attended Catholic school until the beginning of her graduate studies. This, she believes, "made [her] a lifelong feminist rebel." After receiving her B.A. from Boston College in 1974, Caputi attended Bowling Green State University, from which she received her Ph.D. in American Culture in 1982. She has been teaching in the American Studies department at UNM since then.

Jack the Ripper
He was the first.
—cover blurb from a 1988 collection
of stories on the Ripper[1]

Ted Bundy—A Man With Vision
—A Man With Direction
—A Prophet of our Times
—flyer advertising a student program on Bundy,
University of New Mexico, Albuquerque, April 1989

Freddy's [from the Nightmare on Elm Street *series]*
fame—make that notoriety—was confirmed by the
National Coalition on Television Violence, which in a
recent survey found that children ages 10 to 13 are more
familiar with Freddy and his Paramount counterpart
Jason of Friday the 13th *than with such famous historical*
figures as George Washington, Abraham Lincoln or
Martin Luther King, Jr. Jason was recognized by 72 of the
100 children surveyed and Freddy by 66, while poor
Honest Abe was identified by 36.
—Albuquerque Tribune[2]

Recently, as I watched an MTV show, "The Week in Rock" (September 16, 1989), I was taken aback as the announcer commented, "Now for some news from Boston—home of baked beans, BU, and at least one renowned serial strangler." How blithe, normalizing, and easy a reference to atrocity. Yet, why should I have been surprised? Just one year earlier, in autumn 1988, Great Britain and the United States "celebrated" the centennial of the crimes of "Jack the Ripper." Mourning, which might seem appropriate to the occasion, was notably absent (except in feminist demonstrations and writings). Rather, light-hearted Ripper paraphernalia, such as a computer game, T-shirts, buttons, mugs, and a blood-red cocktail, appeared throughout England.[3] Most strikingly, in both the United States and England, the legend of the Ripper was ubiquitously retold and millions were refamiliarized with its elements—in a massively promoted made-for-TV movie, innumerable newspaper accounts, an exploitation thriller, *Jack's Back*, and scores of new books on the master killer.

This recent mythicization of the Ripper continues a process that has been in motion since 1888. Elsewhere, I have argued that "Jack the Ripper" is father to an "age of sex crime"[4] and that his status as an ambiguous (both heroic and monstrous) cultural icon legitimates male violence against women. The crimes of the Ripper have provided a cultural category for a new type of crime (the territorial, ritualistic, nicknamed, serial sex slayer) and acted as a role model for subsequent killers, including "The Boston Strangler," the "Son of Sam," the "Yorkshire Ripper," the "Green River Killer," the "Hillside Strangler," and so on—killers who then go on to generate legends and attract cult-like behavior of their own. Serial sex killers such as these are celebrated (sometimes covertly, sometimes overtly) along a cultural gamut including made-for-TV movies,[5] rock 'n' roll songs,[6] horror fanzines,[7] jokes, pornographic magazines such as *Hustler*,[8] and extreme sadist publications.[9] Simultaneously, a parallel cult can be discerned in the adulation given (primarily by teenage boys) to the fictional screen counterparts of the modern sex killer, such as "Freddy Krueger," the child molester/ murderer from the *Nightmare on Elm Street* movie and television series, and "Jason," the hockey-masked murderer from the *Friday the 13th* series.

While such mythmaking proceeds unabated, serial murder itself has become an increasingly prevalent reality in modern, Western life. Justice Department official, Robert O. Heck, sums up the general situation:

> We all talk about Jack the Ripper; he killed five people [*sic*]. We all talk about the 'Boston Strangler' who killed 13, and maybe 'Son of Sam,' who killed six. But we've got people [*sic*] out there now killing 20 and 30 people and more, and some

of them just don't kill. They torture their victims in terrible ways and mutilate them before they kill them. Something's going on out there. It's an epidemic.[10]

Although Heck's statement is superficially correct, his language works to obscure what actually is going on out there, for the "people" who torture, kill, and mutilate in this way are men, while their victims are predominantly females, women and girls, and to a lesser extent, younger men. As these hierarchical lines indicate, these are crimes of sexually political import, crimes rooted in a system of male supremacy in the same way that lynching is based in white supremacy. That recognition, however, is impeded by longstanding tradition, as Kate Millett noted in her classic work, *Sexual Politics*:

> We are not accustomed to associate patriarchy with force. So perfect is its system of socialization, so complete the general assent to its values, so long and so universally has it prevailed in human society, that it scarcely seems to require violent implementation. Customarily, we view its brutalities in the past as exotic or 'primitive' custom. Those of the present are regarded as the product of individual deviance, confined to pathological or exceptional behavior, and without general import. And yet . . . control in patriarchal societies would be imperfect, even inoperable, unless it had the rule of force to rely upon, both in emergencies and as an ever-present instrument of intimidation.[11]

The most commonly analyzed form of such patriarchal force is rape. Early feminist analysts of rape asserted that rape is not, as the common mythology insists, a crime of frustrated attraction, victim provocation, or uncontrollable biological urges. Nor is it one perpetrated only by an aberrant fringe. Rather, rape is a direct expression of sexual politics, a ritual enactment of male domination, and a form of terror which functions to maintain the status quo.[12] Similarly, the murders of women and children by serial killers are not the result of inexplicably deviant men. On the contrary, sexual murder is a product of the dominant culture. It is the ultimate expression of a sexuality that defines sex as a form of domination/power; it, like rape, is a form of terror that constructs and maintains male supremacy.

Heck's statement invokes shared knowledge of a tradition of serial murder beginning with Jack the Ripper, that, as he puts it, "we all talk about." Indeed, we all do. In this essay, using several representative killers, I will trace some of the ways that modern culture talks about the sex killer. I will survey the folklore and popular culture representations of these killers (both actual and fictional), and interpret these for what they tell us about male supremacy, cultural constructions of monstrosity and horror, as well as fears of the future.

Father to an Age

Two women cops working twice as hard for half the glory. . . .
TONIGHT: Decoys for a Jack the Ripper.
—*TV Guide* ad for the premiere episode of *Cagney and Lacey*,
1982[13]

Imagine . . . a study of feminism from the point of view of Jack
the Ripper . . . a novel that bristles with irony and wit.
—*New York Times*, review of *Confessions of a Lady-Killer*
(1979)[14]

A third class of strangers are so utterly beyond the pale that they
seem alien not only to the group, but to the human species. I
refer to monsters, indicated by names like: pervert, degenerate. . .
psychopath . . . fiend, demon, devil . . . Jack the Ripper.
—Orrin Klapp, 1962[15]

[Jack the Ripper] that great hero of my youth, that skilled human
butcher who did all his work on alcoholic whores.
—Charles McCabe, *San Francisco Chronicle*, 1971[16]

Jack the Ribber—a restaurant in New York City

I need some help here. Some hands. Just send me anybody. Jack
the Ripper. I'll take anyone who's good with a knife.
—Hawkeye on *M*A*S*H, c. 1973*

And Jezebel the nun, she violently knits,
A bald wig for Jack the Ripper, who sits,
At the head of the Chamber of Commerce.
—Bob Dylan, "Tombstone Blues," 1965.

The ghost of Jack the Ripper hovered over Washington today.
—*ABC Nightly News*, 29, Nov. 1984 (in reference to Federal
budget cuts)

> Knock. Knock.
> Husband: Who's there?
> Voice: Jack the Ripper.
> Husband: It's for you dear.
> —*The Benny Hill Show*, c. 1980

> Mrs. Hanson . . . had always worn an extra enforcement of
> petticoats against an ever-potential Jack the Ripper.
> —Fannie Hurst, *Imitation of Life*, 1933[17]

> Traces of the Ripper's presence constantly intrude into urban
> women's consciousness. Walking down my street in Manhattan
> recently, I came upon graffiti emblazoning the Ripper's name on
> a side of a building. That same week the Lesbian Herstory
> Archives forwarded to me a threatening letter from 'Jack the
> Ripper': 'THE ORIGINAL JACK not a cheap imitation. I've
> conquered death itself and am still on this earth waiting to strike
> again.'
> —Judith Walkowitz, 1982[18]

As just this brief sampling of references indicates, the figure of Jack the Ripper preoccupies this culture in the form of a pervasive and particularly all-embracing metaphor (though, obviously, with different meanings for women and men). The mythic Ripper inspires awe and laughter, he is viewed as both hero and monster, and he is hailed by many as a key innovator, not only in the annals of true crime, but also in the imagination of modern horror. In a recent discussion of that genre, two of its practitioners, writers Harlan Ellison and Gahan Wilson, traced the origins of modern horror to Jack the Ripper:

> ELLISON: Everything that scares us today dates back to Jack the Ripper. He is still the operative icon of terror. He may be small potatoes by current standards...but the Ripper started it. He created the form.

> WILSON: Just as no one paints landscapes the same way since Turner, a creative monster like the Ripper changed the landscape of what scares us. He inspired generations.[19]

Wilson and Ellison seem quite vicariously thrilled by the Ripper, if not actually heroizing him as a "creative monster" who blazed their path into the realms of horror. But, of course, this is an expedient and gender-specific thrill; as men, they personally have little to fear from the Ripper and do not have to suffer any consequences of that aggrandizing mythicization.

The crimes of the Ripper occurred in the Whitechapel district of London, an area well-known as a center of poverty and prostitution. The still unknown killer has been credited with as many as 20 murders, although probably only five were the work of the one man; others were imitative or unconnected crimes. The killer made no attempt to cover up his actions. Rather, he left the bodies on display, out on the open street in four instances. Furthermore, he (or, far more likely, someone pretending to be the killer) advertised his crimes by writing letters to police, press, and citizen groups, nicknaming himself in one letter, taunting the police, predicting future crimes, and even mailing in half of a human kidney to the chief of a Whitechapel vigilance group (the letter writer claimed to have eaten the other half). The victims, all prostitutes, were not raped; their throats were slit from behind and then the sexual and other organs were severely mutilated. While similar atrocities indubitably had occurred before, indicated, perhaps, in legends of werewolves and vampires, or tracked as isolated incidents of "lust murder" in the nineteenth century, it was not until 1888 in London that the idea of a sexually motivated criminal, specializing in mutilation, dismemberment, and murder, first took shape as a cultural icon.[20]

Many have asked why Jack the Ripper, more than other sex criminals, has left such a mark? Nigel Morland avers: "The melodramatic name of Jack the Ripper . . . is largely the reason for his immortality, that and the imaginative folk lore which has always surrounded him."[21] In truth, the identity of the Ripper never has been established; this evocative anonymity has been a source for much of the Ripper lore as self-proclaimed "Ripperologists" and "Ripperophiles" continually sift over the known information, proposing improbable and often highly romanticized possible identities (e.g., a member of the royal family).

Another factor, along with this anonymity, further enabled the mythicization process: the crimes of the Ripper stand as one of the first media events. As historian Judith Walkowitz noted: "One cannot emphasize too much the role of the popular press, itself a creation of the 1880s, in establishing Jack the Ripper as a media hero, in amplifying the terror of male violence, and in elaborating and interpreting the meaning of the Ripper murders to a 'mass' audience."[22] A key feature of that elaboration was the wedding of the crimes to traditional horror images and formulae. "Unable to find historical precedents for the Whitechapel 'horrors,' commentators resorted to horrifying fictional analogues."[23] Here are the beginnings of the Ripper mythos—the sex killer as human monster, master criminal, immortal being—as well as the origins of his role as a stock character in twentieth century literature. Jack the Ripper has been a recurring figure in popular and serious fictions (beginning with Frank Wedekind's *Die Busche der Pandora*, 1904, and Marie Belloc Lowndes' story "The Lodger," 1913), in films (e.g., Nicholas Meyer's *Time After Time*, 1979), television dramas, (most notably as an immortal alien entity on *Star Trek*), and songs (e.g., Link Wray's "Jack the Ripper," 1959, Screamin' Lord Sutch and the Savages' "Hands of Jack the Ripper," c.1969).

Still, the reasons why the Ripper has become so solidly entrenched as a cultural icon go beyond his colorful nickname or the fortuitous collaboration of the nineteenth century popular press. His enduring popularity, instead, primarily is rooted in the patriarchal foundations of the modern world and his essential meaning is as an emblem of misogynist terrorism. Horror writers might expediently celebrate the mythic ripper as a "creative monster" who "inspired generations"—I assume they mean of horror writers. Yet, the Ripper legend also has inspired generations of misogynist men, both armchair criminals who enjoy identifying with the Ripper in the various fictional portrayals as well as actual killers who directly indicate that they were emulating the Ripper.[24]

As time goes by, the Ripper's mythic representations have only increased and a bibliographic essay listing all of the forms in which the Ripper makes an appearance would run well into hundreds of items. Three interconnected themes recur in this accumulated Ripper lore: (1) the immortality of the Ripper; (2) the confusion of the historical and fictional criminal; and (3) the establishment of a sex-murder tradition, built upon the Ripper's original crimes.

In 1905, British children jumped rope to this chant: "Jack the Ripper's dead/ And lying on his bed. He cut his throat with Sunlight Soap/ Jack the Ripper's dead."[25] Still, that is one of the very few times the Ripper has died in the popular mind. Rather, his primary persona is that of an immortal and continually lethal presence. This notion was introduced to a mass audience by Robert Bloch in his 1942 short story, "Your's Truly, Jack the Ripper"[26] and subsequently has been imitated countless times. In the 1979 film, *Time After Time*, Jack the Ripper actually travels into the present through his unsuspecting friend H. G. Wells' time machine. The horrified Wells is finally able to dispatch him via that very machine, sending him, as perfectly befits a mythic creature, "into *infinity*, where he really belongs."

A startling juxtaposition of stories in the October 30, 1979, issue of *US Magazine* illustrates both the second and third themes. The first, a news story on a series of sex slayings in Yorkshire claims: "A New Jack the Ripper is Terrorizing England." On the very next page, a headline for a story on the film *Time After Time* reads: "The Stars Really Fall in Love in a New Jack the Ripper Flick." This placement collapses the "New Jack the Ripper" almost imperceptibly into the "New Jack the Ripper Flick," as if there really were no substantial difference between the two. Such juxtapositions may lead us to consider the ways that the incessant mythicization/heroization of the misogynist killer encourages the emergence of "New Jack the Rippers," men eager to fill out the archetype of the criminal genius/monster, whose exploits are reviled but simultaneously celebrated in the popular culture.

A number of writers from a variety of perspectives have surveyed the lore surrounding the Ripper and it is not my intention to recapitulate that material in any greater depth here. Rather, having established the prominence and prevalence of Ripper lore, I want to concentrate on the much less analyzed personae and lores of several men who come from the "generations" inspired by Jack the Ripper, killers such as Ted Bundy and David Berkowitz.

"America's Jack the Ripper"

> So let's salute the mighty Bundy,
> Here on Friday, gone on Monday.
> All his roads lead out of town.
> It's hard to keep a good man down.
> —An Aspen folk singer, celebrating Bundy's first prison escape, 1978[27]

In 1981, when the *Reader's Digest* published an original article on Ted Bundy, its cover blurb announced: "Caught: America's Jack the Ripper."[28] In some ways, this seemed mere hyperbole. The two killers were not that alike: Bundy selected college coeds, not prostitutes, as his victims and he hid the bodies, rather than displayed them. Nevertheless, just as Jack the Ripper seemed to personify the underside of Victorian England, so too Ted Bundy epitomized his society, presenting a persona of the superficially ideal, all-American boy. Ironically, it was just months after the 1988 centennial celebration for the mythic father of sexual murder that the focus effortlessly shifted to that paradigmatic son, Bundy—to the drama leading up to his execution, January 24, 1989, and the revelry that accompanied it. In the days preceding his death, Bundy's story dominated the mass media, memorializing and further mythicizing a killer who had already been the subject of scores of book chapters, articles, five books, and a made-for-TV movie (where he was played by Mark Harmon, an actor whom *People Weekly* once gushed over as the "world's sexiest man"). On the morning Bundy went to the electric chair, hundreds (from photographs of the event, the crowd seemed to be composed largely of men) gathered across the street from the prison. Many wore specially designed costumes, waved banners proclaiming a "Bundy BBQ" or "I like my Ted well done," and chanted songs such as "He bludgeoned the poor girls, all over the head. Now we're all ecstatic, Ted Bundy is dead."

The most common journalistic metaphors for the overall scene were that of a carnival, circus, or tailgate party before a big game.[29]

This sort of spontaneous outpouring of folk sentiment regarding Ted Bundy was not without precedent. In the late 1970s, when he was awaiting trial for the murder of Caryn Campbell in Aspen, Colorado, Bundy managed to escape twice. The first time he was caught and returned to custody; the second time he was successful and traveled to Florida. But upon the news of his escapes (particularly the first) a phenomenal reaction occurred. All observers concur: "In Aspen, Bundy had become a folk hero."[30] "Ted achieved the status of Billy the Kid at least";[31] "Aspen reacted as if Bundy were some sort of Robin Hood instead of a suspected mass murderer. A folklore sprang up out of the thin Rocky Mountain air."[32] T-shirts appeared reading: "Ted Bundy is a One Night Stand." Radio KSNO programmed a Ted Bundy request hour, playing songs like: "Ain't No Way to Treat a Lady." A local restaurant offered a "Bundyburger" consisting of nothing more than a plain roll: "Open it and see the meat has fled," explained a sign. Yet after his second escape, the FBI took Bundy seriously enough to name him to their 10 Most Wanted List, seeking him "in connection with 36 similar-type sexual slayings throughout several Western states."

Just as Bundy's young, white, generally middle-class victims were stereotypically (and with marked racist and classic bias) universalized as "anyone's daughters," Bundy himself was depicted as the fatherland's (almost) ideal son—handsome, intelligent, a former law student, a rising star in Seattle's Republican party. And although that idealization falls apart upon examination— he had to drop out of law school due to bad grades; he was chronically unhappy and habitually abused alcohol; he was a nailbiter and a nosepicker—it provided an attractive mythic persona for purposes of identification. As several feminist analysts[33] have noted, a recurrent and vivid pattern accompanying episodes of sensationalized sex murder is ordinary male identification with the sex killer, as revealed in "jokes, innuendoes, veiled threats (I might be the Strangler, you know)."[34] Such joking followed Bundy's murder of two sorority women at the Chi Omega House at the University of Florida, Tallahassee. As one woman who lived there at the time remembered:

> Probably the most disturbing thing was the series of jokes and innuendoes that men traded about the murders. My boyfriend at the time was a public defender, and it was his office that represented Bundy at trial. He heard a lot of comments by virtue of being male and working close to the investigation that I probably would never have heard otherwise. We talked recently and he said there were basically two kinds of humor about the killings: (1) sorority-related jokes, (2) jokes

which connected the violence of torn-off nipples and bite marks on the victims to Bundy's sexual 'appetite' as in 'eating' the victims sexually or sometimes, literally. One such joke was: 'What do you get when you have a Tri Delt, a Chi O, and a Phi Mu? A three-course dinner for Ted Bundy.' What could possibly be behind this kind of humor? I really don't buy the theory that these jokes help to reduce the stress of a horrible event. I think they just reduce the horror of the event in order to make it acceptable.[35]

After his first escape, the male identification was with Bundy as a rebel, an outlaw hero. When he was on trial for murder in Florida, as the joking there indicated, he provided fodder for some sadistic sexual fantasies. But subsequently, Bundy did the supremely unmanly thing of confessing to his crimes and manifesting fear of death. No longer qualifying as hero, Bundy was now cast into the complementary role of scapegoat. The "bloodthirsty revelers" who partied outside as Bundy was executed, through their objectification and disrespect for the victims and lust for death, still mirrored Bundy, but now delightedly demanded that the all-American boy die as a token sacrifice for his and their sins.

Elements, frequently obscure, of Bundy lore now can be found in various places. Students in a popular culture class tell me that they are sure that the name of the family (Bundy) on the Fox network's parodic sitcom *Married With Children* deliberately recalls the notorious Ted Bundy and is a subtle reference to the down side of "happy" American family life. The punk band, Jane's Addiction, on a 1988 album, includes a song, "Ted, Just Admit It."[36] (This was before Bundy had confessed.) Here, they sing of television news being "just another show with sex and violence" and chant over and over that "sex is violent." But I encountered the most startling mythicization of Bundy last spring at the University of New Mexico in Albuquerque, where I teach. There I found a flyer advertising a program on pornography, held in the dorms and sponsored by a student group, showing the tape of Bundy's last interview. The flyer displayed a likeness of the killer under the logo: *"A Man with Vision. A Man with Direction. A Prophet of Our Times . . . Bundy: The Man, The Myth. The Legand [sic]."* Unfortunately, I was unable to attend this program, having gotten the flyer only after the fact. I was given the names of two male students who organized the program, but my attempts to find and contact them were unsuccessful; they were seniors and the semester had ended. Therefore, I cannot say with certainty what the tone of the program was. The flyer itself combines elements of a seemingly serious agenda, e.g., "film, informed speakers, discussion" with patently "sick" humor, e.g., the references to Bundy as a visionary prophet. The sponsor for the event was the Entertainment Program Committee, a dormitory student group, so I imagine that it was put on primarily as a way for, primarily male, students to get together to joke about Bundy, particularly his claim that pornography led him to sexual violence.

As previously noted, the mystery behind the actual identity of Jack the Ripper has generated a considerable amount of his lore. Although his identity is clear, other factors about Bundy provide legendary fodder. Bundy confessed to 30 murders, yet he also has been implicated in at least 20 other murders by the authorities; moreover, without much corroborating evidence, some relatives of missing women are sure that their loved ones were killed by Bundy. For example, Sophia Mary Healey disappeared at Royal Gorge in Colorado in 1979. *The Denver Post* reports that her mother "clings to the notion her daughter was murdered or abducted by a man seen entering the park in a tan VW immediately after Healey. That man, she believes, was notorious serial killer Ted Bundy, who had recently escaped from a Colorado jail."[37] Like his predecessor, Jack the Ripper, Bundy has become something of a "collective for murder."[38] Finally, Bundy was "illegitimate" and his mother has never revealed the identity of his birth father. Such obscure paternal origins are an open invitation to mythicization as happened recently when an article in *Vanity Fair* (May 1989) broadly suggested (without any actual evidence) that Louise Bundy was impregnated by her abusive father and Bundy was thus a child of incest.[39]

Finally, the greatest myth surrounding Bundy is one that we encounter nearly everywhere in the mainstream press—the concept that Bundy, and others like him, are complete "enigmas." This was constantly reiterated in refutation of Bundy's claim—which he had made consistently since his capture in 1978—that pornography had influenced his evolution into a sex killer. For example, *Playboy* approvingly quotes one of his lawyers, James Coleman: "He [Bundy] didn't know what made him kill people [*sic*]. No one did."[40] Similarly, a *New Yorker* editorialist, after pooh-poohing the "deadly dangers of nude centerfolds, X-rated movies, and bottom-rack periodicals," averred: "I don't believe that Ted Bundy or anyone else understood what made him commit and repeat the crimes he confessed to, which were rape murders of an unimaginable violence and cruelty."[41] First of all, such cruel violences are verifiably imaginable (and even erotic and/or entertaining) in this culture—consider the pornographic snuff film or soft-core snuff, such as the slasher film; Bundy's fame is more than matched, particularly among children, by that of the extremely cruel and violent fictional serial killers, Freddy Krueger or Jason. Secondly, a feminist analysis would not find Bundy and his ilk to be inexplicable deviants, but rather, logical, if extreme, products of a systemically misogynist culture: one that promotes an ideology of male supremacy; objectifies women; repeatedly associates violence and virility; eroticizes weaponry and various forms of violence and murder; and immortalizes and heroizes such men as Jack the Ripper.

Bundy ceaselessly demanded that people see him as just like them, as "sharing a common humanity." As he told evangelical minister Jim Dobson in his final interview: "Those of us who are . . . so much influenced by violence in the media, in particular pornographic violence, are not some kind of inherent monsters. We are your sons, and we are your husbands, and we grew up in regular families."[42] While part of Bundy's appeal is his overwhelming facade of normalcy, another sex killer from the 1970s deliberately cultivated a diametrically opposed persona—that of the inherent and committed monster.

"I am the 'Monster'"

> I am deeply hurt by your calling me a wemon [sic] hater. I am
> not. But I am a monster. I am the 'Son of Sam' . . . I am the
> 'Monster'—'Beelzebub'—the chubby behemoth.
> —David Berkowitz, letter to police (April 1 1977), printed in the
> *Daily News*, June 5 1977

During his spree as the "Son of Sam," the killer who randomly shot young women as they walked alone on the street, or sat in parked cars with other women or men, David Berkowitz wrote highly dramatic and disturbing letters to both police and press, letters which were subsequently printed in the daily papers. One such letter was sent to columnist Jimmy Breslin of the *Daily News*:

> Hello, from the cracks in the sidewalks of New York City and from the ants that dwell in these cracks and feed on the dried blood of the dead that has settled into these cracks.

> Hello from the gutters of New York City, which are filled with dog manure, vomit, stale wine, urine and blood.

> Don't think that because you haven't heard from me for a while that I went to sleep. No, rather, I am still here, like a spirit roaming the night. Thirsty, hungry, seldom stopping to rest; anxious to please Sam.[43]

The first day that just a part of that letter was printed, the *Daily News* sold a record-breaking 1,116,000 copies, a record that stood until the day Berkowitz was apprehended in mid-August. Actually, an extraordinary number of newspapers was sold throughout that entire summer as the *Post* and the *News* vied in a circulations war, turning their most sensationalist attention to this story. So intense was their coverage that the *New Yorker* charged the city's tabloids with what we might think of as "self-fulfilling publicity," of possibly encouraging the killer, or another of like mind, to strike again "by transforming a killer into a celebrity . . . into a seemingly omnipotent monster stalking the city."[44] While such criticism may seem to be merely enacting the social class differential between the prestigious magazine and the tabloids, a few years later, Berkowitz indicated that the *New Yorker* might have been right. He avowed that after his fourth shooting:

> I didn't much care anymore, for I finally had convinced myself that it was good to do it, necessary to do it, and that the public wanted me to do it. The latter part I believe until this day. I believe that many were rooting for me. This was the point at which the papers began to pick up vibes and information that something big was happening out in the streets Real big![45]

The attention of the people of New York throughout the summer of 1977 was riveted on the "Son of Sam." Men wearing T-shirts bearing the police sketch of the suspect's face walked the streets. Talk of the killer had become "the staple of conversation." Then mayor Abraham Beame summed up the melodramatic fascination of that time: "Son of Sam. I even liked the name and that in itself was terrifying. I knew it would stick—would become his trademark—you could see it all building, the fears of the people, including my own, and the headlong rush of the press to create a personality, someone they could build a story around."[46] Significantly, that movement to create a narrative was facilitated not only by Berkowitz's self-articulated monstrosity, but also by his style and choice of victims, for the killer who preyed on parked teenage couples seemed the very embodiment of that most common boogeyman of teenage horror—the stalking maniac of the popular urban legend, "The Hook." In journalistic accounts of the shooting of several of Berkowitz's victims the basic elements of "The Hook" clearly structure the narrative. The boy and girl pull into a lover's lane to neck and begin to talk about the killer. The boy plays it cool but the girl gets scared and begs the boy to leave. The boy doesn't take her fear seriously, but finally agrees. Just then the killer approaches and shoots them.[47]

After Berkowitz was captured in August 1977, reminders of the terror continued to haunt New York women, some deliberately planted by big business. Berkowitz had claimed that he "liked to shoot pretty girls," a remark that was widely quoted in the press. Incredibly, just a few months after his arrest, Max Factor introduced a new face moisturizer called "Self-Defense." As the billboards throughout the city threatened: "Warning! A Pretty Face Isn't Safe in this City.

Fight Back with Self-Defense." In this campaign, the cosmetics firm unabashedly tried to cash in on the fear generated by the sex killer, and, at the same time, implanted some all by itself.[48]

Again, in Albuquerque, I have observed several references to Berkowitz in the local youth subculture. Currently, one of the most popular local punk bands is called "Cracks in the Sidewalk"; it is common knowledge among their fans that the name derives from Berkowitz's "hello from the cracks in the sidewalk" letter to Jimmy Breslin. When Berkowitz was caught, he claimed that he was possessed by demons and under orders to kill from a man named "Sam" who communicated with him through a barking dog. (Later, he confessed that he had made all of this up.) Ten years later, on public access cable television in Albuquerque, a group of local amateur filmmakers showcase their works (frequently short horror films featuring a serial/slasher killer) on a program they call *Son of Sam Theater*. A man, who bears some resemblance to Berkowitz, hosts the show. He holds a dog hand puppet whom he calls Sam and talks with during brief addresses to the audience. Occasionally, another man will enter and chat with him, proclaiming himself to be another serial killer, e.g., Ed Gein (the murderer on whom the killer in *Psycho* was based). The general tone is one of high camp and hilarity, as when "Berkowitz" slashes "Gein" to death with a knife in a mode reminiscent of *Psycho*'s famous shower scene.

This cross referencing between actual serial killers and horror film is itself significant. For the most common monster of contemporary horror film is a serial killer, beginning with Norman Bates in *Psycho* (Alfred Hitchcock, 1960). We now see the immortal or at least regenerated serial killer in *Silent Rage* (Michael Miller, 1982), in the phenomenally popular Freddy and Jason of the *Nightmare on Elm Street* and *Friday the 13th* series, as well as *Child's Play* (Tom Holland, 1988) and *Shocker* (Wes Craven, 1989).

"Pop Culture Heroes"

> Freddy is pollution. Freddy is evil. Freddy is what's wrong with
> the world. . . . Racism, pollution, child molestation, child abuse,
> alcohol, drugs.
> —Robert Englund[49]

> Nowadays, the good guys seem to be fighting a losing battle, and teenagers appear to like it that way. Jason, the goalie-masked, knife-wielding fiend of the *Friday the 13th* series of movies and Freddy Krueger, the hideous-looking killer in the "Nightmare on Elm Street" movies, are pop-culture heroes.
> —*New York Times,* Oct. 1989[50]

> Our heroes and their narratives are an index to our character and conception of our role in the universe.
> —Richard Slotkin[51]

As noted earlier, a key factor in the mystique of Jack the Ripper has been his incorporation into the horror genre as a stock character. Indeed, by the latter part of the twentieth century, one of the most common monsters, as Robin Wood has observed, is a "human psychotic."[52] Moreover, even the traditional monsters—the vampires, werewolves, and phantoms—now are being overtly portrayed as sex killers.[53] If patriarchal legend has immortalized the Ripper (and is in process on Bundy, et al.), his screen brethren too are deathless, surviving seeming demise in feature after feature, resurrecting to dispatch those intrepid teenage girls who vanquished them in earlier installments, and gloating, as does Freddy in *Nightmare on Elm Street IV*, "I am eternal."

Like Bundy and Berkowitz (and their fictional forebear, Norman Bates), Freddy and Jason have identifiable mothers—but not fathers. Jason, the young son of a female cook at a summer camp, drowned while the camp counselors neglected him in favor of sexual satisfaction. His mother begins a vengeance campaign in the first *Friday the 13th* (Sean Cunningham, 1980), only to be beheaded by the sole surviving girl. Jason, however, isn't dead. In *Part II*, we meet him as a deformed teenager who keeps a candle-lit shrine to his mother's head. His first action is to gore to death the surviving girl from the original film and then to begin the silent reign of terror that has lasted through seven sequels (he doesn't even get his famous hockey mask until *Part III*). The loquacious Freddy Krueger of *Nightmare on Elm Street* originated as a child molester and murderer in an affluent suburban community. Tried for his crimes, he was freed on a technicality, so some local parents got together and burned him to death. Now Freddy preys upon the children of these parents through their dreams. In *Nightmare, Part III*, we meet Freddy's mother, a ghostly nun who explains that as a young girl working in a madhouse, she accidentally was locked in with the inmates and repeatedly raped. Freddy was thus, "the bastard son of a hundred maniacs."

It is mythically necessary to leave the paternity of these killers nebulous and even multiple, for their true father is indeed a collective entity—the patriarchal culture that has produced the serial killer as a fact of modern life. Moreover, these deranged sons must themselves stand in for that absent father, assuming the punitive paternal role. As Wes Craven (director and writer of the first *Nightmare on Elm Street*) has indicated: "Freddy is the most ruthless primal father. The adult who wants to slash down the next generation."[54]

In Craven's original conception, Freddy was "the most evil human being you can imagine, someone who goes after children." He had no plans to make Freddy invincible and eternal; rather, as he planned it, the extremely resourceful heroine of the first film, Nancy (Heather Langencamp), defeats Freddy by denying him, by turning her back on him and forbidding him reality. However, producer Nick Shaye wanted sequels and insisted upon a ludicrous ending where Freddy resurrects and the teenagers are doomed. (The heroic Nancy is killed off in *Part III*). Craven points out that under Shaye's direction, the movement was to "soften Freddy and make him a little bit more of a buffoon. . . . Now in a sense, he's embraced by younger kids. And they can make fun of him. In a way he's dangerous and in a way he's a joke. It's probably safer to deal with him that way."[55] Craven's rationale is the same one that is used to explain the disturbing joking about serial killers such as Ted Bundy. Yet, it is women who would most need to find ways to manage fear about sex killers and in my experience women rarely if ever make these jokes. Such joking is a means of normalizing the sex killer and identifying with him. Softening Freddy only softens and makes palatable the sexual abuse and murder of children. Incidentally, Freddy is not the first serial killer to be perceived as ironic and witty; that role was originally written for the mythic Jack the Ripper. Nor is he the first figure to double as buffoon and evil terror. John Wayne Gacy, rapist, torturer, and killer of 33 boys and young men, frequently performed for children as a clown.

Most commentators speak quite loosely about the "kids" who embrace these filmic killers, yet we should be wary of the facile generic and the gender differences it conceals. Although there is no comprehensive study of the demographics of the slasher film audience, all observers agree that it is mostly between the ages of 12 and 20 and largely male.[56] Without undertaking extensive interviews, it is difficult to discern in any conclusive way what Freddy and Jason mean to the, disproportionately male, children and teenagers who are so fascinated by these films in which a couple making love signals an imminent assault, where there are virtually no permanent survivors, and where both sexes are targets, though it is on the women's bodies and (usually more prolonged) deaths that the camera lingers. Film critic Robin Wood discusses the types of identification operating for the slasher film audience, but first distinguishes these current products from traditional horror:

> There the monster was in general a creature from the id, not merely a product of repression but a protest against it, whereas in the current cycles the monster, while still produced by repression, has essentially become a superego figure, avenging itself on liberated female sexuality or the sexual freedom of the young. . . . Where the traditional horror film invited, however ambiguously, an identification with the return of the repressed, the contemporary horror film invites an identification (either sadistic or masochistic or both simultaneously) with punishment.[57]

One element operating in viewers' masochistic identification is to pledge allegiance to the punitive father, hoping quite hopelessly that this will save you. We see this in the stories of those women who "fall in love" with killers such as Ted Bundy[58] (his wife actually married him after he had been convicted of the Chi Omega murders). The other, and probably more common, strategy (the sadistic one) is to identify with the violator and his role, to be titillated by his excesses and turned on by his depredations.

In October 1988, 19-years old Sharon Gregory was murdered in Greenfield, Massachusetts, when an 18-years old white man, Mark Branch, stabbed her over 50 times. Branch, at the time, was undergoing psychological counseling due to his obsession with slasher films; he particularly identified with "Jason" the murderer of the *Friday the 13th* series. When his home was searched, police found over 75 slasher videos and 64 similar books, three knives, a machete, and three hockey goalie masks, like that worn by Jason.[59] Branch eluded the police for about a month and then hanged himself in a local woods. Perhaps significantly, the murder took place around Halloween. This factor created additional havoc in Greenfield and caused town officials to ask parents to cancel traditional trick or treat activities. The officials requested this not because they were afraid Branch would strike again: "Instead, they are afraid pranksters may dress up as Jason . . . and scare young children or cause edgy residents to overreact and hurt someone in the dark."[60] Branch's sadistic identification with Jason (as well as the expected pranksters' identification with Branch) is, assuredly, extreme, yet not completely unexpected. A hero, after all, is a role model, one who acts out the fantasies of his fans, one who inspires emulation.

For obvious reasons, Freddy and Jason are often discussed together: each is a powerful and compelling contemporary symbol of evil. Yet, the two series and the two monsters are quite distinct. The *Friday the 13th* movies are pure gorenography;[61] the thin stories and cardboard characters exist only to give flesh to the slaughter scenes. It is difficult to imagine anything but sadism to be behind an identification with Jason. But, the original *Nightmare on Elm Street* movie (and to some extent the sequels), although not free of the slasher film's fixation on the coupling of teen sex with elaborate female death, is far more visually and philosophically interesting. Freddy is no mere death machine. As Robert Englund (the actor who plays Freddy) puts it: "He is the nightmare in suburbia. He is the nightmare in white America and he's reminding you that you can't escape IT!"[62] As such, Freddy may invite some identification as a completely unrepressed individual, a revolutionary figure who disregards and destroys traditional mores and values, one who exposes as fraud the image of the happy nuclear family and ideal suburban community.

A rather astonishing poem, "A Nightmare on Sesame Street," seems to stem from such a perspective and displays a sense of apocalyptic humor akin to Freddy Krueger's own.[63] It was written by a ten year old African-American boy in 1988 and turned in as a classroom assignment.

> It was a pleasant day, everybody was happy. "Play Ball," shouted Big Bird one bright sunny day. But his friends disagreed. Which game should they play? Grover spoke first. He said, "Please let's play catch." But Henry suggested a quick soccer match. "Hey buddies," said Ernie, holding his bat, "how about baseball?" I'd really like that. "I agree," Betty Lou said, flexing her mitt. But Oscar retorted, "Not enough grit." Cookie completely ignored the debate. While he munched on a frisbee that looked like a plate. "I get a kick out of football," said Bert. But Oscar continued, "Not enough dirt." "My racket is tennis," said Oscar persisting. Big Bird interrupted, "Let's try coexisting!" "We'll take turns," Big Bird said averting a brawl. And that's what they did. And they each had a ball . . . until . . . there he was Freddy Cruger [*sic*]. He said, "A is for Aim, B is for Blades. C is for Cut and D is for Dead." He popped Grover's ball then he sliced him. He stabbed Ernie and threw him somewhere. He stabbed Bert when he said he wanted to play football. He sliced Cookie Monster's cookies. "What's going on here," said Big Bird. "Run," said Henry. "He will kill you." "Nonsense, I'll ask him to be my friend." "Will you be my friend," Big Bird said. Not a chance, ffft ouch I'm dying. Cruger kills the rest of the people at sesame street. And his next stop is Mr. Rogers' Neighborhood.

This piece certainly bespeaks a rage against the TV-version of banally happy children's culture and experience. Yet if this poem is a rebellion, it is one that is programmed for self-defeat. For Freddy Krueger—the child molester and murderer—is no genuine stranger to that world, but a direct product of it. He is the alter ego, not the true opposite, of that other cultural icon, the all-knowing and authoritative suburban "good dad"; Krueger is Ward Cleaver unrepressed, running amok, wielding a cleaver. He is the incestuous/alcoholic/abusive/ murderous father, hidden behind the placid facade of Elm Street, U.S.A. Moreover, he is the consummate "nuclear father," threatening imminent apocalypse.

By killing women and children, Freddy and Jason, as well as the actual killers whom they reflect, are symbolically destroying life and the future itself. Robert Englund tells the (again predominantly young male) readers of the skateboard magazine, *Thrasher*:

> Child Killer? What are children? Children are the future. Freddy's killing the future. Freddy hates beauty. He hates youth. He hates the future. . . . It's kinda political y'know. Freddy hates the future. He's killing the future. Parents are weary. They don't want to defend the future anymore. The kids see it, and Freddy's killing the kids. [64]

Killing the future. Psychologist Robert J. Lifton points out that the fear of "futurelessness" (the belief that oneself and the world has no future) is a condition particularly afflicting children and teenagers in the nuclear age. It is commonly accepted that monsters from 1950s' horror and science fiction—Godzilla or giant ants—were metaphors for "the Bomb." Yet, current film monsters continue to carry those nuclear meanings.[65] As murderer of the future, Freddy is a symbolic evocation, not only of the reality of rampant child abuse and murder, but also of the everyday potential of nuclear annihilation, of radical futurelessness.

The delirious embrace of the sex killer (factual or fictional) is a phenomenon closely related to what Lifton has described as the "nuclear high": the desperate attempt to deny or escape destruction through identification with the agent of that destruction. Thus, the consummately lethal nuclear weapons are mythicized as beautiful, awesome, even divine, as the "only form of transcendence worthy of the age." Lifton illustrates this "nuclear high" by pointing to one of the final images of *Dr. Strangelove* (Stanley Kubrick, 1963), "in which man rides bomb to its target while uttering a wild Texas yodel."[66] Interestingly, an episode of *Freddy's Nightmares*, (a television series spin-off from the films), tells the story of a young girl who dreams presciently of nuclear holocaust. Throughout that episode, our commentator, Freddy Krueger, appears, first with a mushroom cloud coming out of his head, and then out in space, riding a nuclear missile down to the planet Earth to blow it up. He takes off his hat and waves it, calling "Yee ha," clearly in homage to that well-known *Dr. Strangelove* scene. Then, he reconsiders, turns the missile around, and says, "Nah, I'd rather get you little buckaroos one at a time." Freddy, we then realize, is something like a personalized nuclear bomb.

One other fact must be mentioned: in *Dr. Strangelove*, the madman general who engineers world nuclear destruction is the aptly named General Jack D. Ripper. How fitting that these icons of sex murder so frequently merge with those of nuclear annihilation, for both of these atrocities are apocalyptic—both kill the future. Moreover, both are based in male supremacist sexuality and are marked by the equation of "unimaginable" cruelty and violence with power, eroticism, and ecstasy.[67] Freddy Krueger and Jason join Jack the Ripper and Ted Bundy as the founding fathers and sons of an unremittingly apocalyptic culture, pointing to a future consisting of no safe sex ever, beaches spiked with toxic waste, extinct species, global warming, and nuclear war.

Atomic scientist Leo Szilard once commented regarding the heroization of his fellows after World War II: "It is remarkable that all these scientists . . . should be listened to. But mass murderers have always commanded the attention of the public, and atomic scientists are no exception to this rule."[68] Yet, why must mass murderers rule our attention? Like the originally efficacious heroine in the first *Nightmare on Elm Street*, we might instead ourselves take command and deny them that aggrandizing focus. Such denial would not be the passive and self-defeating kind that merely pretends that they don't exist, but an *active* denial, one that negates their lure, deconstructs their lore, and does not perpetuate, but diminishes their reality.

Notes

1. Gardner Dozois and Susan Casper, eds. *Ripper* (New York: Tom Doherty Associates, 1988).

2. "Freddy Items are Vendor's Dream," *Albuquerque Tribune*, Sept. 2, 1989, A18.

3. Debbie Cameron, "That's Entertainment? Jack the Ripper and the Celebration of Sexual Violence," *Trouble and Strife* 13 (1988): 17-19.

4. Jane Caputi, *The Age of Sex Crime* (Bowling Green, OH: Bowling Green State University Popular Press, 1987).

5. One of the worst offenders was NBC's *Ted Bundy: The Deliberate Stranger.* See Peter H. Brown, "Murder Most Glamorized," *Los Angeles Times*, "Calendar," April 2, 1989, 18-23.

6. For example, the Rolling Stone's salute to the Boston Strangler, "The Midnight Rambler." For commentary on this and other songs, see Caputi, *Age of Sex Crime.*

7. For example, see Jimmy McDonough, "I Can Teach You How to Read the Book of Life," *Bill Landis' Sleazoid Express*, 3, no. 4 (1984):3-5.

8. See Caputi, *Age of Sex Crime,* 53-62.

9. For example, *Pure.* See an interview with its publisher, Peter Sotos, in Adam Parfrey, ed., *Apocalypse Culture* (New York: Amok Press, 1987), 125-127.

10. Quoted in Robert Lindsey, "Officials Cite Rise in Killers Who Roam U.S. for Victims," *New York Times*, 21 Jan. 1984, A1.

11. Kate Millet, *Sexual Politics* (New York: Ballantine Books, 1970), 59-60.

12. See Susan Griffin, "Rape: The All-American Crime," *Ramparts*, 10 Sept. 1971, 26-85, reprinted in Susan Griffin, *Made From this Earth: An Anthology of Writings* (New York: Harper and Row, 1983), 39-58; Millet, *Sexual Politics,* 61-62; Diana E. H. Russell, *The Politics of Rape: The Victim's Perspective* (New York: Stein and Day, 1975); Susan Brownmiller, *Against Our Will: Men, Women and Rape* (New York; Simon and Schuster, 1975).

13. *TV Guide*, 20 March 1982.

14. Mark Schechner, "Male Chauvinist Romp," rev. of *Confessions of a Lady-Killer*, by George Stade. *New York Times Book Review*, 18 Nov. 1979, 15.

15. Orrin E. Klapp, *Heroes, Villains, and Fools: The Changing American Character* (Englewood Cliffs, NJ: Prentice-Hall, 1962), 59.

16. *San Francisco Chronicle*, 7 Oct. 1971, cited in Brownmiller, *Against Our Will*, 294.

17. Fannie Hurst, *Imitation of Life* (Cleveland: World Publishing Company, 1943), 97-98.

18. Judith R. Walkowitz, "Jack the Ripper and the Myth of Male Violence," *Feminist Studies*, 8 (1982): 543-74, esp. 570.

19. "In Pursuit of Pure Horror," *Harper's Magazine*, Oct. 1989, 45-53, esp. 47.

20. Caputi, *Age of Sex Crime*. See also Deborah Cameron and Elizabeth Fraser, *The Lust to Kill: A Feminist Investigation of Sexual Murder* (New York: New York University Press, 1987).

21. Nigel Morland, *An Outline of Sexual Criminology* (New York: Hart, 1966), 138.

22. Walkowitz, 550.

23. Walkowitz, 550.

24. See Caputi, *Age of Sex Crime*, 34-35.

25. Iona and Peter Opie, *The Lore and Language of Schoolchildren* (Oxford: Clarendon Press, 1959), 11.

26. Robert Bloch, "Your's Truly, Jack the Ripper," in *The Best of Robert Bloch*, ed. Lester del Rey (New York Ballantine, 1977), 1-20.

27. Cited in Steven Winn and David Merrill, *Ted Bundy: The Killer Next Door* (New York: Bantam, 1980), 217.

28. Nathan M. Adam, "To Catch a Killer: The Search for Ted Bundy," *Reader's Digest*, March 1981, 210-39.

29. See Jacob V. Lamar, "I Deserve Punishment," *Time*, 6 Feb. 1989, 34.

30. Richard W. Larsen, *Bundy: The Deliberate Stranger* (Englewood Cliffs, NJ: Prentice-Hall, 1980), 182.

31. Ann Rule, *The Stranger Beside Me* (New York: New American Library, 1980), 255.

32. Jon Nordheimer, "All-American Boy on Trial," *New York Times Magazine*, (10 Dec. 1978): 46+.

33. Millet, *Sexual Politics*, 62; Suzanne Lacy, "In Mourning and In Rage (With Analysis Aforethought)," *Ikon*, (Fall/Winter 1982-83): 60-67; Walkowitz, "Jack the Ripper."

34. Lacy, "In Mourning," 61.

35. Communication from Cassandra Sitterly, 10 August 1984.

36. Jane's Addiction, *Nothing's Shocking*, Warner Bothers, 1988.

37. Kevin Simpson. "Scenic Gorge Belies What Jumpers See as Final Solution," *Denver Post*, 13 Aug. 1989, 10B.

38. This is Tom Cullen's phrase regarding Jack the Ripper. See Tom A. Cullen, *When London Walked in Terror* (Boston: Houghton Mifflin Company, 1965), 4.

39. Myra MacPherson, "The Roots of Evil," *Vanity Fair*, May 1989, 140+.

40. Playboy Forum, "Ted Bundy's Original Amateur Hour," *Playboy*, June 1989, 49-50, esp. 49.

41. "Talk of the Town," *New Yorker*, (27 Feb. 1989): 23.

42. Quoted in Lamar, "I Deserve Punishment," 34.

43. Quoted in Lawrence D. Klausner, *Son of Sam* (New York: McGraw-Hill, 1981), 168.

44. "Talk of the Town," 15 August 1977.

45. Quoted in David Abrahamsen, "Confessions of 'Son of Sam,'" *Penthouse*, Nov. 1983, 60.

46. Quoted in Klausner, *Son of Sam*, 146.

47. For an analysis of urban legends, including "The Hook," see Jan Brunvand, *The Vanishing Hitchhiker: American Urban Legends and Their Meaning* (New York: Norton, 1981). For reports about the "Son of Sam" which are structured by that narrative, see Klausner, *Son of Sam*, 222-227.

48. This is reported by Pam MacAllister in "Wolf Whistles and Warnings," *Heresies: A Feminist Publication on Art and Politics*, 6 (Summer 1978): 37-39.

49. Robert Englund interviewed by M. Fo, in *Thrasher*, February 1988, 72-77, esp. 72.

50. Lena Williams, "For More U.S. Youths, It's Always Halloween," *New York Times*, Oct. 30, 1989, B1.

51. Richard Slotkin, *Regeneration Through Violence: The Mythology of the American Frontier, 1600-1860* (Middletown, Ct.: Wesleyan University Press, 1973), 564.

52. Robin Wood, *Hollywood from Vietnam to Reagan* (New York: Columbia University Press, 1986), 83.

53. As in *The Howling* (Joe Dante, 1980) where the werewolves are sex killers.

54. Quoted in Richard Corliss, "Did You Ever See a Dream Stalking?" *Time*, 5 Sept. 1988, 66-67, esp. 67.

55. Quoted in Dan Gire, "Bye Bye, Freddy! Elm Street Creator Wes Craven Quits Series," *Cinefantastique*, 18, no. 5, (July 1988) ; 8-10, esp. 10.

56. Carol J. Clover, "Her Body, Himself: Gender in the Slasher Film," *Representations* 20 (Fall 1987); 187-228, esp. 224.

57. Wood, *Hollywood*, 195.

58. One of Bundy's biographers, Ann Rule, says that after NBC's made-for-TV movie, *Ted Bundy: The Deliberate Stranger*, aired, she received "letters and phone calls from women who . . . had 'fallen in love' with Ted Bundy." See Brown, "Murder Most Glamorized," 23.

59. Stephen J. Simurda, "75 Horror Films Found in Slay Suspect's Home," *Boston Globe*, 9 December 1988, 28.

60. Tom Coakley, "After Slaying, Fears Disrupt Halloween in Greenfield," *Boston Globe*, 27 October 1988, 21.

61. I define *gorenography* as non-sexually explicit material that nevertheless sexualizes objectification, subordination, domination and/or violent behavior (e.g., battering, torture, mutilation, dismemberment, and murder) so as to arouse the viewer and to endorse and/or recommend the behavior as described, represented, or documented. It is murder, torture and mutilation presented in a context that makes murder, torture and mutilation sexual. See Caputi, "Advertising Femicide: Lethal Violence Against Women in Pornography and Gorenography," forthcoming in Jill Radford and Diana E. H. Russell, *Femicide: The Politics of Woman Killing* (Boston: Twayne Publishers, 1990).

62. Englund, interviewed by Fo, 72.

63. The poem was given to me by the boy's grandmother. Clearly, he might have copied the first part of the poem from another source, but the part with Freddy coming and slaughtering everyone is the boy's invention.

64. Englund interviewed by Fo, 75.

65. For further discussion see Caputi, "Films of the Nuclear Age," *Journal of Popular Film and Television*, 16, no. 3 (Fall 1988): 100-107.

66. Robert J. Lifton and Richard Falk, *Indefensible Weapons: The Political and Psychological Case Against Nuclearism* (New York: Basic Books, 1982), 77.

67. See Caputi, *Age of Sex Crime*, 140-44, 188-197; Diana E.H. Russell, ed., *Exposing Nuclear Phallacies* (New York: Pergamon Press, 1988).

68. Quoted in Paul Boyer, *By the Bomb's Early Light: American Thought and Culture at the Dawn of the Atomic Age* (New York: Pantheon, 1985), 61.

Caputi attributes learning how to write to her post-undergraduate work at Boston College with philosopher and feminist Mary Daly. Caputi's job was "idea editing" and involved both listening to Daly read a manuscript aloud and responding to the manuscript with suggestions. As for her own writing process, Caputi always begins with a title, trying to put the central theme into it even if she isn't quite sure what that theme is at the beginning. After creating a "very scratchy" outline, she writes, putting everything through numerous drafts and "weathering [the] criticism" of key friends. As far as "The New Founding Fathers" goes, Caputi sees it as a good way to interest people both in popular culture and feminist studies.

For Discussion

1. Make a list of all of the serial killers you know something about. Write a paragraph for each name describing what you know about this person.

2. Make a list of the serial killers Caputi describes in her essay. Write a paragraph for each name summarizing what Caputi says about them.

3. Compare the lists and descriptions from questions one and two. How are the descriptions different? Based on these descriptions, write an essay outlining how you see serial

killers differently than Caputi.

4. In paragraph 11, Caputi argues that the popularity of Jack the Ripper is "rooted in the patriarchal foundations of the modern world and his essential meaning is as an emblem of misogynist terrorism." What does Caputi mean by "patriarchal foundations of the modern world"? What is misogyny and how is Jack the Ripper "an emblem of misogynist terrorism"?

5. Summarize Caputi's argument in your own words.

6. Look at the title of this essay. The term "founding fathers" has a specific meaning for Americans. Describe that meaning in your own words. Why does Caputi use this phrase in the title of her article? How does her use both depend on and change our understanding of the term?

7. According to Caputi, why do we celebrate the "lore and lure" of serial killers? Using specific references from the text, describe what Caputi sees as the lore of serial killers. Describe also the lure of serial killers.

8. Why do you think we are so attracted to serial killers? What drives us to turn these people into legends? Why are they so compelling?

9. Carin Bigrigg's essay discusses childhood myths, whereas this essay discusses more "adult" myths. Compare and contrast how the two kinds of myths function within contemporary culture. What motives drive each kind of myth-making and what are the social consequences? Do you think that one kind of myth is more dangerous than another? Why? Why not?

10. Several essays in this section discuss how who we are and who others think we are tend to be two different things. Caputi uses this concept to illustrate the difference between the serial killer as a real person and as a myth created by society. Discuss the dangers of categorizing people as illustrated in Caputi's article, in "Snow on the Cactus," and in "MTV." Feel free to use your own experience to support your points.

Stare

Wayne Oakes

Wayne Oakes was born in 1945 in Macon, Georgia. He has earned a B.A. in geology and anthropology from the University of New Mexico, as well as an M.A. in library science from the University of Pennsylvania. He currently works at UNM's Valencia Library. His professional history is quite extensive, and includes working for several years in both the Norwegian and American Merchant Marine, for four years as a firefighter with the U.S. Forest Service, and for 15 years as an archeologist in the American Southwest.

The blank stare
is not blank

it is a long look
at a vague place

where fishing line
enters moving water

where embers struggle
to keep burning

where being and shadow
become midday.

Of his relationship to language, Oakes states, "[it] is one of love and hate. There is something calm and soothing about being able to describe aspects of the world I live in, while at the same time, there is something dark and tempestuous about language as a brain-child of self-consciousness." As such, he feels that writing and reading have always been explorations of the self and of the world. His poetry "attempts to use the tangible symbols to describe the intangible—the space between things." These explorations begin in Oakes' mind in the early morning and grow from a few lines into a poem as time passes. Revision, always an ongoing process, takes place "over days, weeks, or months depending on the individual poem."

For Discussion

1. Define the word stare. What kind of looking is Oakes writing about? Describe the difference between "looking" and "seeing."

2. What is the thesis of this poem? Support your restatement with appropriate explanation and examples.

3. If the blank stare isn't blank, what is it?

4. How is hope/desire implicit in a stare?

5. Why and when do you stare?

¿RED OR GREEN?

In the Mountains Dreaming of the Sea
Wayne Oakes

Wayne Oakes was born in 1945 in Macon, Georgia. He has earned a B.A. in geology and anthropology from the University of New Mexico, as well as an M.A. in library science from the University of Pennsylvania. He currently works at UNM's Valencia Library. His professional history is quite extensive, and includes working for several years in both the Norwegian and American Merchant Marine, for four years as a firefighter with the U.S. Forest Service, and for 15 years as an archeologist in the American Southwest.

Sitting by the campfire
I see more than enough reason.
Mountains feel muscled
as if walking too heavily
might tighten canyons
into crevices.

Unknown forms adumbrate
around the fire.
In sleep,
wisdom is taut:

memories of the sea
wrapped around the heart
like seawrack on rocks,

notes from the past
found in bottles
on beaches of the world,

sea turtles tremble
bothered by dreams
of egg thieves,

a sailor more in love
with the memory of a woman
than with the real woman.

At sea, the horizon
keeps its distance.

Of his relationship to language, Oakes states, "[it] is one of love and hate. There is something calm and soothing about being able to describe aspects of the world I live in, while at the same time, there is something dark and tempestuous about language as a brain-child of self-consciousness." As such, he feels that writing and reading have always been explorations of the self and of the world. His poetry "attempts to use the tangible symbols to describe the intangible—the space between things." These explorations begin in Oakes' mind in the early morning and grow from a few lines into a poem as time passes. Revision, always an ongoing process, takes place "over days, weeks, or months depending on the individual poem."

For Discussion

1. In this poem, there is an obvious split between the geography of the mountains and the geography of the sea. Oakes, as man and poet, sits in one and writes of the other. If the mountains can be compared to "reason," which he sees "more than enough of," then what might the sea be compared to? Support your choice with explanation of elements from the poem which led to it.

2. What does Oakes mean when he uses the metaphor of the "sailor more in love with the memory of a woman than with the real woman"? To answer this, think about the split between memory and reality. You may use an example from your own experience to help explain the split.

3. The alliterations of the m and c in stanza one and of the w and the r in stanza three are very noticeable. Read each stanza out loud, and describe the impression that such repetition of sound has on you as a reader. Describe the difference between the sounds in stanza one and those in stanza three.

4. Oakes ends with "at sea, the horizon keeps its distance." What is the implication about the horizon in the mountains?

5. Read Oakes' comments about love and hate which begin the endnote above. Think about the imagery in this poem and explain how it might be a poetic example of the split between that which is "calm and soothing" and that which "dark and tempestuous." Use examples from the poem to support your explanation.

6. Explain the word *adumbrate*, and describe what it adds or takes away from the poem.

7. Campfires and sea shores both seem to cause contemplation in people. How do you account for this?

8. Choose one of the other poems in this text and compare it to this one in as many ways as you can find.

Is This Urban Design?

Mark C. Childs

Mark Childs took his bachelor's degree in architecture from MIT, his master's in architecture from the University of Oregon, and his master's in public administration from the University of Washington. He has taught at the University of New Mexico's School of Architecture for the last three years.

The object of art is to give life a shape.
—*Jean Anouilh,* The Rehearsal

I dug 600 feet of ditch—by hand.

There is a set of one-liners I used to dismiss my mania—it's cheaper than going to the gym; it's my therapy; I like playing in the mud—all of which have a grain of truth but none of which really capture my motivation. The truth is Stanley Crawford made me do it, and Dolores Hayden helped me understand why.

Mr. Crawford is the author of *Mayordomo: Chronicle of an Acequia in Northern New Mexico,*[1] which I read upon moving to New Mexico. His account of the community organized around the use and maintenance of an irrigation canal chronicles the relationship between the natural environment, individuals, traditional Spanish culture and modern American society. Mr. Crawford is a poet of the most powerful sort—he can move strangers to action just for the beauty of it. When I bought a house in Albuquerque's North Valley and found I had an easement for a ditch through my neighbor's backyard, I got out my shovel.

As the weekends wore on, with 20 feet a day of progress, I questioned if there was a border between poetry and lunacy. However, I persisted.

The *acequia* is not just the ditch but also the organization that runs it. In traditional communities the land owners along the watercourse compose the *acequia.* These traditional *acequia* associations are, Stanley Crawford points out, one of the few civic institutions left in which members have fundamental control over an important aspect of their lives. In Albuquerque, experts design our water supply systems; standards adopted by a national organization of engineers dictate the design of our neighborhood streets; developers with their hired urban designers convert fields into "communities"; and the bureaucracy known as the Middle Rio Grande Conservancy District manages the irrigation system.

When I had dug about 80 feet of my folly, a neighbor introduced himself and gave me an extra wheel he had. The wheel opens the gate that floods the ditch, called the Hale, that I was tapping into. He also told me that the Hale was a community ditch—the Conservancy doesn't run it. However, there wasn't an active ditch association. At about 120 feet, another neighbor realigned his fencing to make certain his horse would not ruin my ditch. From 120 feet to 200 feet my five-years old son actively helped me dig. At 200 feet, yet another neighbor roto-tilled my path to make it easier to shovel. At 400 feet, the last neighbor on my route brought in a backhoe and dug the ditch through his yard. I had water. More importantly, I had good neighbors. Six hundred feet of ditch gave me biceps, garden irrigation and the beginning of membership in a community.

I am an architect and thus I draw in order to think about places. Last winter, I mapped the Hale and ownership of the property it floods. A neighbor and I visited all the owners to add their telephone numbers to the map and then gave everyone a copy. This map-making gave form to the relationship of adjacent landowners. The Hale ditch association fell into place.

Two Greco-Roman concepts of the city vie as the dominant influence in how we make our settlements—*civitas* and *urbs*. That is, sometimes we see our towns and cities as reflections of community or *civitas*, the city as a moral assembly of people. Sometimes, we measure the quality of our cities by the efficiency of their form for certain functions, such as mobility or the provision of water. The art of this functional form-making is *urb*an design. Is my ditch, then, urban design?

The March 1996 issue of *Urban Land*, a journal of the development industry, provides an example of what is considered the mainstream of urban design. The urban design projects discussed in the issue are excellent examples of current practice done by famous and talented urban designers and, to their credit, illustrate attempts to address municipal budget, environmental, adjacent community and even "social infrastructure" concerns. They also share critical characteristics: (1) they are large—from 80 to 9038 acres; (2) ownership and control of the land has been centralized; (3) they are treated as sites that have no significant pre-existing community other than the current owner(s); (4) the design has an underlying consistency—it offers *a* view of the world; and (5) the experts' role is to develop a product which does no harm to municipal budgets and can be sold at a profit to consumers. In the current professional world, ditch digging, no mater how poetic in intent and social in outcome, is not urban design.

But what about the places where ownership is fragmented and interwoven, where various, sometimes competing, communities exist? Who does the redesign of existing cities? Dolores Hayden, an architect and historian, writes in *The Power of Place: Urban Landscapes as Public History*,[2] "Indigenous residents as well as colonizers, ditchdiggers as well as architects, migrant workers as well as mayors, housewives as well as housing inspectors, are all active shaping the urban landscape." The incremental and small-scale actions of multiple actors produce the complex social and economic space of a city. When these actions are done not simply as individual exploits, but as part of making a city, then they are a physical manifestation of *civitas*.

This kind of shaping of the city is clearly different from the industry's urban design projects. I would like to rehabilitate and extend the old term, Civic Art, to speak of this work. The term has the advantage of emphasizing both community (*civitas*) and creativity. Civic Art as practiced before World War II has been dismissed as "townscape design," that is, a superficial approach that concentrated on visual play rather than the myriad of economic, political and sociological aspects of a city. However, the principal advocates of Civic Art, the architects Werner Hegemann and Elbert Peets, defined Civic Art as design based in culture,[3] and it is in this manner, *urb*an form serving *civitas*, that I use the term. Civic Art rests on the mores, manners and history of communities and requires individual buildings be thought of as part of the whole city. It is not dependent on large projects or central control of the land. Instead of treating sites as uninhabited natural canvases, Civic Art weaves the cultural and environmental history of a place into form.

Civic Art in this new incarnation is embryonic. The role of civic artist is not well-developed. However, two aspects are clear. First, the civic artist cannot hide from political issues pretending to be simply a technical expert. The autocratic methods of current urban design are not well-suited to a civic artist who favors democracy. Dolores Hayden's work described in *The Power of Place* provides examples of collaborative efforts in minority and women's urban history and public art. Secondly, the civic artist is an observer and weaver of patterns—whether as cultural historian, ecosystem analyst, or urban architect, the civic artist brings to a collaborative effort the ability to see and add to patterns. Making and sharing a map crystallized the transformation of my ditch work from an individual utilitarian task to a congregation of community.

My ditch is not part of the political economy of current urban design practice; nor is it a recreation of a traditional acequia association. But hopefully it is a small example of the cultural-environmental practice of Civic Art. If we value our cities, perhaps we should dig in and do the pleasantly hard work to which Stanley Crawford and other poets of community call us.

Notes

1. Stanley Crawford, *Mayordomo: Chronicle of an Acequia in Northern New Mexico* (Albuquerque: University of New Mexico Press, 1988).

2. Dolores Hayden, *The Power of Place: Urban Landscapes as Public History* (Cambridge, MA: MIT Press, 1995).

3. Werner Hegeman and Elbert Peets, *The American Vitruvius: An Architecht's Handbook of Civic Art* (New York: Princeton Architectural Press, 1988).

Also of interest:

Collier, Jr., John and Malcolm Collier. *Visual Anthropology: Photography as Reseach Method.* (Albuquerque: University of New Mexico Press, 1986).

Cronon, William, George Miles and Jay Gitlin, eds. *Under an Open Sky: Rethinking America's Western Past.* (New York and London: W. W. Norton and Co., 1992).

When Professor Childs started his education at MIT, he majored in planetary physics, and pursued a minor in creative writing. Then, between his freshman and sophomore years, he went to Europe, where he found many examples of buildings which not only served multiple purposes, but spanned many periods of history. In particular, he recalls a farm complex in Switzerland in which the layers of time were evident in the myriad additions and constructions. Seeing this structure encouraged him to switch to architecture. Although, in academia, publications in one's field are necessary for survival, Professor Childs' first publication was a poem. His affinity for writing, which began early in his career, has continued, and is more than evident in the style of this essay. Further, he believes that this piece is an important cultural criticism of the movement away from a connection between people and their places, and toward corporate layers which preclude the individual's involvement in the design and function of communities. In fact, one might say that his essay itself delineates the "border between poetry and lunacy" by demonstrating the beauty of community, and the wasteland that can form without it.

For Discussion

1. Write a response to the first line, "I dug 600 feet of ditch—by hand." Describe the effect of that line (length, placement, etc.). How does the form dictate the impact?

2. Examine the rhetorical structure of the essay. To do this, make a chart where the paragraphs are marked either a) personal experience, or b) scholarly examination. Afterward, look at the pattern—what is Childs doing with the structure? How does the structure support or enhance the content?

3. In paragraph eight, Childs makes a distinction between *civitas* and *urbs*. In your own words, define each term. Then, explore the function of each in your own ideal society.

4. Childs describes the way that he pulled all of his neighbors together both through the physical labor of digging the ditch, and also through the mental labor of creating a map. Describe a situation from your own experience where a group of loosely connected people were pulled together. Who were they? How did it happen? What was the outcome? If it hasn't happened in your experience, pick a situation where it should happen, and imagine how it could.

5. Childs believes that one of the reasons for homelessness lies in the destruction of low cost housing and the zoning which precludes mixed-use developments, which would provide new, low cost housing. Think about Albuquerque and write a letter to the city council which makes creative suggestions for alleviating homelessness.

6. Read Wilde's essay, "Snow on the Cactus," and consider how his experience differs from Childs'. Write an essay which compares and contrasts the two authors' senses of and experiences with "community."

7. One of Childs' concerns is that government (an external, detached entity) controls decisions that once were controlled by individuals/communities (internal, involved entitities). Read Berthold's essay, "The Nature of the University," and consider that he argues that the needs of the one outweigh the needs of the many in certain cases. Divide into groups: some will represent "city government," and some will represent "local neighborhoods." Consider the following:

A new freeway is being planned through the neighborhood. It will bring money in construction jobs and encourage satellite businesses; it will also run next to the elementary school, condemn 30 houses in its path, and destroy part of the bosque. Depending upon what group you are in, argue for or against the building of this freeway.

Missouri Avenue on the Caprock

Jerry Williams

Jerry Williams is a professor of geography at the University of New Mexico. He is also the director of the Southwest Institute in the summer months. Williams was born in Maryland. He received his undergraduate degree from Bridgewater College in Virginia, after which he joined the Peace Corps. Williams studied rural development in Africa before getting his master's degree in geography with a focus on international development from Indiana University. Williams then returned to Africa and lived on a game park for three years. He earned his Ph.D. from the University of Oregon, where he did his dissertation describing his experiences in economic development in the African game park. In 1977, Williams came to UNM as an Africanist.

Lured by reports about grama grass that was so high it tickled the belly of a horse, the settlers poured onto the high plains of New Mexico during the first decade of the twentieth century. Boom towns began to sprout up along the sidings that the single-line railroads needed for intersecting trains and for locating maintenance crews. The towns especially blossomed if the siding was next to a highland area of prairie that appeared capable of supporting dryland farming. The railroad companies, which were provided with large blocks of land to promote settlement, and the merchants of the new railroad towns had a mutual interest and investment in attracting sodbusters to the open grass plains of the eastern part of the state.

Prior to the arrival of the railroads, the high plains had been the homeland for many societies: Comanche buffalo hunters, followed by Mexican sheepherders, and at the turn of the century the highlands were controlled by the cattle companies. Legal right to the land had been contested since 1846 when New Mexico became an American territory. A number of companies and individuals surfaced with documents as proof of lands granted to them by the Mexican government before the arrival of the Americans. Many of the title disputes over land grants covering much of the Llano Estacado and Buffalo Plains had subsided and the federal government proceeded to free areas for homesteading in 1905 and 1906 (although much of the litigation was not resolved until several decades later). Included in this land release was the 1200 square mile southeast-sloping caliche (chalk-base) caprock area bordering Texas and bisected by the southern boundary of Quay County. This area, referred to locally as "the Caprock," is a rimrock area of the Llano Estacado that has been dramatically

Location of the Caprock

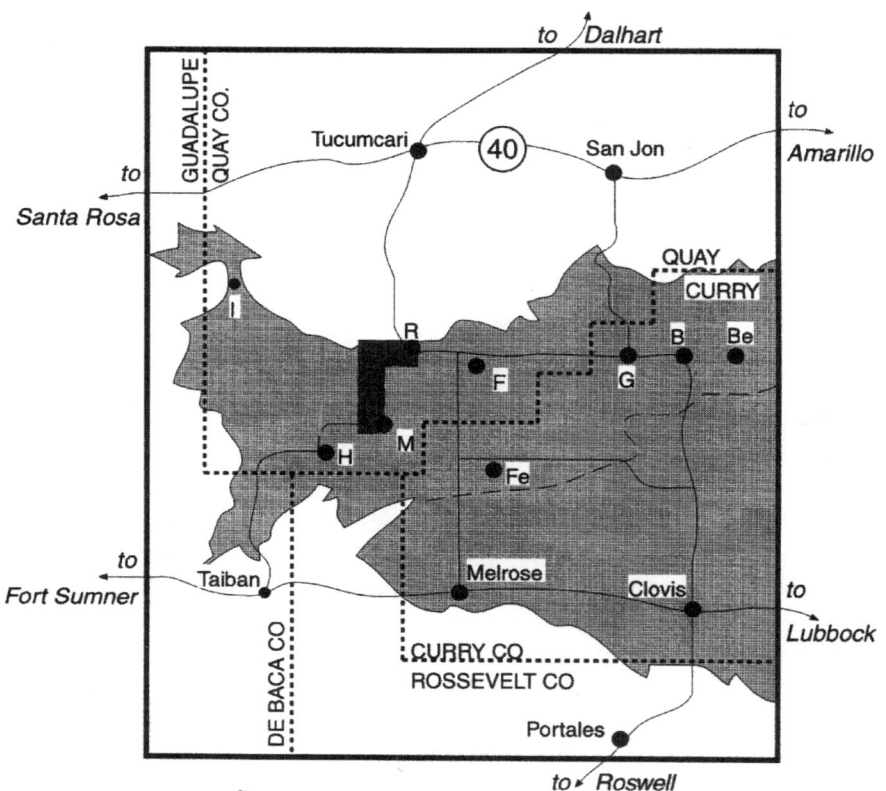

 Limits of the Caliche Base

‒ ‒ 4500' Elevation Southern Limit
of the Highland Cap

B	Broadview	H	House
Be	Belview	I	Ima
F	Forrest	M	McAlister
Fe	Field	R	Ragland
G	Grady		

exposed by downcutting tributaries of the Canadian River on the north and the Pecos River to the west. Moderately thick stabilized sands over the caliche had formed a reddish loam soil which supported a thick mantle of grass dotted with numerous depression lakes. The place must have appealed to the farmers from further east as they wandered onto the vast open space in search of the right quarter section of turf to live on, develop, and, after a time, claim for their own.

Groups of curious farmers began arriving by train at Melrose and Tucumcari in 1905 and 1906. Others came by horseback from Texas, drifting westward from small places like Bovina and Hereford. Many headed to a little spot in the grass called House where a land surveyor and commissioner helped determine places available for filing. These adventurous men came from small towns and rural counties in Texas, Arkansas, Oklahoma, Kansas, and Missouri; several came from as far away as Tennessee, Virginia, and Georgia. Many had procrastinated during the 1890s land rush for Oklahoma and West Texas, and they viewed New Mexico as a last chance for cheap land and the opportunity to acquire their own farm. The land offices surrounding the Caprock were kept busy recording land filings, and there was a flow of commissioners and aides over the plains in search of the elusive section markers to guide settlers to unclaimed parcels of land. The original survey of land in this area was less than scientific, as described by Victor Westphall in *The Public Domain in New Mexico* (Albuqueruqe: UNM Press, 1965). "It was obvious that when the original survey had been made the marked monument rocks had been tossed off each side of a wagon as it traversed a winding route. . . . By tying a red cloth to a wagon wheel and counting the number of revolutions, the team arrived at surveyed distances." Juana Foust, in a little-known but excellent novel called *Prairie Chronicle* (New York: Putnam and Sons, 1932) about pioneering on the Caprock, claimed that it was miraculous that anyone could make proper land filings in the area. In a particularly graphic account of one family's crossing of the Cap in search of the claim, she relates that:

The men made a game out of checking the distance between section rocks. They already had heard tales about how this country was surveyed. The current story was that the surveyor loaded a wagon with rocks, then tied a handkerchief around the twelve-foot rim of the wheel. On the 440th turn of the handkerchief he threw out a rock, if he remembered to.

. . .

'Four hundred and one,' Bugs called back to the women, 'the bastard that laid this out must a been full of Choc [Choctaw beer].'

. . .

The next section would be long, maybe five hundred turns of the wheel and a hundred yards out of line. 'He was thinkin' about his girl when he drove this mile,' Joe said. (Foust, 27)

Between 1906 and 1908 immigrant railcars, freightcars slightly modified so they could carry people, began to arrive at this farming frontier with extended families, household goods, livestock, and farming machinery. Cousins, uncles, parents, friends, and anyone of filing age joined the caravan to begin the process of consolidating the land claims by settling on adjoining parcels or by acquiring nearby patents through private land sales. Land speculators without agricultural supplies also arrived on these immigrant trains. They were after profit by cash sale of land and were not interested in "proving-up," or living on the claim long enough to receive a patent.

Frank Jester, the highly respected late veterinarian of the Caprock, offered a personal account of some of the problems encountered by the first pioneers.

> I came with my grandparents [from Scofield, Missouri] . . . my dad couldn't get an immigrant car. They were a-comin' in here like flies in 1906 and 1907. There was no road up from Tucumcari; that Plaza Largo down in Quay Valley had quicksand. . . . You got stuck in there, you was in trouble. Get to the Caprock and no road up the Cap. . . . Had to put about three or four teams to a wagon and double them up with chains to drag them wagons up the slopes. Hauled most of our lumber then from Melrose, but lord . . . there was a strip of sand between here [Ragland] and Melrose that give us a mess of trouble.

According to Frank, the hostility to the farmers went beyond the physical difficulties of getting onto the Cap. "The cowboys of the Horseshoe Ranch [northwest of Melrose] had burned off the grass on the Spring of 1906. Just as far as you could see it was black as a hat. They said those nesters couldn't survive without livestock feed." But the good rains continued through 1908 and as the new grass sprouted the Caprock quickly filled with dugouts, tents, poleshacks, or frame houses on nearly every 160-acre land plot available for homesteading.

Although the law required that the claimants reside on the land they filed on, there was very little inspection and only random enforcement of this rule. A lot of extended families lived together on a single filing and casually maintained small dugouts and shacks on peripheral land parcels so they could file claims on them. Opal Vance Howard recalls that "[t]hey came on out and homesteaded on the land they had filed on, and they pitched a large tent where all of them stayed until they built their houses on each one of their quarters." Some families, such as the Franklins of Missouri Avenue, were clever enough to immediately consolidate four quarter-section claims of a single section by constructing the house at the midpoint of the section and extending the claimants' bedrooms onto each quarter they were attempting to prove-up. The Caprock had to have one of the greatest rural population densities in New Mexico in 1908, the last year of good rainfall before it began to get too dry to support dryland cultivation. "Every quarter section had somebody living on it," says Roscoe Runyan, "every 160 acres. But when it commenced to get dry . . . there was old maids and old bachelors and every kind of person you can imagine. But a lot of 'em was footloose . . . and when it got dry they went back to where they came from. Somebody else got their places and filings."

But not every family left; some remained and survived the hardships of the harsh climate. And it is they who are responsible for the evolution of over 40 communities on the Caprock, many centered on only some meeting-place like a brush-arbor or a building used for school and church. Most of these with names such as Hope, Frio, Murdock, Ford, and Grand Plains remain only in the memories of the dwindling number of old-timers who fondly recall the prayer meetings, singing conventions, and the few months a year they spent at the one-room subscription schools. A number of communities were able to support stores and post offices which were connected by mail contract routes and wholesale lines to Melrose, Taiban, Tucumcari, and San Jon. Places such as Ard, Hollene, Plain, Hansel, Ima, and Roosevelt are evident on the landscape today only as cemeteries, in varying states of maintenance, in the midst of wheat fields or rangeland. Several places such as Wheatland, Bellview, Forrest, and McAlister were large enough to support a variety of services and became locations for high schools in the 1920s and 1930s. These villages are mainly abandoned today, with numerous building shells and ruins attesting to their previous importance. Only the small towns of House, Grady, and Broadview survive as service centers on the broad expanse of the Caprock. Declining population, especially of young families, threatens their future existence.

The dispersed agricultural population did not live in towns or specific centers. Instead their home sites stretched across the prairie in a linear-grid pattern following the wagon ruts along a survey line. This pattern was sharpened when the nesters erected fencelines to contain their stock and the ruts were transformed into unmaintained rural roads. One such path ran from the north edge of the Caprock (three miles west of Ragland) to a place one mile west of McAlister. This 10-mile stretch of road became the front street for a lot of homesteaders, as did many other similar sand tracks throughout New Mexico. The uniqueness of this one was that the folk along it all came from Missouri; everyone that is

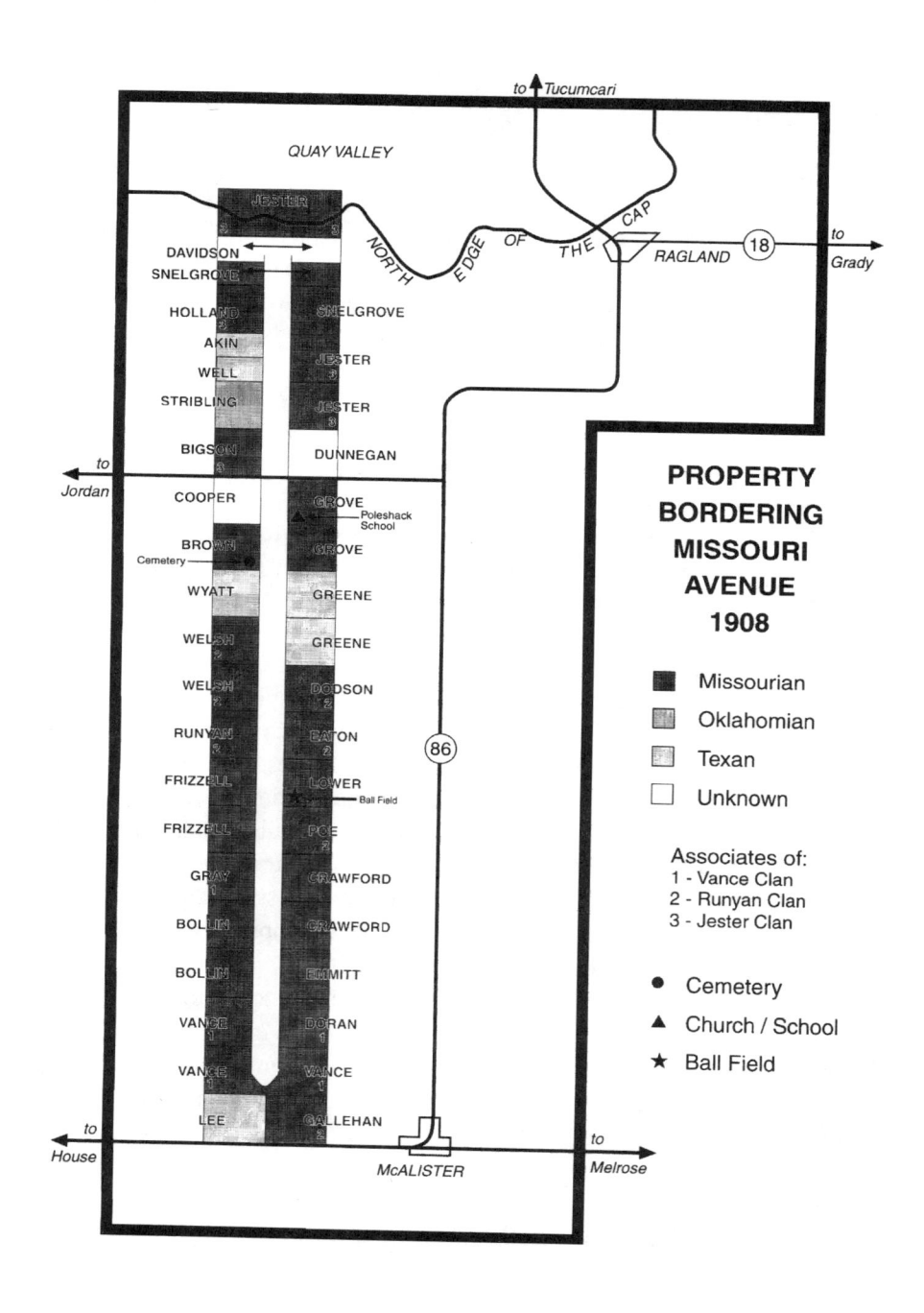

QUAY VALLEY

to ↑ Tucumcari

JESTER

NORTH EDGE OF THE CAP

RAGLAND

18 *to Grady*

DAVIDSON
SNELGROVE
SNELGROVE
HOLLAND
AKIN
JESTER
WELL
STRIBLING
JESTER
BIGSON
DUNNEGAN

to Jordan

COOPER
GROVE — Poleshack School
BROAN
GROVE
Cemetery
WYATT
GREENE
WELSH
GREENE
WELSH
DODSON
RUNYAN
EATON
FRIZZELL
LOWER — Ball Field
FRIZZELL
POE
GRAY
CRAWFORD
BOLLIN
CRAWFORD
BOLLIN
EMMITT
VANCE
DORAN
VANCE
VANCE
LEE
GALLEHAN

86

to House

McALISTER

to Melrose

PROPERTY BORDERING MISSOURI AVENUE 1908

■ Missourian
▨ Oklahomian
▤ Texan
□ Unknown

Associates of:
1 - Vance Clan
2 - Runyan Clan
3 - Jester Clan

● Cemetery
▲ Church / School
★ Ball Field

except the Wyatts and the Greens, who came from Texas. These two exceptions are quickly pointed out by the Missourians who remember the old days, but they add that it was only their land that adjoined "The Avenue." The Texans' houses faced another section line. Courthouse records in Tucumcari indicate that there were a few other non-Missourians but they also were not part of the Avenue (such as the Akins and Wells families from Texas and the Stribling clan from Oklahoma) and had built their homesites facing the next section line to the west.

Of the 42 land parcels that bordered this homestead highway, 31 were proved-up by Missourians, six were granted to Texans, one to an Oklahoman, and four went to those of undetermined home-state origin. Twenty-one of the 23 houses known to front onto Missouri Avenue were occupied by Missourians at the time the first private deed for each claim was recorded. It is of little wonder that so many people from the same general area of the nation should find themselves in clusters on the frontier. Many of the settlers were extended representatives of one family who often came out together as a form of kinship cooperative. This was true of the Vance family on the southern part of the Avenue where Bill and Maggie and Jimmy each had quarter-sections along the road and had acquired four additional homesteads by the mid-twenties. The enterprising Vance family became a prominent economic element of the Caprock when they introduced the Turkey Red wheat stock from the farmlands around Ravenwood, Missouri. As Opal Vance Howard recalls, "They brought wheat and their coal-fired steam thresher. They were the first on the Caprock to raise wheat . . . they were the ones to turn this into wheat country. The Vances were threshers in Missouri and they threshed on the Cap from Ima [on the western edge] into Texas [60 miles to the east]. The Turkey Red stock was analyzed as the best milling wheat of the pioneer period."

In the middle section of Missouri Avenue were the clan and friends of the Runyan family who had come out from Bolivar, Missouri. These included the Eatons, Welshes, Poes, and Dodsons. The Eatons and Dodsons were among the first to drill wells and furnish water to their neighbors. Prior to this the farmers were dependent on unreliable storage in the many depression lakes, or they would have to carry water in barrels from springs or old rangeland wells that were up to 20 miles away. The northern edge of Missouri Avenue was settled by the Jester family and acquaintances from Scofield, Missouri. Frank Jester offered a theory about why so many other Missourians were attracted to the Cap. "It went to raining in the Spring of 1907, and those Missouri boys planted potatoes and corn like they did back in Missouri . . . and they sent it back there (to the county fairs) . . . won prizes. . . . Oh man, those huge potatoes and long ears. . . . They thought [as well as farmers back in Missouri] they'd come to the land of milk and honey."

The concentration of farmers along this one road did have a community focus. Although they would go to Jordan or McAlister for mail and supplies, they also supported a school-church building near the middle of the Avenue. The building was named Browning, retaining the name it had at a former location before it was slid on log-runners to Missouri Avenue. There was also a cemetery that formed in the quarter-section across from the church which became one of a handful of dominant pioneer burial grounds on the Caprock, superceding cemeteries that had begun at Ard, McAlister, Jordan, Curry, and Hartford. As Opal Howard recalls, "the Browning Church also served as a social ground for Missourians, a place where they would have separate picnics. They carried this on for quite a while. . . . It was important for the first generation of settlers where one came from."

There's not much on the Avenue today. Many of the old wood frame houses stand abandoned to the wind and the vandals. A few of the old dugouts can still be found (if one knows precisely where to look) and the plows, wagons, and harnesses that were instrumental in breaking sod and hauling the necessities of life are now visible in the ruins of an old shed or in the clumps of tall weeds on the edge of a wheat field. Rarely does a car travel the path of Missouri Avenue. The county paved the north-south section road a mile to the east which provided a more direct connection between McAlister and Ragland, where the highway drops off into the Quay Valley and to Tucumcari. Only the occasional farm vehicle passes in order to reach land parcels that now belong to consolidated agri-businesses.

The people of Missouri Avenue? Many rest in the tidy rows of Browning Cemetery. But others drifted off the Cap long ago when the dust and sand wasted the farmland and there was no water for stock. A lot have lived out their lives in Tucumcari, Melrose, Clovis, and Albuquerque. Others returned to their hearths of the Midwest or pushed on into other frontiers farther west. There is a diminishing number that did not leave the Caprock and they can still be found in isolated places throughout the high plains. It is from these remaining first generation pioneers that the story of homesteading can be reconstructed and hidden places such as Missouri Avenue can be resurrected.

After doing research for an atlas called New Mexico and Maps *with Paul McAlistar, Jerry Williams realized that there was no significant research on homesteading in New Mexico. This discovery led to his interest in why people located in specific areas of the territory. Williams began by studying New Mexico land title claims and how they changed from 1880 to 1980. He reinterpreted these changes into a sequence of homes and families. He then interviewed more than three hundred descendants of these pioneers. In return, Williams learned about the places, land use, communities, and important events that affected the lives of the pioneers. "Missouri Avenue on the Caprock" is a part of the story that these interviews revealed.*

For Discussion

1. According to Williams, why did the settlers come to New Mexico? What other interests contributed to the settlement of eastern New Mexico?

2. In paragraph two, the author writes: "The federal government proceeded to free areas for homesteading in 1905 and 1906." Who lived on this land before 1905 and why was their land taken away? Write a brief essay on this subject including information from the text as well as your opinion.

3. How was the land divided into homesteads? What were the problems associated with the surveying of the land as well as the claims filed by homesteaders?

4. Locate the personal accounts in the text. Why are the personal accounts of the homesteaders important?

5. How does the author give the article a sense of place and time? Why are time and place important to this article? Find specific examples in the text to illustrate your answer.

6. In paragraph nine, the author states: "It is of little wonder that so many people from the same general area of the nation should find themselves in clusters on the frontier." What evidence does the author provide to support this statement? Evaluate the validity of this statement.

7. How was a sense of community established by the Caprock settlers? Compare this essay with "Is This Urban Design?" by Mark Childs. How are the communities in each brought together? What are the common threads? How is time bridged when comparing the two essays? Write an essay in which you use examples from each text to support your opinions.

8. In paragraph 11, the author quotes Opal Howard who says: "It was important for the first generation of settlers where one came from." Do you feel that this statement is applicable today? Are your family's roots important to you? Why or why not? Write an essay about your family's roots in which you consider Opal Howard's statement.

9. Why, in your opinion, is this piece important to the history of the United States in general and New Mexico in particular?

Los Alamos: Coming Down from the Hill of Certainty

E. A. Mares

Tony Mares was born and raised in plaza vieja *(Old Town) Albuquerque. He attended college at Notre Dame and UNM before taking a B.A. in Spanish from Florida State. An M.A. in Spanish Literature followed, also from Florida State. Working a number of jobs as well as teaching, Mares returned to school for a Ph.D. in European history from the University of New Mexico. In the fall of 1995 he was hired to teach in the English Department at UNM.*

The story of Los Alamos is well-known in terms of the scientific and technological advances and applications related to nuclear physics and other sciences that have been investigated and developed in its laboratories. As a scientific community, Los Alamos was founded during World War II for the very practical purpose of designing and assembling the final model of the atomic bomb. After the surrender of Nazi Germany, only a few skeptics such as the Hungarian-born physicist, Leo Szilard, questioned the necessity of using the atomic bomb.[1] Most of those who supported the Manhattan Project were certain about its necessity and the atomic bomb's ultimate use at Hiroshima and Nagasaki. Debra Rosenthal, among others, has captured this sense of certainty on "The Hill": "The war years in Los Alamos were remarkable, full of purpose, energy, camaraderie, and creativity born of necessity, but the war is long over. The old excitement has been replaced by comfortable routine."[2]

More than 50 years later, the Impact Los Alamos Oral History Project marks, in my opinion, an important step in coming down from the hill of certainty—the hill of intellectual smugness—in order to wrestle constructively with the many and complex issues swirling around Los Alamos. These issues are of vital importance not only to Los Alamos and its surrounding communities, but also to the world-at-large.

The story of the founding of the enigmatic city on The Hill and the aura of secrecy within which the scientists, engineers, technicians, working crews, and their families lived for many years is also fairly well-known. Less well-known, however, is the story of Los Alamos in terms of how silence and secrecy impacted the lives and fortunes of these families, especially in terms of the psychological effects and social consequences for individuals and families involved. There is still much to be done in terms of social and historical research in this area in relation to the lives of those individuals, and their families from the towns, villages, and farming and ranching communities of northern New Mexico who went to work on The Hill. In terms of culture and history, were these people ever able to "return home" again? And what did "home" mean? This is the story that is of particular concern for the Impact Los Alamos Oral History Project.

What I will attempt to do is provide an historical and philosophical overview for this oral history project. My concerns are primarily social, cultural, and historical, and I would like to establish from the outset that I have no bias against science and technology. I am an associate member of Sigma Xi (the national science honorary society), and I have done some research and writing in the area of the history of science in New Mexico. I was a co-author of "Science in New Mexico: Origins and History" with Joseph A. Schufle and McAllister H. Hull, Jr., the first chapter of *From Sundaggers to Space Exploration: Significant Scientific Contributions to Science and Technology in New Mexico* (1986).[3] In 1985, on the occasion of the 40th anniversary of the first atomic detonation at the Trinity Site, I wrote a brief overview of the philosophical trail that led from medieval scholastic disputes to the Manhattan Project. This appeared in the *Albuquerque Journal*'s *Impact Magazine*.[4]

I do not question the validity of the Western scientific tradition, but rather the impact it has had on cultures and communities that were, and are, non-Western. Specifically, I have reservations about how Los Alamos National Laboratory (LANL) has historically related to its surrounding communities in northern New Mexico. These are primarily, although not entirely, Pueblo Indian or Hispanic communities.

Finally, I intend to provide an historical overview and cultural context for discussion of the findings and issues raised and presented by the Impact Los Alamos Oral History Project. In short, I would like to be very clear that I do not see the story of Los Alamos as one in which there are "good guys" pitted against "bad guys." Our individual and collective lives and histories are far too complicated and complex to reduce them to simplistic soap operas. What first strikes me when I reflect on Los Alamos are the historical ironies associated with this community. After centuries, possibly millennia of slow change, Los Alamos suddenly experienced an explosive rate of political, social, and economic change after 1943.

From primordial times until the coming of the Spaniards in 1546, the life patterns of the indigenous pueblo and nomadic Indian tribes were governed by the seasons and the vagaries of weather. Change was very slow. Built into the indigenous communities, so to speak, were patterns of intimate relationship to all aspects of nature. There was, in fact, a striving for and an awareness of the need for harmony in such a cosmos. I tried to capture this sense of wholeness and harmony in my poem "Once a Man Knew His Name." This poem reflects my homage to Popé, an unsung hero of New Mexico. Popé was the leader of the Pueblo Revolt in 1680 that expelled the occupying Europeans. I would like to share a few stanzas with you:

> All is sacred in our world:
> Shimmering Mountain to the north.
> Obsidian Covered Mountain to the west.
> Turtle Mountain to the south.
> Stone Man Mountain to the east.
> All the hills are sacred.
>
> All the shrines are sacred.
> All the plazas are sacred.
> All the dances are sacred.
> All the directions and their colors
> Are sacred for the pueblo
> The Spaniards called San Juan.[5]

Though the coming of the Spaniards in 1546 interrupted native patterns, the rate of change, nevertheless, remained fairly slow. The Spaniards introduced many new animals, plants, and agricultural tools and technologies. The Pueblo Indians incorporated these changes into their world view probably because the Spaniards themselves were not caught up in the major European currents that would lead to the Scientific Revolution, the Enlightenment, and the rise of the idea of progress.[6] Also, because Spaniards recognized, understood, and legally allowed communal patterns of living, such as those encountered among the Pueblo Indians, changes introduced by the Spaniards were gradually incorporated into the native world view.

After the opening of the Santa Fe Trail in 1821, a more accelerated pace of change was introduced into the Southwest by the United States. The Southwest had been the far northern frontier of the Spanish Empire and then Mexico.[7] Even though an abundance of goods came down the Santa Fe Trail, transportation was slow and problematic for a number of reasons. The Apaches, Comanches, and other indigenous cultures also resisted this new and aggressive intrusion into their historic domain, combined with the conflicts of the American Civil War. The net effect was a delayed impact of the industrial revolution on the older cultures of the Southwest. In any case, the rate of technological change was still slow enough to allow Indians and Mexicans (called "Spanish" or Mexican Americans after 1846) to make reasonable adaptations.[8]

After the war of aggression against Mexico in 1846 and its conclusion with the Treaty of Guadalupe Hidalgo, honored more in the breaking rather than the keeping, and after the "trail of broken treaties" with Native Americans, the "old social order" in the Southwest was upset. The Native Americans became, at best, noble savages while the Mexicans, now citizens of the United States, remained by and large unwanted ignoble savages in the new order. Technological change and social uprootedness continued to proceed at a slow rate for a few more years in northern New Mexico.[9]

Life for the Pueblo Indians and the Hispanic population in the Los Alamos area went on much as it had before the United States imposed its political, social, and economic institutions upon their societies, only now the locals were economically dispossessed and their agrarian way of life became confined to ever narrower domains as permitted by the new Anglo-American order. Despite all the upheavals, change was still relatively slow until the coming of the railroad in 1879.[10]

The impact of the railroad on New Mexico and the Southwest was enormous. Curiously enough, however, the railroad had a peculiar effect on northern New Mexico. The route that railroad developers chose swung down from Raton Pass to Las Vegas and then bypassed Santa Fe in favor of a route through Lamy and Albuquerque. It thus transformed a large quadrant of northern New Mexico into an economic backwater. The economic center of the state shifted south to Albuquerque. Santa Fe, Los Alamos, and all of Rio Arriba counties remained isolated and rural for Mexican and Indian inhabitants, but became something of a romantic hideaway for Americans ill at ease with some of the social, economic, and aesthetic consequences of the industrial revolution. Taos and Santa Fe became havens for artists, and the inhabitants of the Los Alamos area continued to live in a kind of splendid isolation. The modern world with all its stresses was just over the horizon to the east and to the south, but it was comfortably removed and would remain so until 1942.[11]

All this changed when J. Robert Oppenheimer and General Leslie R. Groves paid a fateful visit to Los Alamos in October 1942. From the war years and until the present, Los Alamos has experienced a half century of incredible change. An area that changed only slowly over a long period suddenly experienced sweeping transformation in what is historically a very short time. The Western individualistic and analytic world view was suddenly and dramatically imposed upon Los Alamos. Los Alamos had the Indian and Hispanic cultures still intermingled with their own communal values and traditions, as opposed to this Western world view.

In my mind, I keep returning to that journey up the Jemez River Valley undertaken by General Groves, the director of the Manhattan Engineering District (the atomic bomb project), and Oppenheimer, the brilliant, enigmatic, and charismatic theoretical physicist who was the director of Project Y (the code name for the bomb research and assembly part of the Manhattan Engineering District). Oppenheimer, familiar with New Mexico since his youth, had spent much time in the state. His family owned property near Pecos, and he thought that the Jemez area would be suitable for a project that might involve hundreds of scientists, as he then expected.[12] I have often wondered if Groves had the awareness of Oppenheimer, or to what extent either of them really cared as they drove north that they were following the path of a sacred river. They were crossing a territory populated by people of ancient cultures who possessed an utterly different world view. Here, where sacred rituals were performed throughout the year to harmonize the relationship between humans and the cosmos, the general and the scientist drove along old U.S. 85 through rich farmlands and orchards along the east bank of the Jemez River. No one spoke to the locals about what was planned. No one consulted them. No one was interested in what they had to say. No one saw any need whatsoever to consider their input on the momentous decisions underway. For all practical purposes, the dwellers of this land were mere local color. They were, in effect, part of the landscape.

From Bernalillo, Groves and Oppenheimer proceeded along State Route 44 to San Ysidro and on to Jemez Springs. They found the narrow Jemez canyon too confining so they continued their drive into the high country toward Valle Grande. Oppenheimer had long admired the land around Los Alamos, and he wanted the general to consider it as a possible site. As they continued north, the atomic fuse lit by modern physics under the pressure of the modern nation-state was slowly burning its way to Los Alamos. Since 1942, nothing has ever been the same. Not for Los Alamos, the United States, or for planet earth. I think that Los Alamos in its broadest context has forced us, and continues to force us, to try to comprehend the profoundly disturbing irony of how people and communities can be entirely left out of the decision-making processes that forever alter their relationship to land, their families, their cultures, and the entire human ecology.

The existence and demands of LANL have radically skewed all of the social, educational, and economic indices of northern New Mexico's counties. Some of these counties were among the poorest in the nation when the labs opened up. These same counties remain among the poorest in the nation while Los

Alamos county has one of the highest standards of living in the world.[13]

I am not pointing a finger here at any individual or group. What I am doing is raising a serious issue. Los Alamos has had two types of consequences: intended and unintended. The intended consequences involved the creation of immensely destructive weapon systems. The irony here is that atomic weapons development occurred in a spectacularly beautiful and peaceful part of this planet, where the older cultures had at long last learned to live together in relative, although certainly not perfect, harmony. We are now most concerned with the unintended consequences of Los Alamos. Surely one of these was the creation of a vast area of northern New Mexico economically characterized by gross differences in living standards that created a two-tiered welfare system. On the one hand, federal welfare existed for the bright, educated, and outstanding scientists and their coteries who were useful tools for furthering the goals of the nation-state during World War II and the cold war. Great wealth in the form of significant federal infusions of money was brought to northern New Mexico for immensely destructive purposes, even though these purposes were cast in terms of the noblest of intentions. On the other hand, the welfare programs of the New Deal and the Fair Deal were meant to help those who were historically present in the area, for those who were not so useful, and for those who, to put it succinctly, were in the way and had to be at least minimally placated.

As I see it, the three major ironies of Los Alamos are: rapid change introduced to an area where very slow historical evolution had occurred; the sudden imposition of a Western analytic and scientific tradition in a shroud of secrecy upon cultures of the area which had their own unique cultural orientations; and the unintended creation of a large island of social, economic, and educational inequality in the heart of northern New Mexico. These ironies raise questions that need answering.

Los Alamos merits the most serious concern because it is, in a sense, a metaphor for the world-at-large. The problems of Los Alamos are symbolic of the problems of Third World countries in their interactions with the West. To view these problems as opportunities for solutions is to indicate that we have not given up on the dynamics of history and change. Nothing is ever static. We are not necessarily forever frozen into old attitudes and postures but rather we can use our imaginations and intelligence to find solutions to our problems.

For the moment, I want to apply the concept of metaphor to the cultures we are considering here. Let LANL stand for everything we associate with the West, the Tewa world as a representative for New Mexico's indigenous cultures, and the Mexican-American world as a representative for the Hispanic communities in the Southwest. In this reduced frame of reference, several things become clear.

Geographically, LANL, the Tewa world, and the Mexican-American world exist in close proximity in northern New Mexico. These worlds overlap in a complex web of personal, social, economic, political, and cultural interactions. Each of these worlds has its own cosmology—its own highly effective and satisfactory explanatory devices for relating the human condition to the ecology of this planet and to the cosmos as a whole. Each of these worlds needs to protect its sacred precincts—laboratories, kivas, and moradas, respectively—from excessive intrusion by outsiders. Each of these worlds needs to interact with each other (and with all other human communities) in ways that amplify human potential everywhere.

Some useful concepts come to mind here. Murray Gell-Mann, in *The Quark and the Jaguar* (1994), has suggested that it is possible to view a human being as what he calls an information gathering and utilizing system, or IGUS.[14] George Johnson, in *Fire in the Mind* (1995), comments on this notion of an IGUS:

> At the deepest level we are all information gatherers—*Iguses*, in Gell-Mann's term. Dig deep enough through the layers of the mind and surely you will reach rock bottom, an impenetrable floor: the architecture of the brain as it was molded by evolution to find patterns, even if they are not always there. . . . We all share this belief in symmetries, and finding ourselves in a world where the symmetries have broken, we imagine a time before the fall from perfection, whether we call it Eden, the underworld, or the big bang.[15]

Take this concept to a higher level and think of an entire culture, any human community, as an IGUS. If a culture is envisioned as an information gathering and utilizing system, then it might be possible to more clearly describe and develop the most effective means and mechanisms for cross-cultural communication. An expanded and more accurate flow of information might help bring about more equitable political, economic, and social relations. This might realize, in effect, more equitable power relationships.

Recent attempts by Tomás Atencio and his associates in the Rio Grande Institute to develop a computerized communications net—La Resolana Electronica, as it is called—to link rural areas of northern New Mexico on the Internet with some urban areas may be the first significant and sophisticated approach to some of the paradoxes raised by the Los Alamos story as I have discussed here. A recent article by Atencio in *Quantum* reinforces the idea of a culture or a community as an IGUS:

[Places like Taos, Embudo, Dixon, Mora, Abiquiu and Santa Clara Pueblo] were missed by the industrial society at the production end. . . . We never had factories; we never had a working class. We remain peasants tied to the land and it is important that we not lose the energy that makes our ties to the land remain strong. We were missed by the Industrial Age, but we can't afford to be missed by the Information Age. Technology will bring people together.[16]

I would like now to raise some questions. First, we need to identify the issues of power and responsibility for what has happened and what is happening with relation to Los Alamos and the communities it impacts. In other words, what are the institutions and who are the persons who exercise power and authority in the Los Alamos area? Is that authority being exercised responsibly and for whose benefit? This question of power is serious and it needs to be addressed. We also need to address to what extent, if any, the communal values of the Indian pueblos and the Hispanic villages can be brought to bear on the future of Los Alamos. What should the roles be of the local communities in determining their own futures? If, as Gell-Mann argues, there is a central theme that connects the simple and complex, "the theme that connects the quark, the jaguar, and humanity," then what role do the communities have in helping to shape this theme and not merely react to it?[17]

A fourth question is whether any significant dialogue has been established between the various traditional, village-based communities and other communities in the Los Alamos area. Who is talking to whom and is anyone listening? A fifth question, in a broad sense, would be what values are at stake for both individuals and the communities? What I am concerned about are not the stated values that we easily pay lip service to, but rather the operational values such as those that we actually demonstrate through our deeds and actions. Sixth, I would ask what has been and continues to be the environmental impact of LANL? I am thinking of the environment in a larger, social sense as well as the natural. Seventh, what kinds of political, social, and economic interactions must we now consider for the future of Los Alamos? In other words, if a transfer of power needs to occur for the future of Los Alamos, how should that transfer occur? Who should exercise that power? In a sense, we are talking about boundaries. My eighth question would be what sort of boundaries, if any, make sense in the emerging internationalized world where ecological zones are more important than national boundaries? My ninth question would be who is going to make the new boundaries? I am looking beyond the boundaries of the ephemeral nation-state because I think that human cultures and communities are older, more profound, more enduring, and ultimately wiser and more likely to continue, despite their undeniable shortcomings. My last question involves the old way of looking at Los Alamos, national security, hierarchical national values focused on wartime needs, and an imposed scientific community distinct from and much better off economically than the surrounding communities. Is this old way good enough for a world of dubious national boundaries, worldwide communications, and growing ethnic and tribal concerns?

I would urge everyone, but particularly those in the scientific community, to look into their own philosophic and cultural roots for possible solutions to these problems. What wonderful opportunities they present! I would also remind the scientific community, if it needs reminding, that there is a deeply compassionate and humane tradition running through modern physics from Max Planck to Leo Szilard, Richard Feynman and others. In a little-known work of Planck's, *The Philosophy of Physics* (1936), he argues that the scientist, like the rest of us, must make a leap of faith when engaged in the dialogue with nature to understand the world:

> Anyone who has taken part in the building up of a branch of science is well aware from personal experience that every endeavor in this direction is guided by an unpretentious but essential principle. This principle is faith—a faith which looks ahead . . . associations of ideas are not the work of the understanding but the offspring of the investigator's imagination—activity which may be described as faith, or, more cautiously, as a working hypothesis. The essential point is that its content in one way or another goes beyond the data of experience. The chaos of individual masses cannot be wrought into a cosmos without some harmonizing force and, similarly, the disjointed data of experience can never furnish a veritable science without the intelligent interference of a spirit actuated by faith.[18] (#)

I would, then, remind the scientific community and everyone else that a harmonizing force has been present in New Mexico for a long time. Perhaps it is time to recognize the power of that force, its deep roots in alternative cultures and visions of the cosmos, its close association with communication and information, and to grant it the privilege of status, empowerment, and dialogue for the benefit of all of us. I think this harmonizing force appeals to what is best in all of us. I think we should pay it some heed while there is still time.

Notes

1. Spencer R. Weart and Gertrud Weiss Szilard, eds., *Leo Szilard: His Version of the Facts: Selected Recollections and Correspondence*, 2 vols. (Cambridge, Massachusetts: Massachusetts Institute of Technology Press, 1978), 2:186-88, 209-22.

2. Debra Rosenthal, *At the Heart of the Bomb: The Dangerous Allure of Weapons Work* (New York: Addison-Wesley, 1990), 33.

3. McAllister H. Hull, Jr., Joseph A. Schufle, and E. A. Mares, "Science in New Mexico: Origins and History," in *From Sundaggers To Space Exploration: Significant Contributions to Science and Technology in New Mexico*, a special issue of the *New Mexico Journal of Science*, ed. David Hsi and Janda Panitz. Published jointly by the New Mexico Academy of Science and the New Mexico Sigma Xi Chapters and Clubs. 26 (February 1986), 1-24.

4. E. A. Mares, "Los Alamos: From Where the Zigzag Lightning Strikes," *Albuquerque Journal, Impact Magazine*, 6 August 1985.

5. E. A. Mares, *The Unicorn Poem & Flowers and Songs of Sorrow* (Albuquerque, New Mexico: West End Press, 1992), 34.

6. Raymond Carr, *Spain: 1808-1939* (Oxford, England: Clarendon Press, 1966), 69, 76-78; and Roland N. Stromberg, *An Intellectual History of Modern Europe* (New York: Appleton-Century-Crofts, 1966), 169-70.

7. John Francis Bannon, *The Spanish Borderlands Frontier, 1513-1821* (Albuquerque: University of New Mexico Press, 1974), 229-33.

8. Donald Worcester, "The Significance of the Spanish Borderlands to the United States," in *New Spain's Far Northern Frontier: Essays on Hispanos and Indians in the American West, 1540-1821*, ed. David J. Weber (Albuquerque: University of New Mexico Press, 1979), 4-5; Edwin R. Sweeney, *Cochise: Chiricahua Apache Chief* (Norman: University of Oklahoma Press, 1991), 170, 177, 203; Marc Simmons, *New Mexico: A Bicentennial History* (New York: W. W. Norton, 1977), 149-64.

9. Marc Simmons, *New Mexico*, 149-64.

10. D. W. Meinig, *Southwest: Three Peoples in Geographical Change 1600-1970* (New York: Oxford University Press, 1971), 38-52.

11. Ibid., 46-47; George Johnson, *Fire in the Mind: Science, Faith, and the Search for Order* (New York: Alfred A. Knopf, 1995), 11-17.

12. Ferenc Morton Szasz, *The Day the Sun Rose Twice: The Story of the Trinity Sire Nuclear Explosion, July 16, 1945* (Albuquerque: University of New Mexico Press, 1984), 16.

13. See United States Census data for 1940, 1950, 1960, 1970, 1980, and 1990

on population, economics, employment, education, and housing for Los Alamos, Rio Arriba, Santa Fe, Taos, Mora, and San Miguel Counties in the state of New Mexico.

14 Murray Gell-Mann, *The Quark and the Jaguar: Adventures in the Simple and Complex* (New York: W. H. Freeman and Company, 1994), 155.

15. George Johnson, *Fire in the Mind*, 198.

16. Frank D. Martinez, "Sunny Side: One Project Shows That The Cultural Ties That Bind Can Be Electronic," *Quantum* 13 (Spring 1996), 25.

17. Gell-Mann, *The Quark and the Jaguar*, 367.

18. Max Planck, *The Philosophy of Physics* (New York: W. W. Norton, 1936), 121-22.

Tony Mares was aware of Los Alamos and the development of the atomic bomb from the time he was a child. He says there was lots of talk about it in Old Town, and after the war his father was a radiation technician at Los Alamos. As an historian, Mares found himself interested in the impact of Western science on the rest of the world, and found it extremely ironic that the development of the bomb had taken place where earlier cultures had worked out ways to get along. Mares is troubled by the fact that these people were not consulted about the bomb, saying that the scientists might at least have asked the native elders and holy people for their input. Mares sees the scientists' behavior as arrogant, claiming that adults ought not act so irresponsibly. Mares' advice to student writers is to know the grammar solidly, to master it, and to read fanatically and widely, especially the classics and moderns of every culture possible. Writers, he claims, cannot afford provinciality. Finally, Mares adds that for the young, computer literacy is a must, saying hopefully that this generation may be the one to see the dissolution of the nation-state as a result of the computer revolution.

For Discussion

1. Compare and contrast this essay to the one called "Los Alamos: From Where the Zigzag Lightning Strikes." What audience does the author expect in each case? Does the tone differ between the two? How so? Be specific, by referring to examples from both texts to support your points. Do the essays duplicate information, or are there clear rhetorical advantages to writing separate essays on the same topic?

2. What reasons can you give for reading about the bomb more than 50 years after it was developed? Refer to both texts, your own experience and opinion, and other relevant sources in your response.

3. Describe in detail what you understand the writer to be saying through the metaphor he uses in paragraph two.

4. Notice the self-conscious approach to the essay as the writer outlines his purpose and intent in paragraphs five through seven. What are those purposes? Does the writer deliver on this promise in the development of the rest of the essay? Make reference to specific passages from the essay to support your assertions as you formulate your response.

5. Paragraphs eight through 12 summarize thousands of years of history. How is this summary relevant to the writer's main points?

6. Reread paragraph 17 carefully, noting the details to which the author refers. Write for five minutes about your reactions to what you read here. Now read paragraph 18 . What impact does paragraph 18 have because of its relationship to paragraph 17?

7. In the final paragraphs of the essay, Mares lists 10 questions. What effect does ending with so many questions have on the reader?

8. Choose one of the questions Mares lists in paragraphs 23 and 24 and discuss how one could attempt to answer it.

9. What credentials does Mares list for himself as he sets out to examine this issue? Is it necessary for him to do this? Why?

10. Mares ends the essay by suggesting that time is running out. Do you agree? On what do you base your response? Do you feel you need to demonstrate authority to make this argument?

Los Alamos: From Where the Zigzag Lightning Strikes

E. A. Mares

Tony Mares was born and raised in plaza vieja (Old Town) Albuquerque. He attended college at Notre Dame and UNM before taking a B.A. in Spanish from Florida State. An M.A. in Spanish Literature followed, also from Florida State. Working a number of jobs as well as teaching, Mares returned to school for a Ph.D. in European history from the University of New Mexico. In the fall of 1995 he was hired to teach in the English Department at UNM.

An unholy glare as bright as Lucifer, the light bearer, filled the cockpit of a B-29 bomber, the Enola Gay, with an unending surge of light. Down below, at 1,850 feet, a fierce man-made sun, a fiery Cyclops of an eye, vaporized, burned and turned to ashes everything that came within its domain. It was exactly 8:15:43 on the morning of Aug. 6, 1945. The place was Hiroshima, and the first atomic bomb used in warfare had exploded.

In less than a millisecond, a major current of Western thought had reached a brilliant and terrible apogee. The same process of logical analysis that produced the wonders of Western culture, its science, medicine and high standards of living, had now led to the deaths of more than 100,000 men, women and children in Hiroshima. At the core of that logical process was the idea that the human mind could be separated from the consequences of what it imagined and produced.

Never had such immense destruction been produced by so many profound minds. And a significant portion of these talented thinkers had gathered together at a place called Los Alamos, New Mexico, in the spring of 1943.

Is Los Alamos the benefactor of mankind, where the definitive weapons were developed to end World War II and possibly all wars? Or is Los Alamos the beginning of the final chapter in the history of Western civilization? The answers to these questions are not simple. And all answers are haunted by the nuclear threat. "If our God, whom we serve, can save us from the white-hot furnace and from your hands, O King, may he save us," said the prophet in the book of Daniel.

Because of what happened in Los Alamos between 1942 and 1945, the world in its varied tongues is still looking for salvation from the white-hot furnace.

In the beginning, thousands of years ago, Los Alamos was a place where the earth was shattered, not by fissioning nuclei, but by the dancing feet of the Anasazi. These early Indians built their cliff dwellings and their pueblos throughout the area. For those primordial dwellers, Los Alamos was part of the center of their universe, where earth and sky, man and beast and all that was seen and unseen in the cosmos met in the fullness of their need and their mystery. All was sacred and meaningful in this world view—their hills, their shrines, their plazas and their dances.

It was a holistic world view; the early Indian dwellers had not acquired, nor would they for several millennia, that habit of mind that is the glory and bane of Western civilization: a tendency to split and categorize the world, the experience of the world, into myriad separate domains that are treated as if they were worlds unto themselves, with their own theories, their own laws and a sense of absolute separateness that was taken for granted.

In October 1942, two men met in Albuquerque to locate and identify a possible site for the most highly specialized and unorthodox project in the history of science—the building of the first atomic bomb. One of the men was Gen. Leslie M. Groves, director of the Manhattan Engineering District, as the total atomic bomb project was called. The other was J. Robert Oppenheimer, the brilliant, charismatic and enigmatic theoretical physicist who was the director of Project Y, the code name for the bomb research and assembly part of the Manhattan Engineering District.

Oppenheimer was familiar with New Mexico. Since early youth, he had spent much time in the state, and his family owned property near Pecos. He thought the Jemez area, near Albuquerque, would be suitable for a project that might involve up to an hundred scientists, as he then expected.

As they drove north from Albuquerque, Groves and Oppenheimer traveled up the mid Rio Grande valley, the path cut by the sacred river and populated by Indian pueblos whose world view was utterly different from that of the general and the scientist. Here was a land where sacred rituals were performed throughout the year to harmonize the relationship between man and the cosmos.

Groves and Oppenheimer drove along old U.S. 85 through rich farmland and orchards along the east bank of the Rio Grande. From Bernalillo, the two proceeded along SR 44 to San Ysidro and on to Jemez Springs. Oppenheimer and Groves found the narrow Jemez canyon too confining, so they continued their drive into the high country toward Valle Grande. Oppenheimer had long admired the land around Los Alamos, a quiet mountain village, and he wanted Groves to consider it as a possible site.

The Indians were not the only long-established dwellers of New Mexico whose homes and small villages retreated from the moving car as Groves and Oppenheimer drove on. As early as the sixteenth century, Spanish explorers and *conquistadores* had entered the region. By 1600, they were followed by Hispanic settlers who moved up the river valleys and the *cordilleras* extending north from Mexico. The early settlers soon found themselves in conflict not only with the nomadic Indians but with the agrarian pueblos as well. The pueblos revolted in 1680, driving the settlers temporarily from the land. When the settlers returned, in 1692, they learned to live in peace with the pueblos. The Hispanic villagers would pray for rain in their chapels and churches, but they would also consult the Indian religious leaders, the medicine men, on ways to reconcile man and nature in the cosmic voyage. But while their cultural origins were Spanish, at least in part, the Indohispanic settlers found themselves so far removed from those European roots that the European mind-set changed in these Southwestern realms. Perfect cooperation, of course, was never achieved, but there was a blending of peoples and cultures along the sacred river, a confluence of tools, early technologies and human needs that were being worked out in small adobe villages far away from the blazing analytical sun that had been ignited in fouteenth century Europe and had spelled the end of the Middle Ages. Now, in October 1942, the fuse lit by that sun was slowly burning toward the village of Los Alamos, high in the Jemez range.

For the road that Groves and Oppenheimer were traveling stretched back to the medieval roots of Western thought, even earlier. The ancient Greek philosophers had speculated about man and nature and had developed powerful tools, habits of thought, for analytical reasoning. They had even speculated on the structure of matter and had reasoned that the smallest units must be tiny, indivisible particles they called atoms. These early Greek thinkers provided much of the scientific perspective for their own times and for the later Roman Empire.

In the disintegration of that empire, however, a new force, Christianity, arose as a compelling vision of the world. It became the task of the greatest Christian thinkers to try to reconcile the ancient Greek knowledge with Roman law and, above all, Christian theology. The philosophers who engaged in this effort were called scholastic, and by 1274 the greatest of their number, Thomas Aquinas, had achieved a brilliant synthesis of Greek science and Christian theology. Aquinas' *Summa Theologica*, still incomplete at his death in 1274, brought into harmony an hierarchical view of the universe: God, the angels, the saints occupied the highest spheres; man and all his works were at an intermediate level; the plants and animals occupied the lower realms; and all were united for the Divine purpose. Unknown to the Christian philosophers, there were other men— on parts of the planet as yet undiscovered by Europeans—who held quite different views of the world, but with one idea in common: a cosmos characterized by harmony between all its parts in a great chain of being that stretched from the most insignificant scrap of matter to the highest realms of deities and creative forces. For the Indians of the Americas, it was a view of life that was to endure to this day. For the Europeans, it was a mere moment in their development. In less than a century, a new group of philosophers, partially clustered around an English Benedictine monk, William of Occam, was to fire the analytic bullet that split the nucleus of medieval harmony. In that moment, the road to Los Alamos was opened.

Seen in this perspective, Western thought is surrounded by a circle of death that culminated in the atomic bomb. By the middle of the fourteenth century, when William of Occam was challenging the key assumptions of Thomas Aquinas, Europe was under siege from the Black Death that rats had carried from one city to another. In the 1340s, Europe may have lost a quarter or more of its population to the great plagues. While European society crumbled in the face of this disease, so also the edifice carefully constructed by Thomas Aquinas began to crumble. William of Occam challenged the very premises of Aquinas' thought. It was not possible to reason, as Aquinas had done, from the realm of things to the realm of spirit, according to Occam. It was only possible, in Occam's view, to reason about things, objects that could be named, and to clarify their relationship to one another. The higher realms of spirit, for Occam, could be achieved only by faith, and not by reason. Here, of course, are some of the intellectual roots of Protestantism, but there is more to it than that. By suggesting that reason could become a finely honed weapon of the intellect for dealing with things, and things only, Occam's razor meant that precise chains of analytic reasoning could be used to explain the material universe. Here, then, were some of the key insights that were later to come to fruition in the scientific revolution of the seventeenth century. In 1348, Occam perished in the great plague. But he was one of the initiators of that spirit of intellectual excitement that began to assume mythological dimensions as man probed deeper and deeper into the structure of matter. At the beginning of the circle, then a crisis in Western thought occurred at the time of the Black Death. At the end of the circle, after six centuries of sharpening Occam's razor, a major mode of Western thinking led to many of the benefits of modern industrial societies. But it also led to a deadly poisonous black metal called plutonium.

Perhaps such dark thoughts did not occur to Groves and Oppenheimer as they continued to drive toward Los Alamos. It was a beautiful October day, and the mountain air was crisp and clean. By the time they reached the place where *los alamos*, the cottonwoods, grew, Oppenheimer had remembered there was a boys' school and some buildings. Groves was delighted with the location.

Why had the road that had begun in early modern Europe finally arrived at

Los Alamos, so remote in spirit and location from the origins of the science that had led there? The answer is surely one of the great adventure stories of all time. For the dynamic process of inquiry and analysis stirred up by William of Occam and others of his time had eventually led to enormous scientific discoveries and developments.

If the dethronement of medieval scholasticism left European science and philosophy in a quandary after 1348, the sense of insecurity only deepened in the 1400s and the 1500s. Discovery after discovery affirmed that man was no longer the center of the universe, that the silence of the cosmic spheres was terrifying and that the planets did not move, as they were supposed to, in perfect circles around the sun. Rather, they made elliptical motions.

At the beginning of the seventeenth century, the old order of man's relation to the world was in such disarray that a brilliant philosopher hit upon a method to put things right again, a way to bridge the gap between the new science and the old comforts of medieval philosophy. With one foot in the Middle Ages and another foot in the modern world, René Descartes published his findings in 1637, in a little book that continues to have profound reverberations. He called it *The Discourse on Method*. Essentially, this small masterpiece of logic argued that everything could be doubted except the existence of the one who doubted. Starting from this premise, Descartes was able to conclude that since he thought, he must indeed exist. He expressed it in the famous *cogito ergo sum*, I think, therefore I am. Starting from this premise, Descartes went on to deduce that the universe consisted of "thinking stuff," i.e., the mind and all its contents, and "extended substance," i.e., everything outside the mind. This system of thought has been known ever since as Cartesian dualism. It is another milestone on the road to Los Alamos; it was now possible for the European intelligentsia to have recourse to an elegant theory that would justify the separation of mind from matter. This separation meant, in turn, that the objective, material world could be looked upon as separate from man, from the human experience, and could be treated purely from an exploitive point of view. After Descartes, it mattered not what mind could shape out of matter. All that counted was the following of the logical rules for making true statements. If before Descartes, the Christian deity had been a participant in the affairs of man and nature, after Descartes, he was a geometer who watched his designs with aloof indifference. After Descartes, it was possible to think logically and carry out the consequences of that thought without worrying about the consequences.

By the end of the seventeenth century, however, order had seemingly been restored through the work of Sir Isaac Newton. Sometimes referred to as the Newtonian synthesis, what Newton accomplished was the formulation of a precise set of laws that reintroduced the notion of an orderly cosmos governed by celestial mechanics, or the universal principle of gravitation. Newton's discoveries united the disparate work of others such as Galileo and Kepler, into a systematic explanation that took into account all the material phenomena of the universe, or so it seemed. But all thought henceforth would travel under the shadow of Descartes. There was a growing gap between thought and its consequences.

The scientific revolution of the seventeenth century and the Enlightenment of the eighteenth century stand as proud sentinels along the path of development of Western culture. The path reached its summit in the nineteenth century. If ever there was a time of optimism, of rising expectations for the betterment of humanity, it was during the real nineteenth century—the period from the close of the Napoleonic wars in 1815 to the outbreak of World War I in 1915. During that period, especially after 1870, a new Golden Age appeared to dawn on Europe. Levels of industrial production, standards of health and education and public participation in politics were rising throughout Europe.

At the political level, however, there were danger signs that the institutions of Europe were not able to contain the dynamic processes unleashed by the analytic mode of thinking. New ideologies had arisen in the wake of the French Revolution. As the nineteenth century matured, liberalism, nationalism and socialism became increasingly smug and self-righteous. The adherents of these ideologies hardened their stances and became bitter enemies of one another.

Two hundred years after the work of Newton, disturbing currents also began to flow through the scientific community. Critically important to the Newtonian world view were the concepts of absolute space and absolute time. This is the space and time that guides ordinary people as they go about their everyday business. Space was supposed to exist against the background of an elusive substance called "the ether." In 1887, however, two American professors, Albert Abraham Michelson and E. Morley, conducted experiments showing that the ether probably did not exist. The Newtonian world view was flawed. What Newton had predicted about an absolute space and time had not been borne out by experiment.

What began as small doubt in the late nineteenth century became in the early twentieth century a veritable storm of new discoveries that upset the reassuring world view of Newton. Beginning with Albert Einstein's discovery of relativity and Max Planck's formulation of quantum mechanics, the early twentieth century once again saw the placid assumptions of the past bleached white in the glare of the analytic sun.

Most mysterious of all the new discoveries were X-rays and other forms of radiation. Instead of consisting of solid bits of matter, atoms were apparently composed of subatomic particles, of negatively charged electrons that orbited around a core of positively charged protons and electrically neutral neutrons. The atom, then, lost the stability it had long been assumed to have in the Western tradition.

These discoveries led to a sense of unparalleled excitement among the European and American scientists. In keeping with their analytical tradition, they began to probe ever deeper into the structure of the atom.

Almost all the political hopes, the social expectations and the ambiance of general optimism of Europe died in the trenches of World War I. The dashing hero of military romance became the grim statistical entry of one more number added to the millions killed and maimed.

In the terrible aftermath of World War I, new and frightening totalitarian states came to the forefront in Europe. Fascist Italy and Nazi Germany combined bureaucratic organizational techniques with strident nationalism and bitter ideologies that threatened to destroy the humanitarian traditions of Western societies. In Russia, a particularly harsh and militant variant of socialism developed, and the Western powers, by not supporting Lenin and the old Bolsheviks, lost the opportunity to encourage the development of a more democratic type of socialism.

Against this background, the story of Los Alamos takes on a particular poignancy. It began with the fervent efforts of the best scientific minds of Europe and America to beat the Nazis in the race to make an atomic bomb.

A small core of the best and the brightest European physicists had been aware, by the early 1930s, of both the potential of the atom and also the political danger of Nazi Germany. For example, Leo Szilard, a brilliant, idiosyncratic and utterly humane physicist from Hungary, had excellent insight into the Nazis. He kept all his belongings in two suitcases, and after the Reichstag fire in 1933, he fled to England. While there, he remembered a novel he had read a year earlier—H. G. Wells' *The World Set Free*—that talked of atomic bombs. Suddenly the idea of a chain reaction releasing the energy of the atom came to him. Szilard, greatly concerned about the problem of evil in the world, soon began to worry about the prospect of the Nazis' developing the bomb first. Had this occurred, Szilard later speculated, the Nazis would surely have won World War II.

These were not empty fears. One of the three European centers where rapid advancement was taking place in understanding the intricacies of the atom was the University of Gottigen in Germany. A second center was in Copenhagen, which was quickly overrun by the Nazis during the war. The third center was the Cavendish Laboratory in Cambridge, England.

Throughout the 1930s, the European physicists made one exciting discovery after another. James Chadwick, at Cavendish, discovered the neutron, which, because it was electrically neutral, gave promise of being able to penetrate the electron shield around the atom's nucleus and strike it. Were this to occur, then the nucleus might split, or fission, and release an enormous burst of energy. By 1934, Enrico Fermi had bombarded the nucleus of an uranium atom and produced a new set of radioactive elements. He received the Nobel Prize for his work, but he did not perceive that he had actually initiated the fission process. (Years later, Fermi was to remark after seeing an illustration of a scientist that the figure was "probably a physicist not discovering fission.") Fermi never returned to his native Italy after receiving his Nobel Prize. He went into exile with his Jewish wife in the United States.

The exodus from Europe continued. Lise Meitner, a Jewish physicist at the Kaiser Wilhelm Institute in Berlin, fled to Sweden. There she told her nephew, Otto Frisch, about the experiments she and Otto Hahn had been conducting in Berlin. By bombarding uranium with neutrons, they unexpectedly produced the element barium. Meitner and Hahn speculated that they might have split the atom. Otto Frisch contacted physicists at Niels Bohr's Institute for Theoretical Physics at Copenhagen. Bohr, one of the leading physicists of his time, had discovered the structure of the atom. Soon Bohr and his researchers identified the splitting of the atom for what it was and gave an old word from biology an ominous new twist: the word was "fission."

By the summer of 1939, Leo Szilard had become increasingly restless as Europe drifted toward war. He was appalled at the lack of secrecy with which the physicists exchanged information about the discoveries in nuclear science. He had tried to convince the Americans that a serious threat would exist if the Nazis were the first to control the power of atomic fission and, thus, the bomb.

After some adroit maneuverings and with the aid of a fellow Hungarian in exile, Eugene Wigner, Szilard convinced Albert Einstein to send a letter—which Szilard wrote and Einstein signed—to President Franklin D. Roosevelt, expressing the urgency of the matter. The letter clearly stated the developments that had occurred and was somewhat vague about the implications of this new force. "In the course of the last four months it has been made probable—in America— that it may become possible to set up a nuclear chain reaction in a large mass of uranium by which vast amounts of power and large quantities of new radium-like elements would be generated. . . . This new phenomenon would also lead to the construction of bombs, and it is conceivable—though much less certain— that extremely powerful bombs of a new type may thus be constructed."

The peaceful days at Los Alamos were numbered. Shortly after Roosevelt read the letter, Nazi armies invaded Poland. The president then set a slow bureaucratic machinery in motion toward the making of an atomic bomb.

Soon after Groves and Oppenheimer visited Los Alamos, the small town began to be transformed into a secret military base. Although nuclear research had been primarily a European phenomenon, there were excellent nuclear physicists in the United States. And Oppenheimer was an astute choice for heading the project. Because he was steeped in knowledge about physics and had experienced brilliant residencies in major American and European universities, Oppenheimer was both abreast of his field and in contact with major contributors to the development of nuclear science. He had been associated with Ernest O. Lawrence, the inventor of the cyclotron, at Berkeley, and he knew most of the young, bright scientists on a first-name basis. Soon a core had gathered at Los Alamos, the *Who's Who* of the nuclear scientific community.

While Oppenheimer had envisioned a project requiring about 100 scientists, eventually several thousand came to Los Alamos to work on the bomb. Fear of Nazi Germany drove many; others were also attracted by the irresistible urge to experiment with such mighty forces. To be able to unleash and control, or attempt to control, one of the basic forces of the universe is heady stuff.

Besides, there were no real misgivings, initially, concerning the making of the bomb. The Nazi and Fascist menaces had to be stopped. Beyond that, the new weapon held the promise of a devastation so great that it would put an end to all war forever.

Groves had wanted to compartmentalize the bomb research, but Oppenheimer refused to go along with that idea. He sensed, correctly, that for a project so vast and complex, an unimpeded flow of information and exchange of ideas would hasten the goal—an atomic bomb. But no one apparently noticed that to achieve a significant collective goal, one of the processes deeply imbedded in the Western tradition had to be temporarily suspended. The process of analysis and compartmentalization of labor had made possible the type of material growth and development that distinguished the West from other societies. There is a great irony here: it was as if the gap between mind and matter opened by Descartes in the seventeenth century had suddenly to be ignored to bring mind and matter closer together for the explicit purpose of making the atomic bomb. Oppenheimer brought about a temporary harmony of mind, matter and purpose at Los Alamos. He overrode Descartes, in a sense, for a quite specific purpose: the making of the bomb.

Those who have commented on the war years at Los Alamos have pointed out the high morale that was engendered by Oppenheimer's group approach. For three years, then, from 1943 to 1946, a dedicated team of scientists, engineers and technicians, most of them in their twenties and thirties, labored with great idealism to make the bomb, or "the gadget," as they called it, before the Nazis had one.

By the spring of 1945, the Nazis were in full retreat. Their main armies had been smashed, their *festung Europa*, or fortress Europe, was in shambles, and the victorious armies of the Western powers and the Soviet Union were pressing toward final victory over the dying Third Reich. As early, at least, as 1944, some of the scientists involved in the Manhattan Project became concerned about the possible use of "the gadget" if there were no real military need for it. Foremost of these was Leo Szilard. He had initially pressed for the bomb because of the Nazi threat. Once the Nazis were defeated, however, Szilard saw no need to use the bomb against the Japanese, who were facing certain defeat. He now saw the use of the bomb as an unnecessary, inhumane act.

Szilard and a few other scientists, however, were the exception rather than the rule in terms of being concerned about the negative consequences of the bomb. Their thinking was holistic in a way that cuts against the grain of Cartesian dualism. They saw themselves as having a long-range social responsibility. Their colleagues, who thought within the Cartesian mold, separated their work on the bomb from the uses of "the gadget."

Szilard was working at the University of Chicago's Metallurgical Laboratory, the code name for the effort to produce a chain reaction, and he began to address his concerns about the bomb to as many scientists and politicians as would listen to him. He had arranged for a meeting with Eleanor Roosevelt to convey his concerns to the president. Before the meeting occurred, Roosevelt died. Szilard then tried to catch the attention of President Truman but was shunted aside to meet with James Byrnes, soon to become Truman's secretary of state. The meeting was unsuccessful. Szilard continued his efforts. Various committees of scientists were created at the Metallurgical Lab to express their concerns about the future directions of atomic weapons. One of these was the Social and Political Implications Committee, headed by James Franck; it included Szilard. On June 11, 1945, the committee issued its report, known as the Franck Report, expressing the concerns of many of the nuclear physicists and other scientists involved in the Manhattan Project.

Two major concerns dominated the thinking of Szilard and the other scientists who were beginning to have second thoughts about the bomb. One was the impact of the bomb on society after the war. A second concern was the future use of atomic energy. Both concerns were reflected in the Franck Report. Although it was first issued secretly in June of 1945 and not declassified until May of 1946, the Franck Report was amazingly prescient. "We found ourselves," says the report, "by the force of events during the last five years, in the position of a small group of citizens cognizant of a grave danger for the safety of this country as well as for the future of all the other nations, of which the rest of mankind is unaware."

Recognizing the gravity of the moment, the signers of the Franck Report foresaw the stark probability of a nuclear-arms race: "In the absence of an international authority which would make all resort to force in international conflicts impossible, nations could still be diverted from a path which must lead to total mutual destruction, by a specific international agreement barring a nuclear arms race."

The report was specific in its admonition against the use of "the gadget" as a weapon: "We believe that these considerations make the use of nuclear bombs for an early unannounced attack against Japan inadvisable. If the United States were to be the first to release this new means of indiscriminate destruction upon mankind, she would sacrifice public support throughout the world, precipitate the race for armaments, and prejudice the possibility of reaching an international agreement on the future control of such weapons."

As might be expected from young and idealistic scientists, there was an air of optimism concerning the future peaceful potential of the atom. "The large installations and the accumulation of explosive material at present earmarked for potential military use will become available for important peacetime developments, including power production, large engineering undertakings, and mass production of radioactive materials."

The lethal hazards of radiation were only dimly understood in 1945, the problem of accumulation of radioactive waste materials was underestimated, and no one knew what a meltdown was. Seven members of the Social and Political Implications Committee signed the Franck Report. The last name was that of Leo Szilard.

Not all the scientists, of course, agreed. Many believed that a powerful weapon should be used if it promised to end the war quickly. Although Germany had surrendered, Japan still held out, and estimates of American casualties in an invasion of Japan ran as high as 500,000 killed and wounded. Oppenheimer anguished over the use of the bomb, but he was extremely effective in blocking Szilard and others who were set against using it. Perhaps Oppenheimer felt momentarily trapped by the onrush of events. He later expressed regret that the Japanese had not been allowed to witness the Trinity Site test of the first atomic explosion near Alamogordo.

It is early in the morning, May 1, 1985. Driving up from Albuquerque, an aging runner has been quietly humming a tune from the '60s. He parks his car and walks quietly to the small crowd gathered in the pleasant meadow. There is an improvised altar in the meadow, behind it a large cross. Not far from the altar, a river runs full and the current makes a sound of muffled water in the background as a hymn begins to rise from the gathered people: "Holy, Holy, Holy Lord, God of Heaven and Earth, adored."

This is Chimayo, and there will be a Mass this morning behind the Santuario de Chimayo, a holy shrine in northern New Mexico. After the mass, runners will carry a small parcel of sacred earth—believed to have healing powers— from the Santuario to Ashley Pond in front of Fullerton Lodge at Los Alamos. This is a mixed crowd. There are representatives of all major religious denominations. There are Navajos and Hopis. Some people carry placards and petitions concerned with anti-abortion stances, Kent State, the Indians of Guatemala. More hymns begin to rise from the crowd. As the Mass is celebrated by Archbishop Roberto Sanchez, the sound of sheep and goats can be heard in corrals not far away. Across Chimayo River, horses and cattle are standing in rich pasture land. A woman sings off-key, and yet her voice is beautiful and comforting in this setting.

After Mass, Sister Gloria Davis, accompanied by a Tewa Indian, recites a Blessing Ceremony. She scatters corn pollen and her voice rises:

> Blessing is restored to me
> From where the zigzag lightning strikes,
> Blessing is restored to me
> From where darkness rises in the north
> Blessing is restored to me.

Soon the runners are off. Moving in relays, they carry the sacred earth along the road to Los Alamos. For the aging runner, this is a formidable task. His legs quickly become rubbery and his lungs fight desperately to bite into the air. As the runners slowly inch up the steep mountain road to Los Alamos, he is almost overwhelmed by the exertion and by the powerful and hypnotic beauty of the Jemez Mountains.

About a mile from their goal, the runners regroup as an affirmation of their solidarity and run the remaining distance to Ashley Pond together. At least 100 peace demonstrators are waiting at the pond for the runners to appear.

As the aging runner rounds the last bend, he hears the cheer from the crowd and knows he is not running alone. He thinks of Hans Bethe and Victor Weisskopf and the many other nuclear scientists who have come to look upon the weapons designed here as an abomination. He thinks of the tragically flawed promise of nuclear energy, the deaths from radiation whose numbers are legion, and yet the day is bright with promise. The cheers he hears as he and the others approach the finish line remind him of the Greek marathon runners, and he exults in the physical joy of this moment. It is a total experience that defies separation into body and mind, matter and spirit, the inner experience and the outer world, the subjective impression and the objective "matter."

It is a joy come full circle to an earlier time, a mythic time, when man and the world were one. The runner senses there is no going back to that vision, but working together, one and all, there may be a way of going forward to it, a way to heal the old wounds, the old divisions. New forms of thought, action and freedom may give birth to a more fulfilling vision of the world where all people are creative participants and not merely cogs in a mindless machine.

Sister Gloria Davis takes the sacred earth from Chimayo and scatters it over Ashley Pond. Long before Descartes, long before the analytic Greeks, the Anasazi Indians and later the Hispanic settlers saw these particles of earth as wholesome bearers of life. Greater than the circle of death, then, is the circle of life coming back to Los Alamos.

There is still time to stumble on into the future here, where the zigzag lightning strikes and the darkness rises in the north. There is still time for hope at Los Alamos and elsewhere. At least until the last millisecond.

Tony Mares was aware of Los Alamos and the development of the atomic bomb from the time he was a child. He says there was lots of talk about it in Old Town, and after the war his father was a radiation technician at Los Alamos. As an historian, Mares found himself interested in the impact of Western science on the rest of the world, and found it extremely ironic that the development of the bomb had taken place where earlier cultures had worked out ways to get along. Mares is troubled by the fact that these people were not consulted about the bomb, saying that the scientists might at least have asked the native elders and holy people for their input. Mares sees the scientists' behavior as arrogant, claiming that adults ought not act so irresponsibly. Mares' advice to student writers is to know the grammar solidly, to master it, and to read fanatically and widely, especially the classics and moderns of every culture possible. Writers, he claims, cannot afford provinciality. Finally, Mares adds that for the young, computer literacy is a must, saying hopefully that this generation may be the one to see the dissolution of the nation-state as a result of the computer revolution.

For Discussion

1. What rhetorical affect is achieved through referencing Lucifer in the first sentence? Examine the words of this sentence carefully, and show how they establish point of view.

2. Mares makes a big jump through Western intellectual history, as he hints in paragraph two. How effectively has he made his argument by the time he reaches his conclusion? Note the transitions in the essay that mark the development of the argument.

3. Explore the differences in world view briefly suggested in paragraph five. What does it mean to say the indigenous people had an "holistic" world view? Is the characterization of Western culture the writer presents "fair"? What advantages and disadvantages can you see for both ways of looking at human experience?

4. Paragraph nine suggests early efforts to make multicultural coexistence in New Mexico a reality. Is this a romantic view? Examine Mares' examples, and discuss whether you think that kind of cooperation is, can, or should be possible today.

5. Paragraphs 24 and 25 provide a transition from the long examination of European intellectual history to the focus on the development and use of the bomb. Was the creation of the bomb inevitable? How do history and exigencies of the present conspire to create political realities such as the atomic attacks on Hiroshima and Nagasaki? Can you think of other examples in recent history?

6. Mares notes that Oppenheimer regretted that "the Japanese had not been allowed to witness the Trinity Site test of the first atomic bomb explosion near Alamogordo." Speculate for a few paragraphs how the world might have been different if the United States had sent Japan film of the tests at Trinity Site rather than using the bomb on civilian populations in Hiroshima and Nagasaki.

7. Mares returns to his multicultural theme in the final paragraphs of the essay. How important is this to the points he makes in this long essay?

8. Like the essay "Los Alamos: Coming Down from the Hill of Certainty," this essay ends suggesting a shortage of time. What effect does this have on you as the reader?

RIDING THE MAGIC CARPET

When to Forgo the Joe
Bryant Furlow

Born and raised in Oregon, Bryant Furlow first attended Portland Community College before moving to Albuquerque to study biology at the University of New Mexico. He graduated in 1997 and plans a year off before attending graduate school. Furlow expects to pursue a Ph.D., studying evolutionary ecology.

Starbucks and Peet's Coffee have gotten rich dispensing the world's most popular drug. But caffeine—or 1,3,7-trimethylxanthine, as it's scientifically known—does more than keep coffee houses perking. It's used to treat apnea, migraines, even acne. And it reduces the number of fatal car accidents.

So varied are caffeine's uses, in fact, that few blinked when a team of Harvard researchers recently suggested that a jolt of java might prevent suicide. Female nurses who drink coffee are far less likely to commit suicide than those who don't, reported Ichiro Kawachi, M.D., and colleagues in the *Archives of Internal Medicine*. In fact, the more coffee a nurse consumes, the less likely she is to take her own life.

But not so fast. Psychologists worry that amid the flood of praise from scientific circles, coffee's dangers will be ignored. Caffeine, they note, tricks the body into that state of alert known as "fight or flight." The heart races, blood pressure jumps, and—for serious mainliners of mud—hands tremble and muscles twitch. This may be a mere annoyance in emotionally healthy folks, but it can complicate treatment for psychiatric patients, notes the University of British Columbia's Arnold Kruger, Ph.D. Chronic anxiety, panic disorders, and depression can all be exacerbated by caffeine. The drug may also interfere with tranquilizers like Valium.

Given all this, Kruger's advice that caffeine access be limited in psychiatric settings seems sensible. But his suggestion that our all-consuming addiction may justify a caffeine-free society makes him sound like he's well, full of beans.

Bryant Furlow has written a number of articles for Psychology Today *and other scientific journals. He is interested in making science writing more readily available to a lay readership. Furlow notes that there is a great deal of discussion about both the dangers and potential benefits of caffeine. He argues we should be suspicious of moralizing rhetoric, especially in science. Furlow encourages student writers to follow their own interests, to immerse themselves in reading to become familiar with the topic, and to look for common themes as well as side skirmishes. Asked about his audience, Furlow says he writes for his grandmother, who likes science writing, and himself of seven years ago when he discovered his own love of reading and writing.*

For Discussion

1. What tone does the piece take? List the words and phrases that indicate this.

2. How seriously does Furlow take the concern over caffeine? Cite your evidence.

3. What does Furlow's position suggest about society's position on other drugs? That is, if caffeine is a drug that is routinely used in our society, despite evident health risks, might we worry less about certain so-called "recreational drugs?" Use evidence from relevant outside sources to support your answers, going beyond simple yes and no responses.

4. What do you make of Furlow's puns? List them, then discuss what they add or take away from the essay.

5. Are you a caffeine "user?" Have you or anyone you know ever shown the symptoms Furlow lists for reactions to caffeine? Describe how you have seen caffeine affect the behavior of others. Write about any caffeine "addicts" you know. To what extent do you use caffeine on a daily basis?

6. Go to one of the coffee shops on or near campus and note details—types of coffees available, flavors, and prices. What does the place smell like? Describe the people you see. Listen to bits of dialogue and write a short story based on what you see and hear.

On the Chemistry of Learning

G. Dana Brabson

Dana Brabson grew up in Ohio and took a B.S. in chemical engineering at Case Institute of Technology. He did his M.S. and Ph.D. in physical chemistry at the University of California, Berkeley. Brabson spent 27 years in the U.S. Air Force, teaching at the Air Force Academy for several of those years. He has taught in several research universities since leaving the Air Force, and now at UNM researches the chemistry of fire suppression.

> *The remarkable match—*
> *A source of energy,*
> *Capable of illuminating a dark corner;*
> *Able to ignite a pile of aromatic autumn leaves.*
> *A small storehouse of energy awaiting release.*

To a chemist, a match is a classic illustration of a system to which a small amount of energy must be added in order that the potential energy stored in the system can be released. The principal components of the match are carbon, hydrogen and oxygen; additional constituents compose the head. And the primary products of combustion are carbon dioxide and water. Moreover, since these products are more stable than the reactants, burning results in a net release of energy—of heat and light.

If the carbon dioxide and water are more stable than the constituents of the original match stick, what prevents the match from spontaneously igniting? It would seem that there must be some sort of barrier which must be surmounted as a prelude to the ignition of the match.

Indeed, this is precisely the chemist's description of the match. As illustrated by Figure 1, an activation energy barrier lies between the reactants and the products. The friction of striking the match enables a few molecules to surmount the barrier. The net energy released as these molecules reorganize to form products is more than adequate to enable additional reactant molecules to "jump" the barrier, and the process becomes self-sustaining.[1]

It is immediately apparent that life as we know it is possible because of activation energy barriers which provide stable (or at least metastable) residences for the molecules of which we and our environment are composed. It is useful to picture molecules as occupying an ancient volcanic caldera, such as the beautiful, 175-square mile Valle Grande, west of Los Alamos, New Mexico,

ACTIVATION ENERGY DIAGRAM

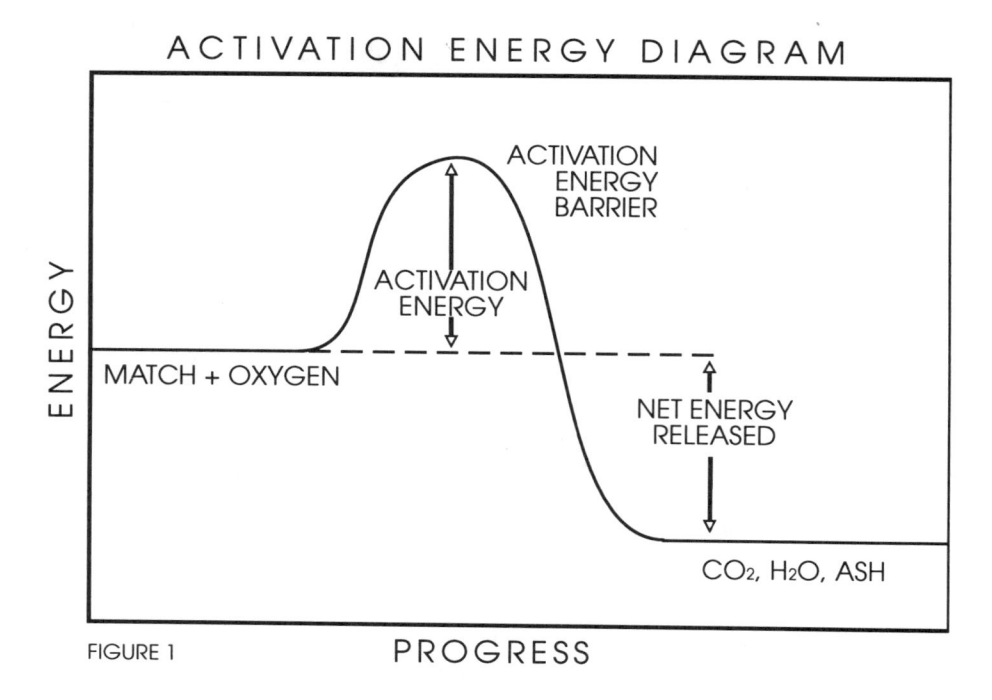

FIGURE 1

surrounded on all sides by a ring of hills.

Given the existence of activation energy barriers, how do we deal with them? As suggested by the match, one technique is to increase the energy of the reactants. We may choose to increase the temperature of the reaction mixture, thus increasing the average energy of all the molecules. Alternatively, we may opt to selectively excite just a few molecules, for example, with a pulse of laser light.

In a sense, raising the energy of the reactants is a brute-force technique. A more subtle approach involves finding an alternate reaction path for which the barrier is not as high, as illustrated by Figure 2. Catalysts are chemical entities which accomplish precisely this objective. A catalyst actually alters the course of the reaction, usually by reacting with one of the starting materials to create a temporary chemical species that subsequently reacts further to yield the products. It is significant to note that a catalyst opens a reaction pathway which otherwise would not be available. Moreover, the catalyst is not consumed by the reaction; after being engaged in its role, it is regenerated. Thus a small amount of catalyst can have a tremendous effect on the course of a reaction. Among the best known catalysts are the enzymes which aid in the digestion of food. Enzymes are known which accelerate reactions by as much as a factor of 1,000,000,000,000,000. It has been said that in the absence of enzymes, it would

ACTIVATION ENERGY DIAGRAM

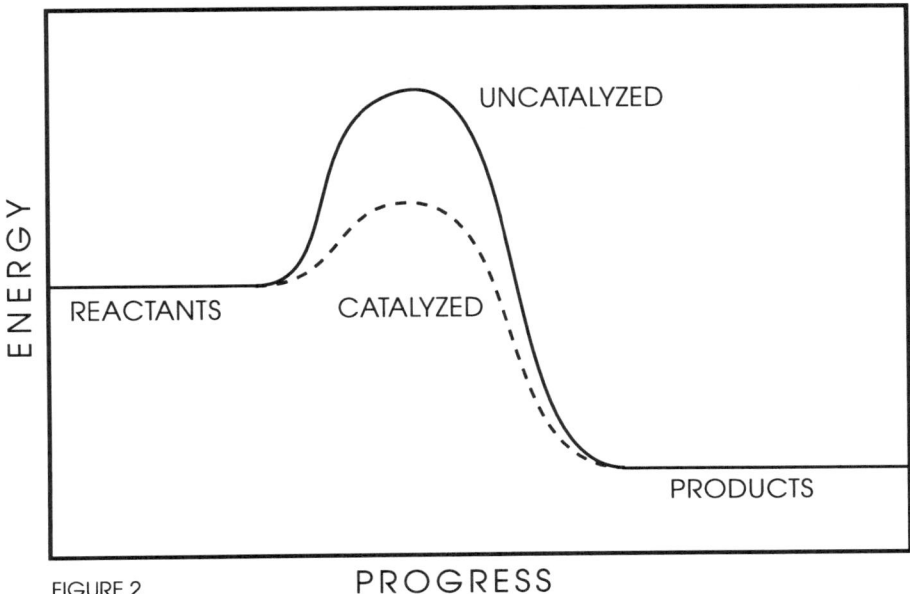

FIGURE 2

take 50 years to digest a meal.

And then there is tunneling. Occasionally, an electron without the requisite energy to surmount the activation energy barrier nevertheless appears on the other side of the barrier. This phenomenon, called tunneling because the electron seems to have tunneled through the barrier, is explained quantum mechanically by recognizing that the wave function of the electron has a finite (though very small) amplitude outside the barrier. Thus there is an extremely small, but sometimes measurable, probability of finding the electron outside the barrier.

For the chemist, the chemical reaction provides an intriguing model of the learning process. We begin by observing that the brain consists of an orderly array of molecules, as suggested conceptually by Figure 3(a).[2] Each molecule in this structure occupies its own potential energy minimum. To change the structure, it is necessary to add energy so that appropriate energy barriers may be surmounted.

It is conceptually useful to compare the structure of knowledge with the structure of the brain. Sensory inputs are transmitted to the brain by sequences of chemical reactions in the nerves. The brain is a zone of continuous activity, generating detectable electrical signals. Indeed, it is difficult to imagine that the structure of the brain is the same before and after introduction of a new bit of knowledge. It is, therefore, suggested that there is a relationship (perhaps direct, perhaps holographic) between the structure of the brain and the structure of knowledge, and Figure 3(a) serves as a useful visualization of the structure of knowledge as well as of the brain. The value of Figure 3 stems, at least in part, from the fact that it yields conclusions in accord with experience. Thus, for example, new information is most readily acquired when it can be attached to existing knowledge, as suggested by Figure 3(b). Moreover, experience suggests that, in many circumstances, new information is incompatible with existing structures and, therefore, either must be rejected or must require revision of the current structure. See Figure 3(c). It is convenient to call these two processes assimilation (attachment of new information to existing structure) and accommodation (revision of existing structure to permit assimilation of new information).[3]

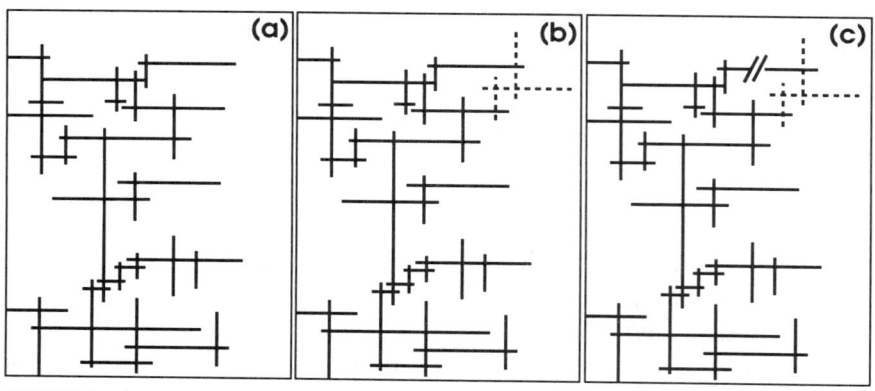

FIGURE 3

Consideration of chemical structures and structures of knowledge leads to the notion that each cognitive structure, like each chemical structure, is character-ized by a potential minimum, and the transition to a new structure is impeded by the potential energy barrier illustrated by Figure 1. As an aside, one is in-trigued by the appropriateness of the phrase "mind set" as a description of a pattern of thought surrounded by a barrier. Phenomenologically, there is ample evidence of barriers to assimilation and/or accommodation of new information, and two classes of barriers may be identified. The first class is encountered when there is a gap in the structure. In this instance, the learner does not have the necessary knowledge to "make sense out of" the new material. We may say that the learner lacks the requisite background or referents. The difficulty might be as simple as not understanding new terminology, or might be as complex as not having the ability to cope with the implied abstractions. The second class of barriers is encountered when the existing structure is incompatible with new information. This class includes the difficulties arising from preconceived notions, misconceptions, and prejudices.

Jean Piaget's concepts of *development* and of *learning* come into sharp focus at this point. It will be recalled that Piaget described four main factors which contribute to the development of cognitive structures: maturation, experience, social transmission, and equilibration.[4] For Piaget, the concept of equilibration plays a central role in the process of learning. Learning is an active response to a stimulus, and involves integration of new structural elements into the existing structure. Moreover, every stimulus is viewed in the context of existing structure. Thus, although learning results in modification of the existing structure, the process is mediated by the existing structure. And the driving force is the propensity for equilibrium. Equilibration, both in the chemical sense and in the Piagetian context, is the "settling" into a new minimum energy state. It is the spontaneous process which, in response to a stimulus, results in learning. Learning is, therefore, a provoked process in which disequilibrium events are encountered and dealt with; and teaching involves intervention ... the generation of disequilibrium events with which the student must deal. At this juncture, one pauses and wonders whether Piaget had the concept of the activation energy barrier in mind when he described the learning process.

Given the striking similarities between the description of a chemical barrier and the description of a cognitive barrier, one is intrigued by the thought that there might be concomitant similarities between the strategies for dealing with these barriers. Consider first the brute force technique of increasing the energy of the sample. In the cognitive domain, we call this motivating the student. There are, of course, numerous motivational tools—from the carrot to the stick. Moreover, as in the chemical case, one can selectively motivate a few students or one can apply strategies designed to motivate masses of people. In either case, the objective is to energize the learner so that he/she is capable of surmounting the barrier.

Alternatively, the teacher may seek to lower the barrier, to catalyze the learning process. In chemistry, the catalyst opens an alternate route having a lower barrier. In learning, the teacher points out errors in the current structure and fills voids in the existing structure. On the one hand, the teacher focuses on the current structure and suggests alternate structures which are in better accord with observation. On the other hand, the teacher assists in extending the existing structure so that it may serve as an attachment point for new information.

And finally, one asks whether there is a cognitive parallel to tunneling.

Tunneling is possible because the electron exists simultaneously on both sides of the barrier. The parallel to tunneling appears to be the intuitive leap by which the student seems to suddenly and effortlessly gain an understanding of a previously difficult concept. A "flash of insight" is strikingly similar to the sudden appearance of the electron outside the barrier, and is not a process mediated by the teacher. The teacher can only observe and marvel.

Yet there is another intriguing aspect of the chemical model. In this model, the products may be more stable than the reactants. This is represented in Figure 1 by the fact that the products are at lower energy. It, therefore, requires a greater input of energy to do something with the products. The cognitive parallel is presented in Figure 4. When we understand a concept more completely, we say that we have a "deeper understanding." When we first grasp a new concept, we often understand it incompletely, and the barriers to alteration are small; but as we grasp the concept more firmly, we develop a position which is firmer and more resistant to attack—a position with a higher barrier.

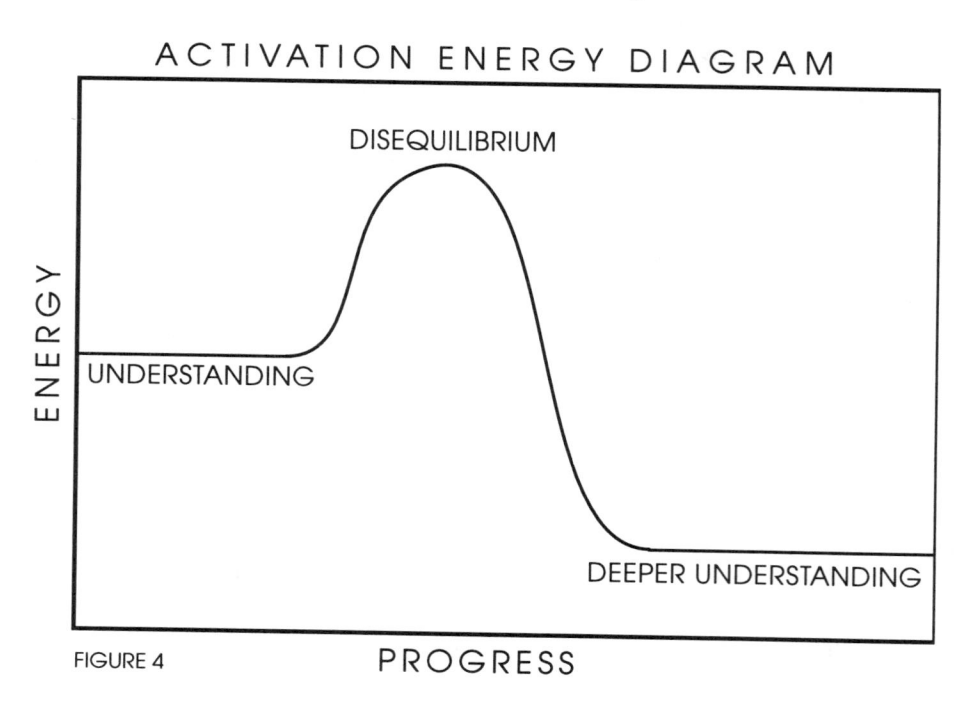

FIGURE 4

Moreover, as a match burns, the net energy released is more than sufficient to sustain the combustion process. Is there not an excitement in learning? Is there not a release of energy which stimulates the student to seek yet more knowledge?

And isn't the ultimate reward for the teacher the realization that a self-sustaining process has been ignited in the student?

Notes

1. Another example, with which the reader is doubtless familiar, is the siphon. Here, the weight of the water falling down the longer leg of the siphon (into the lower bucket) is more than adequate to raise water from the upper reservoir over the lip of the upper bucket.

2. It is hoped that the reader will forgive the author for taking an "engineering" approach, with straight lines and square corners.

3. In the *Journal of Research in Science Teaching* 2 (1964): 176, Piaget defined assimilation as "the integration of any sort of reality into a structure." In this sense, he used "assimiliation" to include both the processes (assimilation and accommodation) which we describe.

Dana Brabson says he came to writing while at prep school in Massachussetts. "Between my junior and senior years," Brabson says, "I was selected to spend two extra weeks at Deerfield Academy during the summer. I never asked and was never told why." During those two weeks, the students involved had to write two essays of five hundred words each every day. It did not take long to find himself searching for things to write about. Brabson argues that writing can be done two ways, either in a vacuum or through knowledge. He stresses that reading allows one to critically analyze one's own writing and lets one know what is new. "On the Chemistry of Learning" has been rewritten several times since its first draft in 1990. Interested in educational psychology, Brabson often ponders how to motivate and influence students. One of his friends in education tested educational processes using students in a class taught by Brabson as subjects. This was his introduction to the work of Piaget, which he noted to be related to his own detailed knowledge of chemistry. This was the impetus for the essay. Brabson sees writing as extremely important for students of chemistry, noting "the publication of data is the only thing to have lasting value."

For Discussion

1. Explain what you understand Brabson to be saying when he refers to "activation energy barriers."

2. Explain how catalysts work.

3. Brabson first focuses on learning in paragraph eight, after discussing the chemical reaction. How effectively does he make the connection in this paragraph? Is the argument convincing by the time you get to the end of the essay?

4. Read paragraph 11 very carefully, and describe in your own words how you understand the connection between chemical activity and the learning process.

5. In paragraphs 13 and 14 Brabson describes the teacher's role in aiding student learning. How closely does this description match your own experience of learning?

6. With Brabson's thesis in mind, read the William Waters poem "Consider Your Ending / To Discover Your Beginning." As you make sense of the poem, note any experience of learning that reflects Brabson's assertions.

7. Try to make connections between Brabson's ideas and those of Berthold in the essays about what the university should be. Based on what you read in the three essays, imagine and write a conversation between the two professors.

The Role of Imagination in Science:
Flying Carpets, Cheap Fuel and Micromachining of Semiconductors
Don L. Kendall

Don Kendall, Ph.D., took his undergraduate degree in physics from the University of Texas, and his doctorate in material science from Stanford University, where his interests included physics, electrical engineering, chemistry and metallurgy. Professor Kendall then worked in private industry for Texas Instruments for 17 years, and afterward spent nine years conducting research for a government laboratory based in Mexico. He is currently a professor of electrical engineering at UNM.

I looked out of the imaginary window. She was a truly beautiful woman. She stepped into this elegant looking flying saucer or something. She reached down and pulled a switch. I swear, the thing leaped into the air! Like whoosh! And she was gone.

Is imagination really important in Science and Engineering? Or is it mostly our ability to analyze and compute and manufacture that is important today? The latter are indeed very important, but I believe that the imagination is ultimately much more important. I cannot prove this in a short lecture, but I will attempt to give you two examples of imagination at work in today's world. They speak to two of the most pressing concerns of today's society, namely the generation and conservation of energy.

The first one involves a new generation method. This will be a new way of looking at the atomic fusion process at *very* low temperatures. The second idea is a possible conservation concept, a very speculative idea of how someone might make an actual flying carpet. I first presented this general concept several years back,[1] but never quite as graphically as you will hear it today.

Before I get into these rather uncommon subjects, let me remind you of what Walt Disney once said: "If you can dream it, you can do it!" I like the spirit behind this statement very much. Of course, if I had to say it to a learned scientific gathering, I might modify it a bit to something like: "If you can dream it through all the physical processes, you can do it!"

Let me illustrate. A number of years back a young teenager stared out of the window and started thinking about trains going in opposite directions at the same speed on the same track. He knew their relative velocity would be twice their individual velocities, and he could visualize the physical processes that would occur if they collided. As his mind wandered, and it often did, he began to think of two light beams approaching each other on a collision course. He said, "Aha, a relative velocity of two times the speed of light. What a collision that must make!" But then he realized that light beams had a chance to collide every day and nothing ever seemed to happen. Besides this, a relative velocity of two times the speed of light seemed a bit strange too. Ten or so years later after years of studying, he had dreamed through all the physical processes. He finally realized that the relative velocity of the two trains mentioned earlier was indeed twice the velocity of each train, but two beams of light could not have a relative velocity greater than just a single speed of light. This opened the floodgates and the theory of relativity and much more came tumbling out of Albert Einstein's fertile imagination, but an imagination that was now very well-prepared. And it all started in the mind of a young boy.

Atomic Fusion at Room Temperature?

With these two famous men in mind, Walt and Albert, let me now return to the first idea I mentioned: the idea of atomic fusion at low temperatures. An incredible dream, since it usually requires many millions of degrees to get two atomic nuclei to fuse together. One of the most ballyhooed press conferences in history took place on March 23, 1989, at the University of Utah in Salt Lake City. Stanley Pons and Martin Fleischmann announced to an incredulous world that they had produced atomic fusion in a test tube at room temperature and that they were getting quite a lot more energy in the form of heat out of the bottle than they were putting into the bottle in terms of electric power.[2] It was simple, or so it seemed.

I heard an interesting story about this. It seems that they had filled up one of their palladium rods with a large dose of heavy hydrogen, or deuterium, D. They did this by simple electrolysis in a test tube full of heavy water, D_2O, and some lithium hydroxide to make the solution conductive. They didn't see much action, so they disconnected the battery and went home. The next morning was Sunday, and one of the professors' children rode a bike into the university and opened the combination lock and went in to look at the experiment. The youngster rushed back home and said: "Dad, the palladium is gone!" "You mean it's been stolen?" he asked. "No it's vaporized or melted or something. It's all over the lab! It's a mess!" To put it mildly, this got their attention.

I should tell you that the excitement has died down very considerably. It has been very difficult to reproduce these results. Some scientists would even say that it has been *impossible* to reproduce them. But in spite of the negative response, especially by the high energy physics community, the idea is still alive (and kicking?). Several labs in several countries have also seen energy in apparent excess amounts, and a group at Los Alamos National Laboratory reported that tritium,T, or "extra heavy hydrogen" has now been detected coming out of the apparatus.[3] This is one of the telltale signs of a nuclear fusion reaction. I can't comment on how significant this is. What I can do is tell you about my own thinking on the subject, which is mostly a dream so far, but the dream has already passed several milestones in terms of understanding of the possible physical processes. Which is to say, it has my attention!

Before sharing my imagination with you, let me remind you again that the "traditional" approach to producing nuclear fusion is to get some D atoms and maybe some T atoms in a container of some kind and to get them incredibly hot. How hot? Only about 10 million degrees or so! That's more than 1,000 times hotter than the surface of the sun! One way this has been done has been by wrapping the container with an imploding atomic bomb to force the D and T atoms to merge or fuse with each other. It works very nicely, but it's hard to find the cup of hot chocolate after you have heated it this way. Another approach is to put the D and T atoms in a glass bubble about the size of a grain of sand, and then zap it from all directions at once with a *two million megawatt laser*. They have to do this so fast that the atoms don't expand very much before the atoms fuse together and give off all of that nice energy. This works too, but they have yet to get more energy out than they put in. However, this has some hope of extracting the energy for some useful purpose, like heating a few hundred gallons of hot chocolate.

Now, let's unfetter our imagination for a moment and try to dream up a completely different approach. Let's try to get a bunch of D and maybe some T atoms and maybe even some lithium, Li, atoms all lined up in a perfect straight line and then somehow trigger the first one in the line and then hope the next one will trigger his neighbor and on and on. In other words, let's play some pool with the atomic nuclei all lined up. The first thing we would probably think of is to try to get the D, T, and Li atoms into a perfect single crystal. We would then remember from somewhere that you can pack a very large amount of H atoms in palladium, or Pd. Also, D and T can be packed into Pd in the same way since D and T are almost the same physical size as H; they are just heavier because of the extra neutrons they carry. And we will also assume for the moment that we might be able to get Li into the Pd in reasonable quantities too. The nice thing about this idea is that all of these small atoms fit in the empty space between the Pd atoms on their normal lattice positions, *and that all of these empty spaces are on essentially perfect straight lines.* Now if the Pd is in the form of rather large perfect crystals, we may have something interesting if we fill up a lot of the empty spaces with these little atoms. All we have to do is get these atoms to sit perfectly still while we get out our little atomic hammer and start our "linear domino reaction." In general, this idea looks interesting because several laboratories have seen "bursts of energy" coming out of of their cold fusion attempts and that *cast Pd rods give many more bursts than do extruded Pd sheets*. The cast rods should have bigger and more perfect crystallites than the extruded sheets, so our idea might explain this unusual observation!

Well the bad news hits us about then. We remember from a physics course that the atoms vibrate all the time so that the incredibly small nuclei will never be in an exactly straight line. So we say: "No problem, we'll take the crystal down near absolute zero where the atomic motion will stop!" And then with our little hammer, we'll get busy. More bad news. We remember that the atoms are still vibrating, even at absolute zero! This is due to the so-called zero point vibrations.

We are now stymied, but being too young and too optimistic to give up, we think about the ways a chain of atoms can vibrate. They can vibrate sideways or they can vibrate along their length, namely as "transverse" or as "longitudinal" waves. We stare out of our window and think of a pep squad at a football game all lined up close together on the fifty yard line. We then imagine them moving *sideways* doing the "wave." If we give the first one a shove, a few neighbors may fall, but they won't continue to fall since they are not in a straight line. On the other hand, if we can get the young energetic squad to move in the wave *along* the length of the fifty yard line, then a shove (from behind, of course) will topple the whole bunch. The drawings may help you see this better, the upper one showing a sidewinder and the other a longitudinal wave for the high school students.

In our nuclear domino case, maybe something will take over at very low tem-

Drawing 1

peratures and the sideway vibrations will somehow be killed off and all the zero point energy dumped into the longitudinal vibrations. If this happens, then all the atoms will be perfectly lined up even though they are vibrating. Then with our little hammer, we will. . . .

Is there any hope of something strange like this happening? Well, superconductivity happens at very low temperatures apparently because the atoms begin to vibrate in a very surprising way to encourage pairs of electrons to stick together. This pairing is very much against the grain for negatively charged electrons, but that's what happens. These paired electrons run around in the lattice for years without ever suffering any collisions with the vibrating atoms or with other electron pairs. Why not something similar to this for our linear chain of fusible atoms? And just to keep the thing going, we may have to build in some *fission* reactions with a few Li atoms. Remember, it is the *fusion* of the D and/ or T nuclei that is the main event. Nevertheless, Li appears to somehow be necessary for some of the cold fusion success stories.[4]

Exactly what are the nuclear reactions that will allow such a linear domino reaction? There are several, and they are all found in a good encyclopedia. I'll leave it as a student exercise. The point I'm trying to make is that almost any of you can understand the general nature of such processes, at least at a level so that you can ask questions and enjoy thinking about them. Do the proton-neutron pairs of the nuclei have to all be lined up "along the 50-yard line" too? Do the neutron portions (rather than the proton portions) of the aligned molecules always face each other in the crystal?[5] (¡*Muy interesante!*) Should we choose something other than palladium as the host lattice? Can we get large enough quantities of these small atoms into semiconductors like silicon or the III-V compounds? (Probably yes, with some subtle techniques.)

And finally we ask, what about the trigger mechanisms? Again, there are several possibilities. These range from natural triggers like cosmic rays, to mechanical stresses, to electrical breakdown, to laser blasts, to radioactive sources, to electrochemical shock, or whatever you can dream through the physical processes. Hey, I didn't say it was going to be easy! If we use Einstein as a model, high school students have at least ten years to get the education to figure it out. And you senior engineers might even do it faster!

Now that we have planted the cold fusion idea deeply into the inner recesses of our brains, let's turn to another completely different kind of idea. This is one of my own personal interests, and it is probably even less developed than the linear domino reaction idea. It's about a way to make a real flying carpet. There are probably a number of ways to do this, but I will discuss only one.

The Flying Carpet

My particular version of the flying carpet came from chemically etching little rectangular holes in a perfect single crystal. I noticed that the walls of the rectangular holes had little steps on them that always faced in the same direction. For example, the steps would always face to the right in a typical set of holes. I stared at these steps for a long time before I figured out what was happening. I

Drawing 2

won't tell you all the details, but it wasn't very difficult. The important point for our purposes is that the steps existed and that they always faced to the right, no matter which of the four walls was observed. What a strange little hole, I thought.

Then I began to think of similar situations. Like a square drawn by a computer. If the square is drawn exactly along the X-Y axes, then the square has perfectly straight sides. But if the square is drawn slightly tilted to the left from the vertical, then the computer always draws the lines with little steps interspersed with straight line segments. And not too surprisingly, all the steps face to the right in these squares. Just like a square hole in a crystal! (In other squares, of course, the steps all faced to the left, but these were simply tilted in the other direction.)

Now let's imagine that molecules bounce off of these right-facing steps and get into sort of a clockwise swirl in the little square holes. At this point we can imagine a special square dance hall with all the walls having right-facing steps on them. The lights are turned down to almost nothing. We then imagine some strong high school seniors hidden inside each step. Every time a dancing couple comes near one of these steps, one of the seniors gives them a shove. After a while all the dancers are moving in a decided clockwise direction around the dance floor.

Now let's return to the molecules in the square hole. They also might somehow be encouraged to swirl around in a clockwise direction, like a little micro-tornado! What does a tornado do? Well, for one thing, it picks things up and moves them. This happens because there is less pressure at the top than at the bottom of the tornado. Could the little tornado in the hole do the same thing? Or could a thin plate with lots of holes with little tornados in them develop a pressure gradient between the top of the plate and the bottom? If the holes really behave this way, the whole plate might take off like a flying carpet!

About this time, the skeptic within me begins to shout. It will never work! How do you get the steps to reflect the molecules better than the flat regions? Won't the much more numerous reflections from the flat sections kill the swirl? Yes they will, *unless* we can heat up the steps so they reflect better than the flat parts of the walls, like the high school seniors hiding in the steps. Maybe we can pass current down the steps in fast pulses. The fast pulses will help keep the heat localized to the steps. What will we use for our power input? Current? Light from lasers? Sunlight? Can we make the steps absorb the light and the flats reflect it? How do we make the steps have the unique properties we want? Can we calculate the effects so we will know how big to make the steps? Or do we need the possible quantum effects of a single or a double *atomic thickness* step? There are many unanswered questions. But they will never be answered unless we start peeling away the layers of complexity. And both the cold fusion and the flying carpet are "rich" ideas in the sense that they involve many fields of science and engineering. *Don't be afraid of any of it!* If you don't understand all of it, get help from someone and keep the idea alive!

Would such a flying carpet type process be useful? Yes, certainly(!) Even if we can't say exactly how to manufacture it at this time. For example, we can imagine an airplane wing with billions of little holes in the surface. This has already been tried by McDonnell-Douglas as a means of reducing localized turbulence. It results in a 10 to 20 percent fuel saving on long flights. All we now ask is for them to add little steps in the holes. Then interlace the wing surfaces with electrical connections to pulse current down the little steps. Then when local stress detectors on the wings feel a strong downthrust of wind, extra power is called for in that region of the wing to activate the little whirlwinds to compensate for the downthrust. The cost of the extra fuel is the least of your worries at this point since the lives of everybody on board are at stake.

Before I close, let me tell you about discussing the flying carpet idea with a well-known scientist a while back. He broke into a big grin and said, "So that's how they did it!" This struck some sort of chord based on something he read when he was a boy. This reminds me that we are all molded by our dreams and aspirations, as well as by our imagination. Yet it is also true that most of us will have to make serious compromises with reality. Albert Einstein went to work in the patent office to make a living. Yet he didn't let his dreams die. I can't give you a formula as to how to do this, but some of you will succeed in spite of everything. I hope you will keep your imagination alive and well and that you will get enough of the right kind of education so you can act on it when opportunities arise. A great deal of the joy of life resides on this single premise.

So whether it is cold fusion or flying carpets or DNA molecular marriages or something else that gets your adrenaline flowing, I beg you to devote some quiet time to thinking about it. Write and save it on a computer. Or write it down in a bound notebook in pencil and put a date and signature on it. A pencil doesn't inhibit as much as a pen. If you think it may be patentable, write it in ink and get two witnesses to sign and date every page after the words: "Read and understood." Be scrupulous in dating things correctly. If you want to change something later, write in ink and date the change. This writing things down is a *minimum* discipline that will encourage you to think through the physical processes. The small stack of notebooks (or floppy disks) will make good reading in later years. You will be surprised how good (and also how bad!) some of your ideas are even now, although you may not yet have the ability to think them all the way through.

If one or more of your ideas is really worth pursuing, either commercially or scientifically, I believe that God will give you the energy, the initiative, the opportunity, and yes, the imagination to get the job done, somehow.

I looked out of the window again. I saw her slide into one of the seats of the thin wing and pull the deuterium initiator. The wing lifted straight up. There was barely a rustle as the air swept through the wing from top to bottom. She spoke some coordinates and it tilted forward and headed for home.

Notes

1. D.L. Kendall and G.R. de Guel, "Orientations of the Third Kind: The Coming of Age of (110) Silicon," in *Micromachining and Micropackaging of Transducers*, eds. C.D.Fung, et al., (Amsterdam: Elsevier B.V., 1985), 107-125; also D.L. Kendall, "A New Theory for the Anisotropic Etching of Silicon and Some Underdeveloped Chemical Micromachining Concepts," *Journal of Vac. Sci. Tech.*, A8 (1990): 3598.

2. M. Fleischmann and S. Pons, "Electrochemically Induced Fusion of Deuterium," *Journal of Electroanal. Chem.* 261 (1989): 301.

3. E. Storms and C. Talcott, *Proceedings of the First Annual Conference on Cold Fusion*, 28-31 March, 1990, Salt Lake City. Also in *Fusion Technology*, (July, 1990), along with several supporting (and other) papers.

4. I appreciate the comments of Ed Storms (Los Alamos National Laboratory) during proof of this paper, especially on the occasional alignments of D atoms that occur during very high temperature fusion (The Oppenheimer-Philips Effect).

5. Again, the comments of Ed Storms (Los Alamos National Laboratory) during his preliminary reading of this paper proved especially helpful here.

Postscript

Present work in our laboratory involves trying to fabricate and test small chemical microchambers made out of chemically micromachined silicon. We use integrated circuit technology and we hope to do interesting and useful chemical reactions in complex structures that cannot be done by other means. An example of a very desirable reaction would be to convert methane to methanol. Methane is the main constituent of natural gas, and it is very expensive to transport from the oil fields, so billions of dollars' worth of gas is burned off every year all over the world. If some inexpensive way could be found to convert this gas to liquid methanol, we might delay the next energy crisis by several decades. Methanol is an efficient fuel for many purposes, and it is much cheaper to transport than is natural gas.

We are fabricating thin semipermeable membranes in complex three-dimensional structures based on silicon technology, which could in principle perform such complex functions as discussed above. Trillions of very small pores, as small as two or three atoms in diameter, are introduced into the membranes. Then several different catalysts are introduced into different membranes throughout the structure, and specific chemical reactions are performed. The incredible flexibility one has in such structures opens up possibilities only dreamed about previously. Or so our imagination and our lab notebooks say. My graduate students—Bill Eaton, Ron Manginell, Caroline Matzke, and Gregory Peake—and I are trying to make some of the simpler structures and test them. One of our problems is that we don't know enough chemistry to select the most appropriate reactions to try. Our other big problem is that the work is too new to be "in vogue" with funding agencies. Again, we try to be imaginative in getting something significant done anyway, while teaching classes and doing all the other things a professor and graduate students must do.

Although Professor Kendall is firmly rooted in the hard sciences, he regularly indulges in interests as diverse as teaching elementary school children and song writing. When working with the children at Chelwood Elementary, who range from grades one through five, he focuses on finding new perspectives to both motivate the children and to give them ways to understand science. A recent project was the writing of a rap song which taught counting in binary numbers. The most important element of teaching, he believes, is Fun, with a capital F. As a scientist, Professor Kendall believes that academic freedom is essential to research. In fact, he left private industry for the university because he found that business practices encouraged restriction. At UNM, he has found a place to follow his unusual and creative research, although the need to be competitive for grant money places practical constraints on his work. Still, for Don Kendall, the magic in the world is found in the beauty of the imagination, because "if you can dream it through all the physical processes, you can do it!"

For Discussion

1. Examine the title. If you had come upon this without knowing anything about the article, what would your reaction have been to seeing "flying carpets" next to "very cheap fuel"?

2. Reread the essay, looking for shifts in the narrative from external quotes to stories to scientific descriptions. First, write a short response about the effectiveness of these shifts. Do they enhance the reading experience or do they detract from it? For either opinion, give support for your view from the text.

3. This essay was actually the keynote speech for the Twentieth Southwest Junior Science and Humanities Symposium given in Albuquerque in April of 1990. It was later delivered as a speech in Mexico in 1991. Knowing that it was designed as a speech, instead of a formal essay, how does your response to question two change? Write a revised response, addressing the same questions.

4. In paragraph nine, Kendall writes about an atomic bomb explosion, which he follows by "[i]t works very nicely, but it's hard to find the cup of hot chocolate after you have heated it this way. . . ." Discuss the possible purposes for putting humor into a scientific discourse. Do you think it helps with the understanding of information that might otherwise be difficult to absorb?

5. Kendall believes that, in order for science to be more accessible to a wider population, scientific writers must use creative analogies to illustrate their points. Go through the essay, and make a list of all of the different analogies which Kendall uses. In what ways do these analogies make comprehension easier? Or do they? If you don't think that they do, explain why.

6. Write out a detailed explanation of some particular thing that you know about or can do, in language that is technical to that thing and without extras like humor or analogies. Then write that same explanation using a combination of humor and analogies. Exchange that first writing with a partner, and discuss its impact. Then exchange the second writing. What, if anything, was changed with regard to comprehension?

Does Administrative Protection Protect?
A Reexamination of the U.S. Title VII and Escape Clause Statutes
Wendy Hansen and Thomas Prusa

Wendy Hansen grew up in Indiana and did her undergraduate work at Lawrence University in Wisconsin. At the suggestion of her undergraduate advisor, Dr. Hansen went to graduate school at the California Institute of Technology where she was awarded her master's and doctoral degrees in social sciences. After teaching at SUNY Stony Brook from 1988 to 1994, Dr. Hansen came to the University of New Mexico where she teaches political science. Thomas Prusa is a faculty research fellow with the National Bureau of Economic Research in Cambridge, Massachusetts. Dr. Prusa received his undergraduate degree from Georgetown University in 1983 and completed his master's and doctoral degrees at Stanford University. Dr. Prusa teaches economics at Rutgers University.

Faced with the rising pressure of increasing foreign competition, many U.S. industries turned to Washington during the 1980s with demands for import relief. Often they argued that they needed protection to offset unfair trade practices or simply to gain time to adjust to the new international trading environment. Industries demanded that Congress do something about the supposed negative impact of imports on U.S. industries and the economy as a whole. But obligations stemming from the General Agreement on Tariffs and Trade (GATT) significantly limited Congress' ability to legislate targeted, sector-specific protection in the form of tariffs or quotas. Consequently, U.S. industries turned to the so-called administrative protection of the trade remedy laws and filed an unprecedented number of trade complaints.

There are two general classes of trade laws under which U.S. industries can apply for import relief: "unfair trade" laws, with antidumping and countervailing duty laws being the primary examples, and "escape clause" or "safeguard" protection under section 201 of the Tariff Act of 1930. While both types of laws provide relief to injured U.S. industries, in recent years industries have resorted almost exclusively to the unfair trade laws. From 1980 to 1988 U.S. industries seeking protection from foreign competition filed over 700 petitions under the antidumping and countervailing duty laws but only 19 escape clause petitions. By way of comparison, from 1963 to 1979, domestic industries filed 532 unfair trade petitions and 75 escape clause petitions.

Why is protection sought much more frequently under the unfair trade laws, and why has the escape clause declined in importance? Part of the explanation may lie in the fact that the laws have different purposes. "Unfair" trade laws are designed to correct for the injurious effects of foreign dumping and government subsidization of exports. The escape clause, on the other hand, is designed to allow industries to seek trade relief merely on the basis of injury from foreign competition. One might thus conclude that U.S. industries battled more foreign dumping and government subsidization in the 1980s than in previous years. That is not the entire story, however.

The preference for invoking unfair trade laws is also the result of how Congress has amended the trade laws over the past 15 years. Each revision contained in the past three major trade bills has increasingly facilitated U.S. industries' use of the unfair trade laws. In fact, the rules governing antidumping and countervailing duty procedures are now so biased in favor of U.S. industries that it is often questionable whether any "unfair" trade act was actually committed—a fact that has led many observers to believe it is more accurate to refer to antidumping and countervailing duty laws as "Title VII" laws (for the section in which they appear in the trade statutes) rather than "unfair" trade laws. From our perspective, the changing filing patterns is due in large part to the fact that Title VII actions are substituting for safeguard actions. Because Title VII actions are now so much more likely to result in protection, an industry will choose to file a Title VII petition although the facts of the case may make it more appropriate (according to GATT standards) to file an escape clause petition.

The dramatic rise of administrative protection over the past decade and explosion of unfair trade cases call out for some evaluation of the effects of such import relief. What are the costs of administrative protection? How much have domestic industries really benefitted from that protection? Since trade protection comes at a high cost to U.S. consumers, it is well-worth examining what that protection buys in terms of saved jobs and revived industries. We shall show that administrative protection does not protect very effectively: industries continue to perform very poorly even after receiving protection. Accordingly, it is difficult to justify the significant burdens that such protection imposes on the rest of society.

An Overview of the Trade Laws

In many nations, including the United States, domestic industries injured by import competition have a number of legal and political channels through which they can seek relief. We can broadly classify those channels into two policy mechanisms: safeguard policies and policies used to correct "unfair" trade distortions. Safeguard policies are any government actions taken in response to import levels that are deemed to "harm" or injure the importing country's economy or domestic competing industries. Of interest to our study is the particular policy tool known as the escape clause, which is built into both U.S. law and international rules of the GATT. It is important to note that import-restraining actions regarded as safeguard actions are justified for economic adjustment and political reasons and do not require that trade be unfair in any way. GATT founders felt a safeguard provision was valuable since nations would be more likely to agree to trade concessions if there were a way to temporarily "escape" from their obligations, regardless of whether the injuring imports were fairly or unfairly traded. "Nondiscrimination" is a crucial characteristic of trade relief under the escape clause; since escape clause actions are aimed at providing "temporary" relief from injury resulting from trade, rather than relief from any particular unfair behavior, escape clause protection is applied to imports from all countries.

Whereas the escape clause is concerned primarily with injury to domestic competing industries regardless of the cause of that injury, the second type of GATT-sanctioned policy tool is designed to offset the effects of unfair trade distortions that foreign firms or governments create in their attempt to promote exports. Antidumping and countervailing duty laws are two specific examples of that type of policy tool; they are used to counter the practices of dumping and government subsidization, respectively. In contrast to the escape clause, antidumping and countervailing duty protection is generally discriminatory in the sense that the duty is applied specifically against imports coming from particular countries singled out as unfair traders. Because the procedures and provisions of antidumping and countervailing duty laws are quite similar, we shall refer to actions filed under either law as "Title VII" actions.

A key feature shared by Title VII and escape clause actions is that the import-competing domestic industry usually initiates the petition for trade relief. Industries thus have a more direct role in their quest for protection than was possible under traditional methods of protection such as tariffs and quotas. Not surprisingly, some industries have been much more aggressive than others in that endeavor. Table 1 lists the industries most frequently using the trade laws from 1980 to 1988. The iron- and steel-related industries have been preeminent users of both Title VII and escape clause laws, followed by producers of agricultural products, chemicals, and machinery.

In contrast to the nondiscriminatory scope of escape clause cases, Title VII cases target a specific country's firms or government as unfair traders. From

1980 to 1988 U.S. industries filed 51 dumping cases against Japan, 26 against West Germany, 25 against Taiwan, and 23 against Brazil. With regard to the practice of government subsidies, Brazil was the most widely cited country with 30 complaints, followed by Mexico (27), Spain (24), and France (19).

Although well over 100 different manufacturing industries have used the laws, the top 15 petitioning industries listed in Table 1 account for almost 70 percent of the cases filed. Interestingly, those top industries share certain characteristics that may account for their using the laws. First, they are large industries as measured by value of output and number of employees: the average petitioning industry has almost four times the sales and three times the employees as the average manufacturing industry. As has been widely recognized, an industry's size may be related to its ability to lobby effectively for trade protection: larger industries have greater resources and can exert greater political pressure on the relevant administrative agencies. Second, industries filing petitions face much geater import competition than the average industry: foreign producers' share of the domestic U.S. market is about 30 percent, as compared with the national average of about 13 percent.

Table 1: Most Frequent Petitioners*

Industry	Total number of petitions
Blast Furnaces and Steel Mills	323
Misc. Fabricated Wire Products	23
Ornamental Nursery Products	21
Ball and Roller Bearings	18
Fabricated Metal Products	17
Valves and Pipe Fittings	16
Industrial Inorganic Chemicals	14
Copper Rolling and Drawing	13
Motor Vehicle Parts and Accessories	13
Hydraulic Cement	12
Potash, Soda, and Borate Minerals	10
House Furnishings	10
Wet Corn Milling	9
Fabricated Textile Products	9
Medicinals and Botanicals	9

*By four-digit S.I.C. classification

Table 2: Key Features of the Trade Laws

Industry	Comment
Injury Criterion	Escape clause's "serious injury" standard more difficult to satisfy than the "material injury" standard required under Title VII.
Presidential Discretion	Reduces desirability of escape clause. During 1980s the president rejected 30 percent of the cases that the ITC recommended for protection.
Scope of Protection	Nondiscriminatory escape clause offers stronger protection. Discriminatory Title VII leads to the filing of multiple petitions.
Length of Protection	Favors Title VII actions.
"Unfair Practices" Test	Should favor escape clause but in practice a nonfactor due to biased Commerce Department procedures.

Why Are the Unfair Trade Laws so Popular?

To a large extent, differences in procedures for seeking and being granted protection under the escape clause and Title VII laws can explain the disparitites in their usage. In Table 2 we list some of the key features that distinguish the laws. As the table makes clear, the differences between the laws make Title VII actions more desirable to industries seeking protection. For instance, the criteria used by the International Trade Commission (ITC) for determining injury, as specified by both GATT and U.S. law, differ significantly for safeguard versus unfair trade actions. Under section 201, the law requires that imports cause or threaten to cause "serious injury" and that they be a "substantial cause" (meaning a cause that is "important and not less important than any other cause") of that injury. In contrast, under the unfair trade laws, once dumping or subsidization has been established, the ITC need only find "material injury" (defined by Congress as "harm which is not inconsequential, immaterial, or unimportant") or the threat thereof to provide relief to the domestic industry.

The unfair trade laws are also popular because the president has no formal role in their application. In escape clause cases the ITC investigates and decides the merits of the petitions, but the president has final decision-making authority over whether to grant protection under that law. In contrast, the president has no formal role under Title VII; for those petitions the ITC determines whether there is injury to the industry, and the Department of Commerce determines whether there are unfair practices occurring in trade. Both agencies must rule in favor of the petitioner for protection to be granted.

The fact that the president has the power to disapprove or alter the ITC's suggested remedy makes escape clause petitions more uncertain and thus discourages industries from filing those petitions. Under section 201, the president may consider the "national economic interest" in his decision whether to grant relief; accordingly, he has very broad discretionary authority over the outcome of escape clause petitions. Furthermore, GATT rules allow affected countries to retaliate against protective relief imposed under a safeguard action. That is, affected countries can levy a tariff or quota on an equal dollar value of U.S. exports. This built-in allowance for retaliation further complicates the president's decision.

Moreover, escape clause cases are less desirable than Title VII cases because escape clause protection is meant to provide only temporary relief from injury resulting from trade. Thus, until recently protection was limited to five years (the 1988 Trade Act extended escape clause protection to eight years). Protection under Title VII, by contrast, is reviewed annually and may continue indefinitely if the unfair practices are determined to continue to exist. As a practical matter, duty orders imposed under Title VII are often difficult to revoke; it is not uncommon for them to remain in place for a decade or more. The limited nature of escape clause protection may further deter industries from seeking relief under that law.

There is, however, one key feature that would seem to deter industries from frivolously filing Title VII actions: the Commerce Department must determine that foreign firms or governments have engaged in an unfair trade practice before dumping or subsidy duties can be levied. In theory at least, such a requirement should increase the probability that the petition will be rejected and thus make pursuing a Title VII remedy less attractive. As has been widely recognized, however, the rules governing how Commerce determines "unfair trade" are slanted in favor of domestic industries, making the determination quite easy to satisfy. For instance, from 1980 to 1988 Commerce rejected only six percent of antidumping cases, while the ITC's rejection rate was 31 percent.

There are numerous examples of Commerce Department procedures that are biased against foreign industries. For example, duty margins are often calculated by using the "best information available," which usually means relying on information provided by the domestic complainant. In antidumping cases, the Commerce Department's method of comparing average home market prices to individual transactions in the U.S. market leads to positive dumping margins even when the prices are the same in both markets. It is noteworthy that Congress transferred jurisdiction over unfair trade determinations from the Treasury Department to Commerce in 1980 largely because Congress disapproved of Treasury's handling of cases and wanted the job done by a body that would work as an advocate for domestic industries.

Industry Performance before Filing for Trade Relief

To evaluate the economic performance of the industries that seek administrative protection, we have examined trends in employment, output, market share, and new capital spending during the three years before the industries filed a

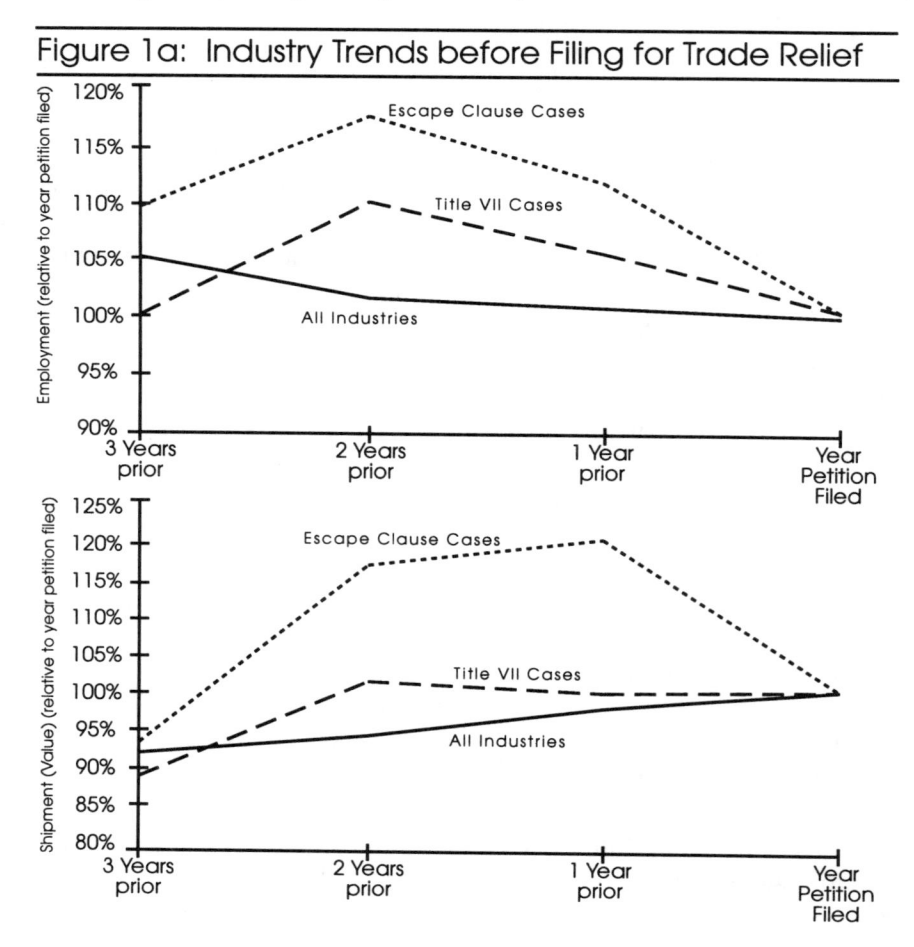

Figure 1a: Industry Trends before Filing for Trade Relief

petition for protection. Consider, for example, the state of the cellular telephone equipment industry in 1984. Employment fell by over 22 percent from 1981 to 1984. Although shipments increased by almost 12 percent during that time, the domestic industry still lost ground to foreign producers: imports' share of the U.S. market increased by over 17 percent. Domestic producers filed an anti-dumping case against Japanese producers of mobile telephones and claimed that those recent trends were evidence of material injury.

Rather than focus on trends on a case-by-case basis, we show in Figures 1a and 1b the trends for the four economic criteria for all industries that filed Title VII and escape clause petitions from 1980 to 1988. To establish a benchmark and to account for overall trends in the economy, we also show those trends for all U.S. manufacturing industries. To better view the trends in the data we measure each criterion relative to its value in the year the petition was filed. (There-

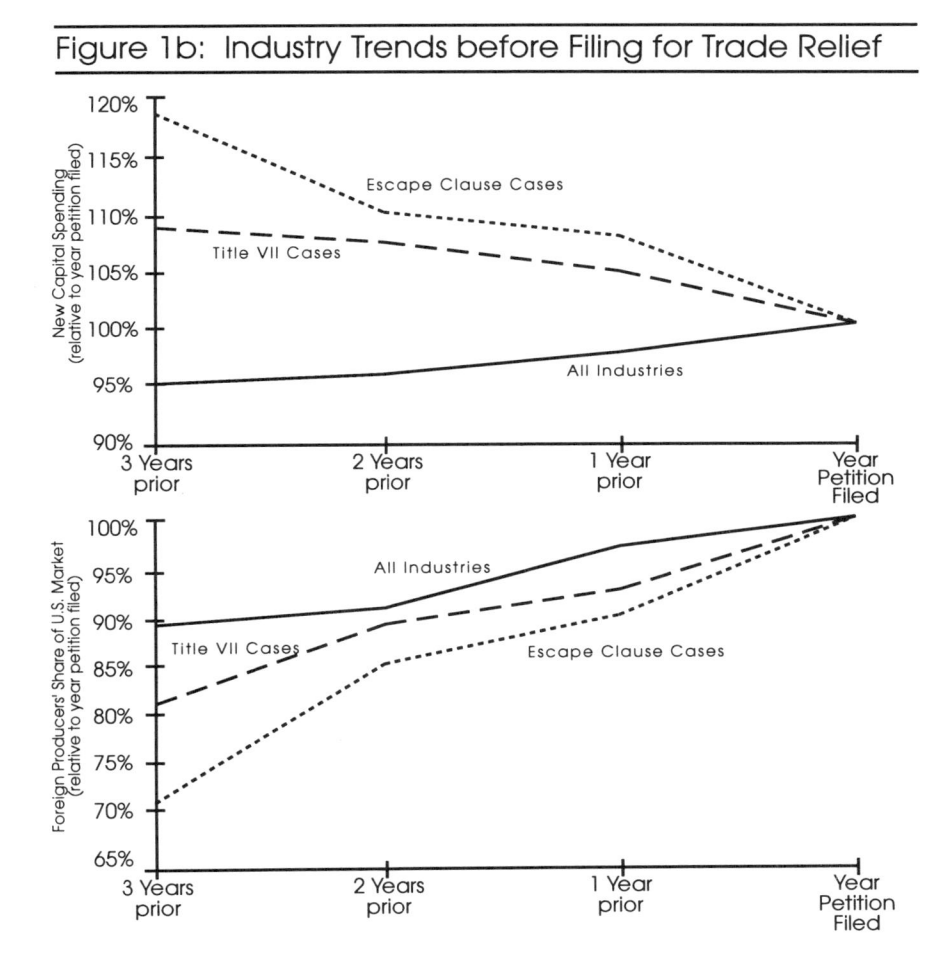

Figure 1b: Industry Trends before Filing for Trade Relief

fore, all the data will have a value of 100 in the year the petition was filed.)

The trends for all the economic criteria are consistent with the notion that the industries suffered poor economic performance during the years immediately before filing the petition. There are a number of trends worth noting. For example, looking at the top panel, we see that on average employment in escape clause cases fell by about 10 percent over the three years before the filing of a petition. Moreover, the rate of decline in employment reached about 18 percent during the final two years. For Title VII cases the petitioning industries' employment also falls dramatically during the final two years before filing for relief. Comparing those trends with the trends for all manufacturing industries in the same years, we find that industries filing for trade relief experienced a much more drastic employment decline than the typical manufacturing industry—a trend the petitioning industries surely used as evidence of injury.

The next panel in the figure displays trends in the value of shipments (output). While on average all industries experienced moderate increases in shipments during the period, industries using the trade laws experienced an initial rise followed by a rather sharp decline immediately before filing the petition. Once again, the pattern is consistent with the industries' claims of injury.

The other panels display trends that are consistent with the above findings. In particular, foreign producers' share of the U.S. domestic market grew much more rapidly in those industries that file trade complaints. For example, industries that file escape clause petitions experienced almost a 30 percent increase in the market share held by imports. In contrast, on average all manufacturing industries experienced only a 10 percent increase during the same time period. Also striking is the rapid decline in new capital spending by petitioning industries, especially relative to the increasing trend displayed by all manufacturing industries.

While those trends demonstrate that industries filing either Title VII or escape clause petitions are performing worse than the average industry (trends consistent with the notion of injury), it is also clear that industries filing escape clause petitions demonstrate an even greater decline. That is consistent with the more stringent injury standard required under the escape clause. It is also consistent with our belief that many industries file Title VII actions because they know they will be unable to prove "serious injury."

The Effect of Protection on Import Trade

Once an industry has decided to file a petition, the ITC must decide whether the injury standard has been satisfied. If injury is shown (and, for Title VII cases,

Commerce confirms the existence of an "unfair" act), the U.S. Customs Service is instructed to levy a duty or quota against foreign imports. That trade restraint imposes a cost on U.S. businesses and consumers: it raises the price and reduces the supply of imported merchandise.

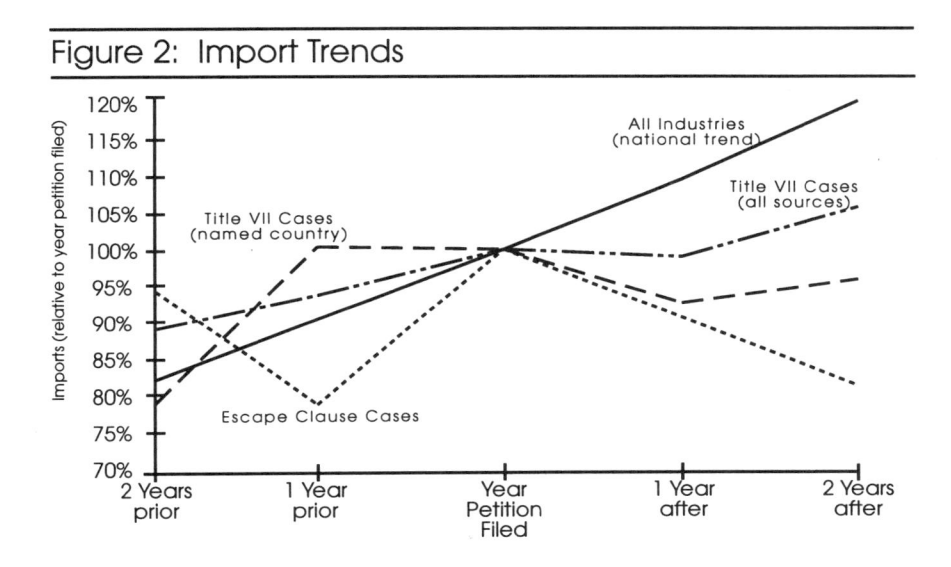

Figure 2: Import Trends

In Figure 2 we show the import trends for industries receiving Title VII and escape clause protection—the five escape clause cases that received presidential approval and the 467 Title VII cases that were settled or had duties levied. Once again, we measure each criterion relative to its value in the year the petition was filed. We see that imports grew at a steady rate for all industries. Using that as the benchmark, we can evaluate the effect of protection. Both escape clause and Title VII protection significantly decrease imports relative to the national trend: import growth in import categories receiving protection is 20 to 30 percent less than the national average during the two years following the imposition of protection.

More specifically, the trend under escape clause protection shows that imports in industries receiving escape clause protection fall sharply after protection is granted: they are about 10 percent lower after the first year and about 20 percent lower after the second year. Further, we find that those percentage decreases are not based on a small import trade volume. Import trade averaged well over $1 billion in industries receiving escape clause protection. Clearly, that protection significantly affects U.S. consumers.

Import trade is also reduced in industries receiving Title VII protection, but here we need to be a bit more careful about how we evaluate the import effect. As discussed above, Title VII protection only affects imports from specific named countries (for example, color televisions from Japan, Korea, and Taiwan). Thus, Title VII protection is discriminatory. Once protection is granted, trade is often diverted from "unfair trader" countries to other countries not subject to the duty order. (For example, imports of color televisions from Japan, Korea, and Taiwan have fallen while imports from Mexico have risen.) Therefore, it is useful to measure the effect of Title VII protection on imports from duty-subject countries as well as overall import volumes.

As Figure 2 shows, import trade from named countries grew very rapidly before protection; afterwards, however, import trade fell significantly. Imports from all sources are likewise reduced, but by far less than those from named countries. By either measure, though, Title VII protection imposes substantial costs on affected U.S. businesses and consumers.

How Effective Is Protection?

The significant negative impact on imports caused by administrative protection is generally not matched by a corresponding beneficial impact on the protected U.S. industries. In other words, administrative protection does not protect very well. Accordingly, it exacts large costs for very little benefit.

Consider once again the 1984 antidumping case against Japanese producers of cellular telephones. The ITC ruled in favor of the domestic industry and levied a weighted average dumping margin of 57 percent. Despite that high rate of protection, the U.S. industry continued to flounder. For example, the share of U.S. sales accounted for by all foreign producers increased by more than 25 percent from 1984 to 1987. Also, employment and output fell by almost one-third during that period. Moreover, capital expenditures in the industry fell dramatically. Thus, it seems doubtful that the costs imposed on U.S. consumers were worthwhile.

In Figures 3a and 3b we consider the same four economic criteria, but once again we restrict ourselves to only those industries that received protection. The figure depicts the industries' performance during the three years following trade protection. As seen in the figure, protection is not a panacea for the industries' ills. By almost every measure, the industries granted protection continued to perform poorly.

With respect to employment, we see that industries receiving trade protection experienced a much sharper decline than the national average, especially for escape clause cases, which experienced a 25 percent decline in employment. The protection did not preserve jobs in the industry.

The picture is not much rosier when we look at the value of shipments. While on average manufacturing industries experienced a 10 percent growth during the period, industries receiving protection showed little, if any, improvement. The porous nature of protection partially explains that result for industries receiving Title VII protection. Recall that Title VII protection applies only to imports from specified countries. Thus, a successful Title VII case often results in other foreign producers increasing their share of the U.S. market (as in the cellular telephone case). As the figure shows, foreign producers' share of the domestic market increases faster than average for those industries receiving Title VII protection.

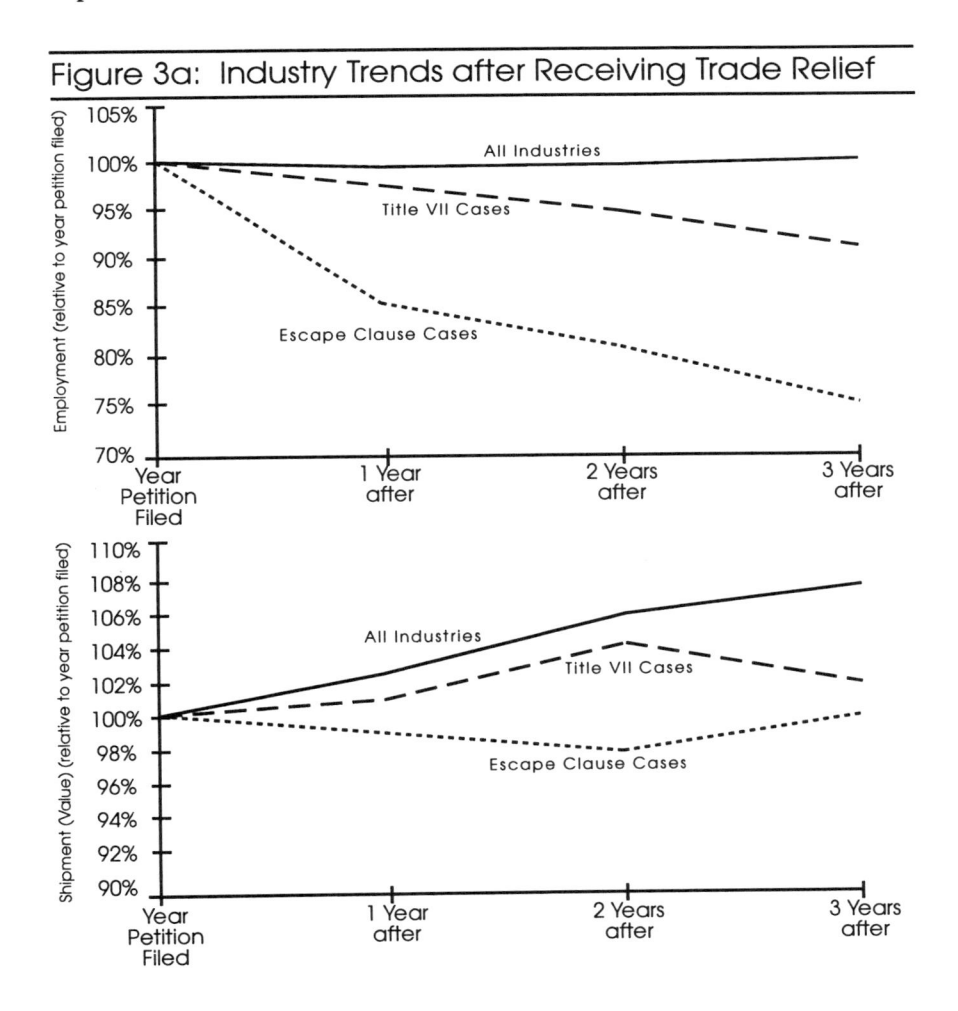

Figure 3a: Industry Trends after Receiving Trade Relief

Note, however, that this does not help to explain the decline in output of industries that received escape clause protection since all foreign producers faced sanctions in those cases. In fact, for escape clause cases, foreign producers' share of the domestic market actually fell after protection was granted. Thus, industries receiving escape clause protection still declined despite the powerful non-discriminatory nature of their protection.

Industries often claim that protection will enable them to retool their factories. While that argument sounds plausible, the evidence is to the contrary. Three years after receiving protection, capital spending by affected industries was 15 percent lower than it was during the year that the petition was filed. In contrast, the average manufacturing industry increased capital spending by about five per-

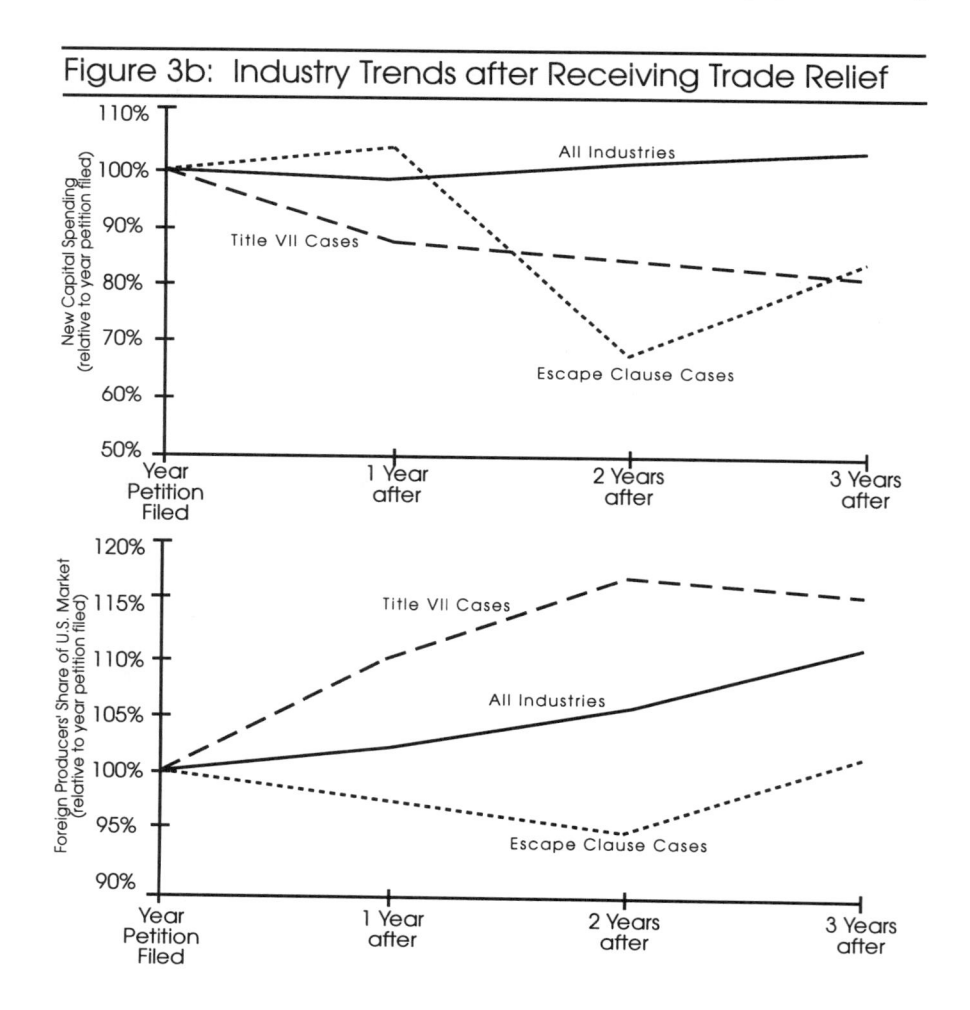

Figure 3b: Industry Trends after Receiving Trade Relief

cent during the same period. Thus, industries receiving protection do not appear to achieve the recovery policymakers anticipated.

Concluding Thoughts

The 1980s witnessed an explosion in the popularity of administrative protection as a means to address troublesome foreign competition. The drop in escape clause actions was more than compensated for by a dramatic expansion of Title VII protection. Yet when we consider what the granting of that protection has accomplished for U.S. industries, the picture is bleak.

Why do the laws perform so dismally? Defenders of the unfair trade laws have argued that they are not enforced vigorously enough, that the discriminatory protection they provide is too easily "circumvented" by import-shifting. Our analysis of escape clause actions counters that argument. In those cases, even where the protection granted is comprehensive, U.S. industry performance continues to deteriorate.

Surely a major factor in explaining the limited benefits of administrative protection is the type of industries choosing to file petitions. Independent of any problems associated with foreign trade, industries using the laws are declining industries, and restraining foreign trade does not reverse their decline. Declining industries are the ones most likely to file complaints, not only because they are desperate to fend off competition, but also because they have the best chance of proving injury and thus prevailing. Unfortunately, those industries may be performing so poorly that mere trade restraints most often cannot reverse their downward course. It may also be the case that easing competitive pressures through imposition of protection dulls the incentives for protected domestic industries to take the steps needed to revive their fortunes.

Suggestions for Further Reading

Baldwin, R.E. *The Political Economy of U.S. Import Policy.* (Cambridge: MIT Press, 1985).

Boltuck, R. and Litan, R.E., eds. *Down in the Dumps.* (Washington, D.C.: Brookings Institution, 1991).

Jackson, J.J. *The World Trading System.* (Cambridge: MIT Press, 1989).

Wendy Hansen feels strongly that writing is a crucial part of any profession. Her realization of language's importance stems from her high school foreign language classes where she learned the necessity of being able to communicate. Dr. Hansen believes that reading other people's work and seeing how they use language is a major part of the writing learning process. Dr. Prusa also stresses the importance of writing well. He realizes that many academic and professional articles are poorly written and tries to avoid similar mistakes in his own writing. In their articles, Dr. Hansen and Dr. Prusa feel that it is important to write in a clear manner. They revise extensively so that their work is very readable. "Does Administrative Policy Protect?" was written with policy-makers and students of political science and economics in mind but is communicable to a larger audience.

For Discussion

1. What tone does the article take in the first paragraph? What specific words signify the authors' position on this issue? Why do you think the authors take this tone? What are their reasons?

2. What is the purpose of "unfair trade" laws and "escape clause" laws? Why do the authors suggest that "unfair trade" laws are more appropriately called "Title VII" laws?

3. In paragraph five, the authors state: "We shall show that administrative protection does not protect effectively." How do the authors support this statement? Refer to specific examples in the text.

4. In "An Overview of the Trade Laws," the authors provide general explanations of the function and use of "escape clause" and "Title VII" laws. Briefly summarize these laws. What are their differences and similarities?

5. Summarize the information in Table 1. What characteristics do the industries in Table 1 share? Why?

6. Why is it important whether or not the president has a formal role in granting trade protection? What role do you think the president's political party has in influencing his decision?

7. Summarize the trends in industries filing for trade relief in terms of employment, output, market share, and new capital spending.

8. As a president of a large corporation experiencing output, employment, and capital spending decreases, would you file for trade protection under "Title VII" or "escape

clause" laws? Write a short essay explaining your choice. Refer to specific passages in the text to support your decision.

9. Do the "unfair trade" and "escape clause" laws work? What are the authors' conclusions? What is your opinion? Write an essay in which you discuss this question using examples from the text. Be sure to talk about the effects each type of law has on the industries and how the effects are similar and/or different.

10. How aware are you of administrative protection? Do you think that this is hurting the consumer? What foreign products have you bought recently?

AMA
Richard Rubin

Richard Rubin is a general internal medicine physician at the University of New Mexico Hospital. Dr. Rubin attended Columbia University where he completed his undergraduate work. He continued his education at Albert Einstein College of Medicine in the Bronx, New York, where he earned his M.D. Dr. Rubin did his internship at the Bronx Municipal Hospital and completed his residency training at Rutgers University Hospital before coming to the UNM Hospital in 1990.

They wheeled him into the emergency room just as my shift was ending, light spraying from silver siderails as the gurney flew past. Laid out that way—mottled, unmoving, a clear plastic tube arching upwards from his open mouth—he seemed so much smaller than yesterday, fragile, almost breakable. Was such a change physically possible? Despite that, there could be no mistake: the gurney streaked by and I knew it was him.

My father still sees patients in the town where he was born, a town that has revered him for a third of a century and rightly so. When I was younger, he would take me on his housecalls, perhaps a half-dozen stops on a winter's evening, each visit marked by a cup of hot cocoa and a dimly-lit glance at my father's world. I would stand motionless in the shadows, in the room's farthest corner, as he would prod and probe, tap and listen, methodically going about his business as the wind outside hissed and drowned out my thoughts.

That's the way it was that night in the ER: I hovered in the background as the new shift took over, running the code with a calculated frenzy, the tangle of IV lines swaying to the cadence of their breathless orders. I seemed to be watching all this through a window, a shield which distanced me from everyone else in the cubicle. At one point a student nurse backed into me; she looked up as if to apologize, but there must have been something in my stare that told her to slide silently away. The cubicle suddenly grew warm, and for a brief dizzy moment I thought the code team's attention would soon need to shift in my direction.

I had seen him the day before and, at the time, it had all seemed so very ordinary. Even looking back, what could be more straightforward? He was a man in his fifties complaining of chest pain, brought in by his daughter. I had taken a cardiology rotation last year, as a fourth year medical student, so if there was one complaint I felt confident evaluating, it was chest pain. For chest pain, the history was everything, and taking a meticulous history has always been my strength, a skill which brings forth approving smiles from all my supervising physicians. Most likely they think I've modeled myself after their example, but on that score they're way off the mark. My true mentor, of course, is someone much closer to home; don't forget that my father was carefully transcribing his patients' stories at a time when many of my professors were still reciting the alphabet, and I know only too well that I've been sitting at a true master's knee for as long as I can remember.

So what about my patient? His discomfort was "atypical" for a heart attack, and in that way *he* was typical of most of the patients I had seen that month in the ER. The pain was both sharp and pressure-like, sometimes made worse by breathing and sometimes not, helped by Sprite as well as nitro-glycerine. It was a strange melange, neither here nor there in terms of a specific diagnosis. My decision to admit him to the hospital was based less on the parts than on the whole: mostly, I was impressed not with how sick he looked, but how stoical he was trying to appear. This gruff and gnarly man in front of me obviously cared very little for doctors and hospitals; he was, as my father would put it, "your classic denier." To my mind, if he was sick enough to come to the ER, he was sick enough to be admitted.

I capped my pen after scribbling a few hurried words.

"You'll need to come in the hospital," I announced.

He blinked twice, then folded his arms across his chest. His fingers were yellow and wide at the nails.

"What are you talking about?" he shot back. "You haven't even examined me."

I squeezed down on my pen but kept my voice the same.

"You've already told me all I need to know."

His fingers curled into fists. The yellow turned white.

"There's no way in hell I'm going in the hospital today."

His daughter frowned and shifted in her seat. She was 18, maybe 19, a thin and sad-eyed girl who'd spent most of the interview staring at the floor.

"Daddy, please. The doctor's only trying to help you."

He twisted to face her, the cords of his neck tensing as he looked to his left.

"No way I go in today. You of all people should know that."

I tried to make my voice as low as possible, smoothing it with sincerity.

"Trust me, this is very important. It's your heart I'm concerned about."

He sat up in the gurney so he could better see my face.

"I can't come in today. Maybe tomorrow."

I leaned forward in my chair.

"I think it's very important you come in today. If this is a heart attack, there's no telling what might happen if you leave."

"Look, I'll make a deal with you. I'll promise to come back tomorrow. I just can't stay here today, that's all."

"What's going on today that's so important? What's more important than your heart?"

He lay back on the gurney, his fingers rolled into a clench. They looked like pillars of ivory. His eyes stared beyond the fluorescent lights above his head.

Suddenly, his daughter addressed me.

"It's my brother . . ."

The man stirred, shooting her a dark glance through narrowed eyes.

"Theresa!"

Her eyes, too, became slits and, for the first time, I saw how much she resembled him.

"Stop it, Daddy! The doctor has to know why you're fighting him so much."

The man's eyes moved back to the ceiling, to the lights above. The girl cleared her throat and continued.

"It's my brother. They're saying he broke his parole. We're all due in court at two o'clock."

The man's eyes remained on the lights but his words flew by like spears, aimed somewhere inside his daughter.

"These are family things, Theresa. No one else has to hear this."

He sat up with a jolt, his eyes scorching first the girl, then me.

"It's time we left."

My throat suddenly felt very dry, and for some reason I found myself thinking of my father.

"Maybe we could talk about this some more. Trust me, it's important that you stay."

But by then he had already flipped his legs over the side of the gurney. He was upright in an instant.

"No. *You* trust me. Right now, it's more important that I leave."

I left the cubicle to confer with my ER attending. He was suturing a twelve-year-old's chin, and we spoke as he made loops with a thread that was nearly invisible. We had no choice, we decided: the man would have to sign out AMA, against medical advice. We saw no other option.

By the time I brought in the papers the man was already dressed. He wrote his name slowly, his signature surprising me with its neatness.

* * *

"Eric?"

The charge nurse was in front of me, appearing out of nowhere.

"Eric, are you all right?"

The code was over. The man had been flat-line in the ambulance and we all knew it was hopeless from the start. The cubicle was littered with alcohol swabs and plastic IV sheaths, and the floor crackled as the crowd headed out.

"I'm fine. Just a little tired."

Her eyes scanned me.

"It's been a long shift. You should go home and get some rest."

I slipped around the curtain as the nurses sponged away the sticky remnants of our efforts. One by one, catheters of every diameter were pulled out and quickly discarded.

My car was in the parking lot in front of the hospital, and walking through the waiting room would save me some time, get me to my bed a few moments faster. To an intern, this was everything. My life was a series of shortcuts.

I saw them as soon as I entered the waiting room. A senior resident, his hands in his pockets, was explaining what had happened. The girl was standing up, sobbing into a ball of Kleenex. Next to her, his arm around her, was a young bearded man, tall and knife-like, a black leather jacket still buttoned at the neck. His hair was long and parted in the middle, and a tiny earring flashed at me from yards away.

I have no recollection of walking across the room, but before I could turn around I found myself at their side, just as the senior resident was leaving. The girl looked up at me and nodded in recognition. I burrowed deep to find words that would somehow be right.

"Everyone did the best they could. We're all sorry we couldn't do more."

She swept an errant strand of hair from her forehead.

"I know you tried," she whispered. "It's no one's fault."

The bearded man suddenly snapped upright, his eyes meeting mine for a fiery instant, then turning, still smoldering, to hers.

"Is he the one?" he asked her. "The one you saw yesterday?"

I could barely hear her voice.

"Yes, he's the one."

He turned to me again. I noticed that the veins in his scalp were coiled and by now almost purple.

"You knew this would happen. Why'd you let him leave?"

"I wanted him to stay. I urged him to. He wouldn't listen to me."

"You should have forced him to stay here. If you had done that one simple thing, this never would have happened."

The girl grabbed his arm and started to speak, but the man's eyes never wavered from mine.

"Cut it out, Bobby. It's not his fault."

"Stop making excuses. The two of you were here. You both should have done something."

All at once I found the words I thought I wanted.

"We couldn't keep him here against his will. He signed out against our advice. We told him not to go, but he had a right to leave. A legal right."

His face tightened, and he aimed a finger within an inch of my throat.

"A legal right? What are you, a doctor or a freakin' lawyer?"

The girl's sobs grew louder, and he led her away from me, cursing me under his breath.

As I watched them move away, I heard the strange cackling of distant voices. A security officer, walkie-talkie in hand, approached me from the side.

"Things OK here, Doc?"

I started for the parking lot.

"Yeah," I said. "Everything's under control."

That night I tried reaching my father, but he was out on another housecall. I tried to imagine what his advice to me would be like. Years earlier, when I first announced my intention to follow in his footsteps, he told me how much happiness he took in my decision, how medicine had stamped his own life with such meaning. "The parade of people you'll take care of is almost endless," he told me. "All types, from every walk of life. You'll see them all sitting in the waiting room and wonder what on earth they could possibly have in common, and then you realize it's you. The only thing they have in common is you. The fact you're doing the best you can for each of them."

Images of Theresa, Bobby, and their father converged on my ceiling for much of the night. Finally, at about three-thirty, I was able to drift off to sleep and for that I was extremely grateful. After all, my next shift in the ER was only a few short hours away.

Richard Rubin's own reading has led to a respect for writing as well as a sense of appropriate language patterns and word choice. In his stories, Dr. Rubin writes about what it is like to be a medical student or doctor. He likes to show how physicians deal with difficult situations. Dr. Rubin begins his pieces by deciding on a specific point which he then expands into the story itself. He experiments with narrative voice to discover what effect it can have on the story. Dr. Rubin enjoys working with medical students and is active in teaching both inpatient and outpatient medicine at the University Hospital.

For Discussion

1. How does the author establish a sense of place in the story? Find the places in the story where the narrator describes the setting. What role does the setting play in the development of the story?

2. In paragraph two, the narrator reminisces about his childhood. Why might the author have included this? Do you think that this works in the story? Why or why not?

3. In paragraph four, the narrator says that he is confident in his abilities to evaluate chest pain. Is he as skilled in patient relations as in diagnosis? How does his confidence hinder him with this patient?

4. In paragraph four, the narrator reminds the reader: "Don't forget that my father was carefully transcribing his patients' stories at a time when many of my professors were still reciting the alphabet." Here, he seems to direct the reader to respect elders. How is his tone with the patient in opposition with this statement? How is the narrator more concerned about the reader audience than the patient audience?

5. Eric says, "My life was a series of shortcuts." How do we see this reflected throughout the story?

6. Eric is earnest in his desire to help the patient but is not skilled in explaining his motives for wanting to admit the patient to the hospital. Does this shortcoming result in the patient signing the AMA form? After the patient dies, the family blames Eric even though the patient signed out against medical advice. In your opinion, who is responsible? How could Eric have explained himself in a way that would have convinced the patient of the danger of his condition? Imagine that you are Eric. Defend your actions and treatment of the patient.

7. Medical ethics often involve complicated issues and emotions. In this story, Eric is not legally responsible for the death of the patient yet feels partially to blame. Break into groups and discuss the ethical issues in the greater community that you are aware of (Dr. Kevorkian, for example). What are your opinions about these ethical issues? How are medical ethics similar to and/or different from the ethics of education? Present your answers to the class.

Wrestlers and Doctors
David Sklar, M.D.

*David Sklar is an emergency medicine physician and Chairman of the Emergency
Medicine Department at the University of New Mexico. He lived in Massachusetts
before attending Stanford University where he earned his undergraduate and medical degrees. Dr. Sklar then came to the University of New Mexico where he
completed his residency training. Before joining the faculty at UNM in 1980, Dr.
Sklar did a fellowship in emergency medicine in San Francisco.*

The congressman called the dean, who called the chairman, who called me.
"Dave, they need a doctor for the fundraiser at the coliseum. Some kind of
wrestling match."

"Are you kidding? Seriously?"

"Yep. Hell, it's for a good cause. Youth at Risk Scholarships."

"But I hate wrestling. It's disgusting. And it's fake."

"Oh, it won't be so bad. Easier than a shift in the emergency department."

"Well, can't anyone else do it?" I pleaded.

"No, Dennis is on nights. Jim is out of town, and I've got an important dinner. And Ed is in the ED."

Minutes later, I was receiving the directions to the coliseum. I began to imagine what a wrestling doctor might be called upon to do, what organs were injured by claw holds, knee drops, sleep squeezes, and falls from the ropes. I
remembered performing some of these holds on my younger brother as a child
and could still hear his cries of agony. And I didn't even know the correct way
to apply the deadly holds.

I arrived at the side door as instructed. A man with a clipboard checked for
my name. "I'm the doctor," I volunteered, showing my stethoscope and blood
pressure cuff.

"Oh good. The forms are on the table. Just sign them at the bottom."

I paused, but then walked over to the table and found physical exam certifi-
cation forms for each wrestler. "Oh," I thought, "so they want me to do physical exams on the wrestlers."

I was actually impressed that some degree of physical health would be required of professional wrestlers. I snatched the forms and pushed through a door
into the dressing room.

They were all big—not just tall, but large in other ways. Big, pot-bellied,
sweaty, with foul language pouring out of square-jawed mouths. Hairy chests
and backs and arms. My stethoscope and blood pressure cuff could barely

accommodate them.

General Justice glared down at me. "I don't need no physical. Just sign the paper."

"I can't do that," I explained. "After all, what if you had a heart attack during your match. It would be my fault."

"Look, doc. You just sign the papers and we go and wrestle. They never put that thing on me," he pointed to the stethoscope.

"Just let him do his job," yelled the Barbarian—six feet, seven inches of fat, muscle and bleached blond hair—who lay prostrate across a bench. General Justice grunted and let me listen to his heart.

"Sounds fine," I reassured him. But when I tested his joints, his elbow could not fully straighten.

"Yeah, it's been like that. No big deal."

"Well, I don't know," I hesitated; "maybe you should see a bone specialist. It could be a sign of arthritis."

"Hell, you land on your elbow like I do and you'd be lucky to bend it at all. It ain't no arthritis; it's just from wrestling."

I signed his paper and moved on to the Barbarian. He lay passively across a bench, and I listened to his heart quickly before examining his belly. It hung down over the bench in layers. I was already past and moving to his knee when my mind clicked. Something was bulging in his belly. I returned and found the same hard lump—a swollen liver. "Uh, Mr. . . . ."

"—Barbarian," he answered.

"Well, your liver seems enlarged," I began. "I can feel the edge way down here." I pointed to near his belly button. "Do you drink any alcohol?" I asked.

"Just beer," he said.

"How much?"

"About a six pack after my match."

"Yeah, and two more six packs before bed," interrupted General Justice.

"Well, I think your liver is enlarged. It could burst if you wrestle."

"No, it's not gonna bust. Anyway, it don't hurt."

"You could die," I continued.

"Hell, I got to wrestle the General here tonight. I don't get paid if I don't wrestle. So don't you worry about me, doc." He sat up and stared at me. "Just sign the paper." I put it in my hands, shaking nervously, trying to decide.

Suddenly two men approached me. One was bald with thick glasses. The other, younger, in a suit with a cowboy hat and moustache. He spoke first. "I think there's been a mistake, doctor. You are supposed to be the doctor out there." He pointed to the auditorium. "Take care of any problems out there. The audience—

people who faint, you know? This here is Dr. Weinberg. He's the doctor for in here, for the wrestlers. He'll take over on the physicals."

Dr. Weinberg stepped forward slowly, almost sheepishly. He received the papers from me and began signing his name at the bottom. I watched for a moment and then shuffled to the door, feeling strangely sad, as if something I had not wanted, that had been taken away, suddenly had become important to me. I walked out to where the audience sat and found my place in the second row, far enough away so that a wrestler flung from the ring would not crush me. I watched the matches with the detachment of an anthropologist observing a strange primitive tribe. The exhortations from the audience, the obvious crowd favorites, the ethnic stereotyping, all were registered in my memory unemotionally. And then General Justice and the Barbarian entered the ring. Suddenly I was no longer detached. No matter that they had rejected me and my advice, they were my patients.

The match began with a body slam that landed the Barbarian on his stomach. I envisioned his swollen liver stretching under the strain. Then General Justice attacked with punches to the face and head. I could barely watch, but continued staring in fascination, as if waiting for the inevitable. The match took a new turn as the Barbarian appeared to gain the upper hand and almost pin General Justice. But then, in some kind of illegal maneuver that went undetected by the referee, Justice escaped and lifted the Barbarian into the air for a final match-ending body slam. The force of the impact shook my seat, and I was sure that the Barbarian's liver had ruptured. I jumped to my feet as the referee counted to three for the pin. Staring at the Barbarian's lifeless face, I knew he was dead. And then Dr. Weinberg hurried to the ring, followed by men carrying a stretcher. Dr. Weinberg did a few compressions on the Barbarian's chest. Before I could yell, "ventilate him," or jump into the ring, I noticed the Barbarian wink almost imperceptibly in my direction. A few more chest compressions and the Barbarian's arms and legs were moving. Soon the Barbarian was shaking off the effects of the body slam and looking to resume the match with General Justice, who was parading around the ring to the loud boos of the audience. I cheered for the Barbarian as he broke a chair over General Justice's head and screamed at the referee as he awarded the match to General Justice.

The rest of the matches that night were punctuated with a few requests for aspirin, one drunk teenager, and a woman who wanted her blood pressure checked. A tame night compared with my typical shift in the emergency department.

As I walked out behind Dr. Weinberg, I couldn't help thinking about the pedestal on which I place truth, scientific validity, and logic—where did Dr.

Weinberg, General Justice, and the Barbarian fit into that? Certainly, they could be considered frauds at one level. But sometimes it's fun to suspend critical judgments and experience the fantasy of a world where heroes and villains do combat, where good and evil actually exist with some certainty and even a vanquished hero will return for another battle. A world without cirrhosis of the liver or heart disease. A world where every resuscitation will succeed. And perhaps a glimpse of this fantasy world makes it a little easier to accept the uncertainty of chest pain, the unfairness of an automobile crash, or the finality of a failed resuscitation.

David Sklar's interest in writing is stimulated by his experiences in the emergency department, a meeting place full of diversity as well as tragedy. This environment provides him with a unique perspective which is translated into his writing. He sees his writing process as continually changing and growing. He is interested in how other writers use language and stylistic techniques, and these, in turn, influence his own writing decisions. Dr. Sklar generally writes with a medical audience in mind. He believes that the sharing of experiences and tragedies can help relieve the stress that results from working in the medical profession.

For Discussion

1. In the beginning of the essay, the narrator says: "But I hate wrestling. It's disgusting. And it's fake." A few sentences later, he recalls applying "deadly holds" on his younger brother. How are these statements in opposition? Why do you think the author included both statements? What effect does this have on the narrative?

2. Discuss the theme of responsibility. Legally, the physician signing the form is responsible but should the responsibility also lie with the wrestlers/producers? How are both the patient and physician responsible? Write a paragraph explaining your answer.

3. Does the narrator resolve the issue of the Barbarian's physical form? How?

4. How does the author feel when he is relieved of his duties as a physical examiner? How do you know he feels this way? Why do you think he has this reaction?

5. How is the narrator drawn into the wrestling match between the Barbarian and General Justice? Does he still see wrestling as *disgusting* and *fake*? How is his attitude in the last paragraph different from his feelings in the beginning?

6. In a brief essay, compare and contrast "Wrestlers and Doctors" with "AMA." How

are the personalities of the patient in "AMA" and the Barbarian the same? How are they different? Compare and contrast how the narrators handle their patients. What are the legal and ethical aspects of each case?

7. In the last paragraph, the narrator suggests that fantasy helps people cope with the problems and tragedies in life. In your own experience, do you find this to be true? List ways in which we escape and examine them in relation to one another. Which ways are more destructive? What do we do to escape as children? As adults? How are they the same/different?